Our dear sister, Mrs. Diana Hagee, tenderly bridges the gap of the hearts of sisters of all ages, stages, phases, and even faces. As you read her work, you will sense the goodness and pleasantness that comes through unity . . . for when we dwell there (in unity) God commands a blessing . . . On behalf of the many sisters who have tears in our hearts; thank you for sharing yours . . .

> Perfect peace to my friend, Diana, and those who love her,
> Lady Serita Jakes

I have enjoyed a personal friendship with John and Diana Hagee which goes back more than 20 years. I can therefore affirm with confidence that Diana's teaching is sound and scriptural. *The King's Daughter* will call forth in women the kind of attitude and lifestyle which should mark those whom Paul describes as "women professing godliness" (1 Tim. 2:10).

> Derek Prince
> Head of Derek Prince Ministries Worldwide
> Jerusalem, Israel

The
KING'S
DAUGHTER

DIANA HAGEE

THOMAS NELSON PUBLISHERS®
Nashville

A Division of Thomas Nelson, Inc.
www.ThomasNelson.com

Published by Thomas Nelson Publishers, a Division of Thomas Nelson, Inc., P.O. Box 141000, Nashville, Tennessee, 37214.

Unless otherwise noted, Scripture quotations are from THE NEW KING JAMES VERSION. Copyright © 1979, 1980, 1982, Thomas Nelson, Inc. Publishers.

Scripture quotations noted AMPLIFIED are from THE AMPLIFIED BIBLE: Old Testament. Copyright © 1962, 1964 by Zondervan Publishing House (used by permission); and from THE AMPLIFIED NEW TESTAMENT. Copyright © 1958 by the Lockman Foundation (used by permission).

Scripture quotations noted KJV are from THE KING JAMES VERSION.

Scripture quotations noted NASB are from the NEW AMERICAN STANDARD BIBLE®, © Copyright The Lockman Foundation 1960, 1962, 1963, 1968, 1971, 1972, 1973, 1975, 1977. Used by permission. (www.lockman.org)

Scripture quotations noted NIV are from the HOLY BIBLE: NEW INTERNATIONAL VERSION®. Copyright © 1973, 1978, 1984 by International Bible Society. Used by permission of Zondervan Publishing House. All rights reserved.

Scripture quotations noted TLB are taken from *The Living Bible*, copyright © 1971. Used by permission of Tyndale House Publishers, Inc., Wheaton, Illinois 60189. All rights reserved.

Library of Congress Cataloging-in Publication Data

Hagee, Diana
    The King's daughter : becoming the woman God created you to be / Diana Hagee.
        p. cm.
    ISBN 0-7852-6644-5
    1. Christian women—Religious life.
  BV4527 .H335 2001
  248.8/43 21   2001044826
                                                                        CIP

Printed in the United States of America
02 03 04 05 VG 5 4

This book is lovingly dedicated to
My King, who has loved me from the beginning
My husband, who is God's cherished gift to me
My children, who have enriched my life beyond words
My parents, who helped mold me
My mother-in-law, who is my spiritual mentor

ACKNOWLEDGMENTS

I want to personally express my gratitude to:
Janet Thoma, who gently and patiently guided
me through this author's journey;
Scott and Sandy Farhart, whose professional wisdom
and personal testimony will impact the lives of many;
Teresa Weaver and Nina Rodriguez,
who continually help me achieve my goals;
and the Women of Esther at Cornerstone Church,
whose prayers and support I cherish.

CONTENTS

chapter one

The King's Daughter

*E*very woman desires her husband's complete and undivided attention when she speaks. I, like many, don't receive that precious commodity as much as I'd like. However, flying in an airplane with my husband at 30,000 feet and at 500 miles per hour seems to gain me that luxury. First, the distractions are few, and second, he can't leave the room.

On one particular trip, I was intently reading the entire book of Esther, not just the selected verses we often memorize. I was amazed by the complexity of God's plan surrounding Esther's life, the discipline and the obedience of who she was and who she was to become. Closing my eyes, I saw this beautiful Jewish woman with glistening black hair, flawless skin, and ruby-red lips that curved upward, revealing a radiant smile that evolved from her heart. Most of all, I saw a breathtaking beauty emanating from her eyes, a beauty so pure, so sincere, that its source could only have been her very soul.

As God positioned Esther to become the queen of Persia, the most powerful nation on the earth at that time in history, she had to prepare herself. *Preparation* is a word that means "to make ready in advance"—usually for a particular use— "to equip" or "to endow." *Why do we not prepare to present ourselves before our King?* I asked myself. The question seized my mind.

Soon my unassuming husband was awakened from a deep sleep with an abrupt poke to the ribs. "What do you think about a class at church for the young women of thirteen to nineteen to equip them to become women of God?"

He quickly said, "A great idea." Too quickly, I thought!

"Did you just say that to shut me up, or do you really mean it?"

"Yes, I mean it!" was his resounding response.

With those words I began an incredible journey. When I returned to Cornerstone Church, I locked myself in a room with my two assistants, Nina Rodriguez and Teresa Weaver, and within hours we had created the curriculum. God's inspiration came quickly for a life-changing program that would dramatically impact the lives of hundreds of women.

The seminar, to be called Becoming a Woman of God, would last twelve weeks, symbolizing the twelve months of preparation for Esther. After King Xerxes called for his men to gather the women of the province for the purpose of choosing a new queen, the women were taken to the "beautification" palace. There they prepared themselves with beauty treatments for twelve months—six months in frankincense and six months in myrrh. King Xerxes would select his queen from among these young women. The word *beauty* is defined as "perfect in physical form, flawless in symmetry, brightness, and fairness." According to Hebrew tradition, Esther was chosen for her inner beauty more than her outer beauty. I knew instantly that the program we were putting together needed to concentrate on the inner woman.

I expected twenty-five to fifty young women to register for the class. Instead more than three hundred girls flooded the registration tables. I was both amazed and scared. The feelings of insecurity that had hindered my life rose within me. I remember calling my precious mother-in-law, Vada Hagee, and asking her to pray for an anointing over me for the first session. She prayed a beautiful prayer, which released the direction and power of the Holy Spirit. With God's help I knew this would be a life-changing experience for all of the participants.

In the theater so perfectly clear in my mind, I saw these young women preparing themselves for twelve weeks to be presented before the church on Mother's Day night, the thirteenth week, in beautiful gowns. As I explained the curriculum in our first session, the girls shrieked with excitement. I was on a roll.

But when I spoke to them about graduation night and the attire they would wear, silence followed. I could not understand what had happened. I looked into their quiet faces, and their eyes spoke back to me. They owned no such garments and had no resources with which to buy them. I was crushed. Soon after my discovery I ended the first meeting and drove quietly home.

Lord, what have I done? I prayed. *I wanted to bless these young women; instead I made them feel inadequate.* I arrived home and cried on my husband's shoulder. As always, he had an answer for me. He would arrange to buy at least one hundred dresses for these precious girls from the benevolence fund of our church, and I would borrow the other dresses from the more affluent families. I was determined not to exclude anyone from my class.

The following morning I went to the largest bridal and formal dress shop in town. I met with the owner and his wife, who attend our church often. I explained our Woman of God class and the need to buy at least one hundred evening gowns at a very discounted price. Then I held my breath.

The immediate response was, "And why don't you take 325 dresses?"

"I can't afford 325 dresses!" I answered.

"I see," he said. "What you don't realize is that I can, and I want to donate them."

His response overwhelmed me. I could hear God's words in my mind: *I own the cattle on a thousand hills. What's 325 dresses?* I began to tear up with emotion. I also began to give the man and his wife abundant thanks for their generous donation.

His next question surprised me even more. "What shoes will these ladies wear?"

I answered with a natural assumption: "Whatever they have at home."

In his typical manner, he replied, "My dresses can't be worn with just any shoes. I will also provide the shoes. It is important that my dresses look the best they can."

One of my many dreams for the class was coming true before my eyes. I was in awe of God's work through this man and his precious, smiling wife.

After profusely thanking them, I went to my car and shut the door. Then I let out a loud scream of joy and thanked the Lord for His miraculous provision. My confidence soared and so did my boldness. You see, now Jesus and I were on a roll!

I remembered that I wanted "makeovers" for these young women. Where would I get them? While I was still in my car, the name of the largest hair salon-chain in town came to my mind. I had gotten my hair cut there several times and heard that the owner knew the Lord, so I called the shop from my mobile phone. As I dialed, I asked the Lord to prepare her heart.

Luckily she was available and took my call. I explained the vision of the class, and when I got to the "outer beauty" portion of the seminar, she interrupted my soliloquy with "Praise God! This is where I come in!"

Once again I began to shake. God had prepared her heart. He was in the car with me, giving me confidence and the words with which to "ask." And He was in the office with her, quickening her to provide the needed resources. God is truly omnipresent.

She offered to close her shops early the day of the makeovers and bring twenty stylists to our church to cut and style everyone's hair. In addition, a team of stylists would select six young girls from the class and give them complete makeovers, which would include facials, manicures, pedicures, and makeup applications as examples for the rest of the group. All of this would be provided at no charge. I knew I was in the will of God!

I called John, and he was amazed at what had happened. Together we prayed a prayer of thanks. The vision that was born in my heart was coming to pass.

Now my mind began to overwhelm me with ideas to equip these young women with the most important tool created for man: God's Word! *Lord, I need 325 Bibles!* I prayed.

When I called a publisher and asked for a deep, deep discount, the company provided the best discount possible. Still I needed more.

Little did I know that the owner of the publishing company was scheduled to have lunch with my husband in the next two days. His company published not only the Bible I wanted, but also another book, on dating.

One of my many responsibilities at Cornerstone Church, the church my husband pastors, is organizing special events and catering. The meeting with my husband and the owner of the publishing company and his staff was to take place in our executive dining room. I thought of Esther and the banquet she had before the king. I prayed, *Father, let me find favor with this powerful man. He has the Bibles and books I need!*

My staff prepared a sumptuous meal, which they would serve on our best china atop beautiful linen. Then before I entered the dining room as the hostess, I joined hands with Teresa and prayed for God's favor.

After the blessing, we all exchanged pleasantries and began our meal. Soon I proudly announced, "I have a testimony!"

My husband almost dropped his fork. That was not my usual style, to speak out among such an auspicious group. "Then let's hear it!" proclaimed the owner of the publishing company, who was my "angel unaware."

I told my story of the Woman of God seminar. All were impressed and moved by God's vision, but more so by His provision.

"That is a wonderful story," he said. Little did he know what would come next.

I took a deep breath. I glanced at my husband, whose mouth was still open. His beautiful brown eyes were as round as I had seen them in a long time.

I proceeded. "I called your staff requesting a discount for 325 Bibles as well as 325 more books on dating. They did the best they could. However, I felt I should ask you to present them to my girls as a gift."

There, I had done my part; the rest was up to God.

He was stunned with my boldness and also took a deep breath before he responded. Then a sparkle appeared in his eyes, and he gave his answer: "Woman, you have your Bibles and your books. I will donate them."

Sweet Lord, You did it again. As Esther had done, I had found favor with the king. My mission was accomplished and God's purposes had prevailed. I have since prayed countless blessings for the many people who allowed God to use them to provide for these precious young women.

Our second Woman of God meeting was the following Tuesday, and I was excited to tell the class what their Father in heaven had provided for them. As I gave them the miraculous account of all that had transpired, I could see hope rise in their eyes. By the end of my story, they were on their feet shouting for joy. Now was a very proper time to describe the God I knew and the God of their provision. The one and only true God. The God of my salvation. As I spoke about the sinner's prayer, I could see conviction upon their faces. The Holy Spirit was in the room. Fifty-two young women stood to pray the sinner's prayer and receive Christ.

The class was God's vision, and His provision met its needs. Graduation was a dream with a happy ending. The young women had completed twelve weeks of classes ranging from self-esteem to sexuality to hospitality to the infilling of the Holy Spirit. The graduates were presented before the church in their gowns. As they bowed before the congregation, they bowed before their Father and their King. I knew that almighty God was pleased.

HOW WE GOT HERE

I could go on for several chapters describing one incredible moment after another as these young women were saved, liberated, restored, and made whole. In today's society, there is a lethal weapon that destroys so many of our young people: hopelessness.

The Word of God says that the helmet of salvation is hope. Jesus Christ is the blessed hope, and whenever Satan can separate us from our hope, he has destroyed our future. The hope of these young women had been restored. If for no other reason than this, the class was a fantastic success.

In the beginning of the Woman of God sessions, approximately fifteen to twenty mothers sat at the back of the auditorium waiting so they could drive their daughters home. After each teaching session, I would break the class into groups of eight to ten young women with an older woman, who had been through our church leadership class, acting as a facilitator. This idea was directed by Titus 2:3–5: "The older women likewise . . . that they admonish the young women to love their husbands, to love their children, to be discreet, chaste, homemakers, good, obedient to their own husbands, that the word of God may not be blasphemed."

These facilitators would lead the younger girls in the "action points" designed for each class, and I, in turn, would facilitate the mothers. Whenever there was an altar call for inner healing or new beginnings, they, too, were at the altar, weeping and asking God to intervene in their lives. I began to ask many questions of God: "Why are these mothers coming with such hunger? We are ministering to them as much as to their daughters. And why aren't they teaching their daughters? How did our society get to this point?"

I remembered a lecture I had attended several years ago, which centered on the evolution of the family. America from its birth was an agrarian society. Children lived on farms with mothers and fathers, grandparents, and often great-grandparents as well. The fathers took their sons into the fields and taught them to provide for their families as they worked side by side. And the mothers taught their daughters to tend to the house and family as they accomplished daily chores together. Evenings were spent around the dinner table. In the summer, mothers and fathers, sons and daughters, and grandmothers and grandfathers sat on the porch, eating cool watermelon and listening to the grandparents tell stories of their own childhood. By hearing these accounts of their elders, young people knew that they, too, had hope for their future.

However, with the arrival of the industrial revolution, fathers realized they could make more money for their families in one week working in the factories than they could working the fields for a month. The migration to the cities began. Young men were no longer working side by side with their fathers. Soon more influence was coming from their peers than from anyone else.

The transition for the women came a bit more slowly. The onset of World War II demanded that all able-bodied men of America serve on the front lines to defend their country. Instantly women were needed in the workplace, not only to keep the nation supplied with goods and services but to provide for their families. Young girls found themselves in the care of their grandmothers or at home on their own.

Our country was never the same after the war ended. Men came back home to children they hardly knew. Some women did not leave their jobs in the workplace. Young girls had less and less teaching from their mothers. The new instructors in their lives were their peers, a new invention called television, and ultimately the world.

Divorce soon became an epidemic as couples found the term *irreconcilable differences* sufficient reason to end covenants. Children lost confidence in the family structure. What was once a mainstay in their lives was no longer as parents were divided into separate homes, often with new husbands or wives and other children. Their heroes now came from a "Leave It to Beaver," make-believe world that had no pain, no separation, and no disappointments.

Today our heroes are those who can make news, not those who form the world by "rocking the cradle." Marketing controls what we eat, what we drive, where we live, what we look like, and ultimately who we become. The values of our society have been so convoluted by the latest craze that we find ourselves longing for something or someone stable in our lives, something or someone who is the same yesterday, today, and forever. Something or someone who will never leave us or forsake us. Someone who is a promise keeper, not a covenant breaker. That Someone is Jesus Christ. It is time we come back to the God of our fathers.

While I was teaching the Woman of God class for the young women, Derek Prince, one of the foremost Bible scholars of our time, came to minister in our church. He has spent the majority of his eighty years on this earth studying and teaching the Word of God in a simple, yet profound, manner. One afternoon he was captive in my car, and I began my testimony about God's provision for my young women. Brother Prince began to weep as he told me of a revelation in the Word that coincided with my class.

He explained that for years the body of Christ has been trying to bridge gaps. Whether they were denominational, racial, or social, it was done in the name of unity. However, God purposely created certain gaps: those between good and evil, between light and dark, between sweet and bitter, and between men and women. Brother Prince felt very strongly that women had gravitated more into a man's world in the name of equality and freedom than men had entered their world. In the search for equality women lost their own identity and their identity in Christ. We were never meant to be equal. *We were meant to be unique.*

Before hearing of my class, he said his biggest frustration was identifying the problem without providing the solution. These classes, he said, would be a way of teaching women the value they had in God's eyes and keeping in place the gaps that He had created.

Unfortunately we have embraced the world and its values so long that the lines between good and evil and light and darkness are dim, so we have difficulty making godly decisions. My husband uses the illustration of entering an upscale restaurant and trying to read the menu under the dim mood lighting. Right after you come in from the sunlight, it is virtually impossible to do so, but after a few minutes in the dark, your eyes become adjusted. So goes the soul. We have been around spiritual darkness and moral decadence so long that what we once considered unacceptable is now the norm.

Through tolerance we have allowed a moral cancer to grow within us to the point that we now mirror the world. Our children are killing each other in the schools. Teenage pregnancy and abortion are at epidemic levels. Fathers have abandoned their homes in search of pleasure. The church in America demands the "feel good" gospel instead of the gospel of truth and conviction. We mirror the world in the statistics of divorce, pornography, abortion, homosexuality, and the other diseases that infect our society. The church in America has become the Laodicean church in Revelation of whom God says, "I will spew you out of My mouth!"

After hearing Derek Prince speak, I knew this class was to be much more than a finishing school. It was to be a class that would provide the hope, security, and sense of self-worth that can come only from the rivers of living water.

Brother Prince has written a wonderful book titled *God the Matchmaker*. He looked into my eyes and asked if he could donate 325 of his books to my girls. This book would equip them, through God's Word, with the principles of choosing a mate. He also said he would do something he had not done in a long time: he would hand-sign every copy.

The girls were blessed by his gesture—as were the mothers who were auditing the class. During this first Woman of God class, something unique occurred. Those fifteen to twenty mothers who were sitting at the back of the class grew week by week. By the time the twelve weeks ended, more than 150 mothers were auditing the class.

What is the Holy Spirit telling me in all of this? I asked the Lord. As always, He answered. My husband suggested that the next Woman of God conference be directed to the older women of our church. Let's equip them to teach the younger women, he said, and also fill a gap in their lives.

The next week in church I announced the class, and again I was surprised. More than five hundred women between the ages of twenty and seventy-eight registered. (Isn't it wonderful to serve the God of "it's never too late"?) Their eagerness to learn more about their King led me to choose the direction of this book. It is written to the woman who has forgotten—or never accepted—the fact that she is the King's daughter. It is written to the woman who does not realize that the King wants to give her every good and perfect gift, not because she is perfect but because He is good.

Once we have accepted the Lord Jesus Christ as Savior, we are daughters of the King. However, we must claim that position. We must represent Him in every facet of life. The beauty of walking with Him is that it is never too late to claim that position in His heart. We are all King's daughters.

A KING'S DAUGHTER

When I was praying about the title of this book, the Lord brought to my mind an important conversation I had with Him several years ago. In sharing this very intimate moment with you, I pray it will impact you as it did me.

In 1981, John and I were invited to meet with Prime Minister Menachem Begin because of my husband's support of the nation of Israel. It was a special honor to meet the man whom God used to form the Jewish state. Needless to say, I was very nervous. As we were being cleared by Israeli security, the Great Accuser began to attack my mind: *Who are you to meet with this head of state? You are a hindrance to this meeting. You should not even be in the room.*

I felt he was right, and I became overwhelmed with feelings of insecurities, as if a huge wave of water had suddenly grabbed me in its undertow. I could not breathe. I began to walk toward my husband to ask to be excused from the meeting. All of a sudden I could hear a voice in my mind that was louder than that of my Accuser: *Why are you leaving something I have ordained?*

Because I am not worthy to meet with such an important person, was my faint response. *I am about to meet with the leader of Israel!*

Immediately that same strong voice made a statement that would change my life forever: *And he is about to meet the King's daughter.*

The wave of insecurity and fear dissipated. I squared my shoulders, entered the room, walked over to the prime minister, and extended my hand. I remember it as if it were yesterday. I shook his hand firmly and said, "I am Diana Hagee. I am honored to meet you."

Unless you knew me then you can't comprehend the miracle of that moment. I would never be the same again. Not because I was in the presence of one of the most important men in history, but because I had taken my place in the society of the kingdom of heaven, the eternal society of the Lord Jesus Christ. I was then and will always be the King's daughter. And so will you. Our King has a divine destiny for us all.

OUR DIVINE DESTINY

Every woman has a divine destiny that a sovereign God determined from the foundations of the world (Eph. 1:4). God called Sarah to have Isaac, the Son of Laughter, when her womb was barren to prove once and for all to humanity that "with God nothing will be impossible" (Luke 1:37).

God called Ruth, a Gentile, to leave her country following the death of her husband and to look into the haggard, tear-streaked face of her mother-in-law, Naomi, and say,

> Entreat me not to leave you,
> Or to turn back from following after you;
> For wherever you go, I will go;
> And wherever you lodge, I will lodge;
> Your people shall be my people,
> And your God, my God. (Ruth 1:16)

Ruth's destiny was to demonstrate that God is a God of hope. As a Gentile coming into a Jewish nation, she had no hope. Yet her destiny was to marry Boaz, a mighty man of wealth, and to have a baby, Obed, the great-great-grandfather of Jesus of Nazareth.

God called Mary to submit her body, her life, and her reputation to give birth to the Son of God, which determined the destiny of all mankind (Luke 1:31).

And you, too, are a very important person in the kingdom of God. The purposes of God will prevail in your life once you have surrendered yourself to His will (Prov. 19:21). Your speech will bless your children, your actions will strengthen your marriage, your loyalty to His call to holiness will allow you to experience His fullness as a single woman, your prayers will move mountains, and your character will influence others for Christ.

In this book, which is a journal of our journey to become King's daughters, you will begin to decipher your divine destiny.

We will look at God's will for you in the three parts of your nature: your soul, your spirit, and your body. In the next chapter we will begin with your soul, your emotions and feelings. Too many of us suffer from low self-esteem. In that chapter we will learn about God's impression of us (isn't it truer than our own since He is omnipotent and omnipresent?). Then we will consider your spiritual life—your testimony for Christ and your relationship to the Holy Spirit. Finally we will examine your physical nature, which includes your goals, your sexuality, even your finances and your hospitality.

The book is interactive in that you will record your thoughts and experiences as you work through the twelve chapters. I suggest that you take a chapter a week. Read the chapter the first day or so. Then use the next three or four days of the week to complete the action points.

ACTION POINTS

The Word of God is about taking action. Our salvation, the infilling of the Holy Spirit, discipleship, and any other facet of the Christian walk take action on our part. So at the end of each of our sessions the teenagers split into small groups, as did the older women when we held the second Woman of God conference. During this time they worked through action points with their facilitators, since it was important for the women who participated in the Woman of God class to immediately respond to what they were taught.

The action points at the end of every chapter will help you learn the concepts presented each step of the way in the journey to becoming a woman of God. By the end of this book you will have a new concept of what it is to be a King's daughter. We are about to embark on a journey that, I hope, will change your life forever.

chapter two

My Value in God's Eyes

Throughout my life I have seen myself as unattractive and inadequate. My mom and my dad did not tell me I was ugly. I simply chose to look in the mirror and see ugly. I was too skinny. (I've gotten over that!) My nose was too big, my teeth were too crooked, and my hair was too curly.

I grew up in the sixties and seventies when straight hair was in style. Girls wrapped their hair around huge curlers or orange juice cans. I couldn't put my hair around an orange juice can if I tried; it was just too curly. I didn't even put on makeup until I was seventeen because I felt there was nothing to enhance.

If there was a party, I was the one in the corner. My sister Sandy was the one who said to the boys, "Hello, I'm here. Let's dance."

Sandy and I went to the same high school, and one day she came home from school and announced that she had been accepted into the Anchor Club, an elite social club. By this time I was in college, but I was truly pleased that she had been chosen for such an honor.

"Were you in the Anchor Club?" she asked me.

"No, I was in the Science Club and the Spanish Club."

She replied, "Don't ever let anyone know that."

Two different people, from the same family, the same circumstances, but I chose to see ugly. She chose to think, *Hey, buddy, if you dance with me, you're lucky.*

My mom and dad sensed my problem, so my dad asked my mom to talk to me. She would say, "You're beautiful." And I would answer, "Yeah, Mom, you say that because you're my mom." It didn't matter what anyone said.

I remember a moment when my dad was barbecuing in the backyard, and I asked, "Daddy, why did God make me ugly?"

"He didn't. He stopped the whole world and He made you, and you're beautiful."

And I thought, *My daddy's lying to me!*

When I was in junior high, I didn't wear a bra. Not because I was liberated. Because nothing was there to support. My father endearingly called me, *"Tabla de planchar."* Translation? "Come here, Sweetheart, my little ironing board."

My mother decided I was going to wear a bra anyway, a padded one, of course. Do you know how hard it was to find a size 28 AA?

The next day I put it on and went to class with my notebook clutched tightly against one side of my chest. Finally about fifth or sixth period I forgot that I had on the bra. I was walking down the hall without the notebook in front of me, and everyone kept staring at my chest.

I thought, *Maybe I've grown.* My mom had said if you support yourself, things start to happen. Well, I looked down. When you have nothing to put into rubber and you press something hard against it . . . One side was well formed, the other side caved in.

Fleeing to the bathroom, I took off the bra and stuck it in my purse.

When I got home that day, my mother was so excited. "Well, how did it go?"

I opened my purse, I handed her the bra, and I said, "I'm never going to wear this again."

I saw ugly.

Maybe you have also seen ugly. Maybe you still do.

CRACKED POTS

I began the session on self-esteem in the Woman of God conferences by pointing toward two covered objects that were on a table at the front of the room. "We have been made by the Potter," I said. "He has made a beautiful, beautiful vessel."

Then I uncovered the first object: a lovely urn-shaped vase with brownish gold speckles. I held up the vase for everyone to see as I said, "This is a vessel. It's created almost perfect. Inside there is a lamp," and I lit a candle in the vase.

Nothing happened. Same lovely vase, but no change once the candle was lit.

"Can't see anything out of that vessel, can you?" I said to the women. "But it's a perfect vessel and it will hold water and . . . it can be lit."

Then I uncovered the second vase, a duplicate of the first, but this one was broken and cracked. A couple of the cracks were large and triangle-shaped; others were small slits. "And here's another vessel," I said. "Broken. Cracked . . . Anyone recognize herself?"

Then I pointed to the cracks. "Maybe this is sexual abuse. Maybe that's mental or verbal abuse. Maybe this is an abortion. Maybe that's a divorce. Who knows, but there are huge cracks. So the devil says, 'What is that good for? You can't hold water; it would totally seep out.' You've been rejected so much, you think God doesn't even want you.

"But when you realize that there's nothing in the world that can hurt you anymore and you finally yield to Jesus Christ . . ." I held the sentence there as I asked that the lights be dimmed.

Then I lit the candle within the vase. The light flickered, then took hold and shone brightly from the vase. "What do you see coming from there?" I asked the attendees.

A few answered, "Light."

"Where's it coming from?"

A few others answered, "From within."

"And how?" I asked.

"Cracks!" other ladies responded. "It's coming through the cracks."

"That's what we're going to do. We're going to take a journey to identify the cracks, and we're going to let the light of the Lord Jesus Christ shine through those cracks.

"We're going to identify ourselves in Christ, not in a relationship, not with a man, not with children. Not with anything else but Christ, because when that happens, we become strong in Him. When that happens, we can identify who we are in Christ, and we become closer to the image He created. We can fulfill the destiny He has for us.

"My purpose is to show you the beautiful woman God created," I said. "How many of you see beauty when you look in the mirror?" No one raised her hand, even when I coaxed them by saying, "Now don't be shy. Be honest."

Then I asked, "How many see ugly when you look in the mirror?" Most of the women raised their hands.

"Satan is using this weakness to keep you from God's best for your life," I told the women, "and you, like me, have allowed him to do so."

And so have many of you who are reading this book.

The well-known psychiatrist Carl Jung stated,

> Acceptance of one's self is the essence of the moral problem and the acid test of one's whole outlook on life. That I feed the beggar, that I forgive the insult, that I love an enemy in the name of Christ. All of these are undoubtedly great virtues, but what if I should discover that the least among them all, the poorest of the beggars, the most impudent of all offenders, yes the very fiend himself that these are in me, and I myself stand in need of my own kindness that I myself am the enemy that must be loved? What then?[1]

Are you the enemy who must be loved?

Esther was a Jewish orphan, a virtual nonentity, raised by her cousin, Mordecai. She had no particular promise. Yet the book of Esther records, "Now the king was attracted to Esther more than to any of the other women, and she won his favor and approval more than any of the other virgins. So he set a royal crown on her head and made her queen instead of Vashti" (2:17 NIV).

Why are we reluctant to accept the favor of God in our lives, as Esther did? We have no problem praying for other people's needs and desires but have much difficulty believing God's promises for our own. Could it be that we believe we don't deserve them?

OUR VALUE IN GOD'S EYES

As I mentioned, self-worth was a constant struggle in my life. After I accepted Jesus Christ as my Savior when I was nineteen years old, my opinions about myself seemed to improve. But as the "honeymoon" period with Jesus passed, I found myself dealing with feelings of low self-esteem more than ever. Every time I tried to do something for the Lord, Satan would remind me of my weaknesses. I struggled with my inadequacies. Satan saw to it that I would get confirmation from the people he controlled to bring his message to me.

When I was about to marry my husband, I received an anonymous letter that declared I would ruin my husband's ministry because "as a Mexican-American I was a second-class citizen." The letter went on to say that no one would come to our church because of who I was. I was devastated! I decided I would not marry him for fear my accuser, sent by the Prince of Darkness, was right. I am thankful that John Hagee finally convinced me that the letter was ordained by the force of evil and should be ignored. I listened and married one of the most cherished gifts God has provided for me.

I look at our congregation now and proudly describe it as a "people's church," filled with brown skin, white skin, black skin, and yellow skin—all God's people—and we love every one of them.

One Sunday morning my husband was preaching a sermon on righteousness. As the pastor's wife, I play two roles when sitting in the pew on Sunday morning. The first and most obvious is that of a helpmate to my husband, who is the shepherd of seventeen thousand sheep (and much is required to meet their needs).

Second, I sit as a member of the church, eager to hear the fresh word of God that comes from the pulpit. That particular Sunday I found myself tuning his message out of my mind; righteousness was a topic I could not fully comprehend. Because of the doctrinal teachings in my childhood church, I had difficulty seeing myself as the righteousness of Christ.

While John tried to perceive whether people in the congregation were following him so they could understand God's righteousness, I saw his frustration mount. Suddenly I saw the birth of an idea come to his eyes. He asked for a volunteer to come from the pews and stand in front of the altar facing him. Then he eloquently described a sinner saved by grace coming to the throne of God with a petition. Instantly, he said, Satan comes to the throne and begins to recount all the sinner has done to bring shame and dishonor to the name of Jesus. Satan reminds the sinner of his unworthiness to receive anything good from God because he is so undeserving.

Immediately John had my attention. He was describing me. Even as my husband, he had no idea of all the insecurities I dealt with, almost on a daily basis. No one knew but God.

I have never been the typical pastor's wife. I was saved at nineteen and had absolutely no theological training nor did I have a role model who even remotely resembled that of the wife of a minister. When I married my husband, I felt as if I were pledging a sorority. Sad to report, I soon began to believe that I was not passing the initiation process.

Older women of the church would approach me and ask, "Do you play the organ?"

"No," I would answer sheepishly.

"Oh, then certainly you must play the piano."

"No, I can't play any musical instrument." (My major at the university was biology, and I dared not give them that training as a qualification for the ministry.)

"Then certainly you must have a singing ministry," they replied, with a sense of interrogation that absolutely intimidated me.

"No, I'm afraid I can't carry a tune."

"Oh, I see, well, we can hardly wait to hear you teach the women of the church."

I was trapped, and I knew I was failing the test. I remember thinking, *Maybe I can attend another church. Surely no one will miss me. I certainly can't contribute anything to John's ministry.*

The Great Adversary was having his way with me.

An incident I will never forget occurred when a woman in our church came to me and asked if she could speak to me about something very personal in her life. I thought, *This is it! My gift is counseling!* So I answered with an immediate yes. But my eyes opened wide with astonishment as she began to recount her sexual escapades. My husband was the only man I had ever dated. He was the only man I had ever held hands with or kissed, so this was new territory for me.

I tried hard not to let my inexperience show. If counseling were truly my gift, I assumed the Holy Spirit would equip me with the proper response.

Finally the poor woman ended her litany and awaited my answer. I opened my mouth, expecting to be given the perfect words that would free this lady who made the woman at the well look like a Sunday school teacher. I could not believe what came out of my mouth. With no forethought I said, "You did all of that?" Where were You, Holy Spirit?

Needless to say, it was time to scratch another gift off the list. I was not equipped to do anything that would enhance my husband's ministry.

Could it be possible that John's teaching that Sunday morning on the righteousness of God would free me from such feelings of insecurity? I edged to the end of the pew and listened with every fiber in me.

John then took a white robe and draped it over the shoulders of the person standing in front of him. He went on: "Whenever a person comes to the throne of God, Satan begins to accuse him of all the sin he has ever committed. But the Father responds in His infinite wisdom, 'I see no fault in this man, only the pure white robe of My Son, Jesus. I see the goodness of My Son imparted to those who call themselves My children. I see the righteousness of My Son. I will grant him the desire of his heart.'"

God could not see the ugly me. He could not see the imperfections and the failures. He could see only the perfection of His Son. I was wearing that covering. I had been afraid to come to my Father for fear of rejection.

Finally I understood the righteousness of God. It was nothing I had done or not done. The goodness of the Son of God granted me blessings. I went forward to the altar and wept as I asked my Father to forgive me for all the good things I had refused to receive from Him because I was waiting to deserve them.

OUR PERCEPTION—CORRECTED

Psychologists say that we form opinions of ourselves early in our lives. These opinions are often developed by positive or negative experiences, by others' comments about us, or by our perception of ourselves. Our society has given us role models through fashion models, sports figures, and movie stars. We compare our self-worth to the standards set by a world of which Christians are not a part.

Yet the world cannot even maintain its own standard for beauty. Women spend millions of dollars on plastic surgery worldwide with doctors who will alter their bodies to conform to their standard of beauty. Pictures of the "beautiful people" are touched up by computers to create the image of "perfect persons." The image that the world presents does not exist. It's an illusion. A facade! Yet we try to attain it because we look at ourselves through the eyes of a very secular society, not the eyes of a loving Creator.

We are on the path of self-destruction. Satan is not in our lives just to give us a bad day; the Bible says he has come "to steal, and to kill, and to destroy" (John 10:10). He will steal what God has already provided for us free of charge. He will kill any form of hope that lies within our spirits.

Our insecurities manifest themselves in many forms: inferiority, inadequacy, guilt, rejection, and unworthiness. These feelings become characteristics that do not resemble the God to whom we belong. They breed contempt, jealousy, gossip, and a critical spirit. We walk a subtle, yet destructive, path when we listen to the voice of the father of lies.

The apostle Paul warned against this. He told the early Christians, "I, therefore, the prisoner of the Lord, beseech you to walk worthy of the calling with which you were called, with all lowliness and gentleness, with longsuffering, bearing with one another in love" (Eph. 4:1–2).

Lowliness of mind means that we accept all things that God says about us without argument. The Word of God tells us that as daughters of the King, we are blessed (Deut. 28:1–14), we are strong in the Lord (Eph. 6:10), we are the firstfruits among God's creation (James 1:18), and we are the light of the world (Matt. 5:14). That's what God declares about you and me. Once we believe that, we certainly can accept ourselves as we are.

Gentleness means that we accept all of God's dealings with us without resistance or bitterness. This enables us to accept God and His purpose for our lives.

Long-suffering means that we accept without retaliation all of man's dealings with us. This enables us to accept our enemies and truly forgive them.

And forbearance means that we accept people with all their faults and differences. This enables us to accept our friends and love them as ourselves.

We must watch our thoughts because they will become our words. We must watch our words because they will become our actions. We must watch our actions because they will mold our character. We must learn to see ourselves through the eyes of a loving God. When we see the potential He sees, then our character will mirror His.

When you stop to think that God made the universe and all that is in it, you become overwhelmed by His power. When you realize that He stopped all He was doing to make you, you are overcome by His loving nature. He made your face in His image to carry the Light of the World within your eyes. He made your smile to draw people to Him with the power of your testimony. He created your soft touch to soothe the fevered brow of a loved one. He designed your knees to bend in prayer so you could intercede for the lost, and your lips to part in praise for the Father. You are special in the eyes of God because He fashioned you in strength, in purity, and in love. You are special because you were created as an extension of Him. He recognizes your cry and understands your desires. For man represents God's image, but woman represents His heart.

As I ended this first session of the Woman of God class, I remembered a prayer that releases the Word of God in our lives, which was tucked away in my files. That night we prayed the prayer, which I simply titled "Releasing the Word in Your Life," as a proclamation of God's provision for us. I asked the women to turn to the prayer whenever Satan came to them with words of accusation and discouragement. And I ask the same of you. Read through the prayer, which is found on pages 23–24, and then copy it and place it on a mirror or in your Bible.

The only prerequisite you need to become a woman of God is the desire to live by the Word of God. Our God sees the desires of our hearts long before He hears our voices. He knows that we long to please Him, and that brings Him pleasure. He will give us strength when we are weak. He will give us direction when we become confused. Jesus will smile when He mentions our names before the Father. No matter how hard it is for you to believe, God made no mistakes when He formed you. You are beautiful to Him, and the more you believe this truth, the more beautiful you become.

And He loves you, just as you are. Hear Him speaking directly to you in this letter:

> When I created the heavens and the earth, I spoke them into being. When I created man, I formed him and breathed life into his nostrils. But you, woman, I fashioned after I breathed the breath of life into man because your nostrils were too delicate. I allowed a deep sleep to come over him so I could patiently and perfectly fashion you.
>
> Man was put to sleep so that he could not interfere with the creativity. From one bone I fashioned you. I chose the bone that protects man's life. I

chose the rib, which protects his heart and lungs and supports him, as you are meant to do.

Around this one bone I shaped you. I modeled you. I created you perfectly and beautifully. Your characteristics are as the rib—strong, yet delicate and fragile. You provide protection for the most delicate organ in man: his heart. His heart is the center of his being; his lungs hold the breath of life.

The rib cage will allow itself to be broken before it will allow damage to the heart. Support man as the rib cage supports the body. You were not taken from his feet, to be under him, nor were you taken from his head, to be above him. You were taken from his side, to stand beside him and be held close to his side.

You are My perfect angel. You are My beautiful little girl. You have grown to be a splendid woman of excellence, and My eyes fill when I see the virtue in your heart. Your eyes—don't change them. Your lips—how lovely when they part in prayer. Your nose, so perfect in form. Your hands, so gentle to touch. I've caressed your face in your deepest sleep; I've held your heart close to Mine.

Of all that lives and breathes, you are the most like Me. Adam walked with Me in the cool of the day, and yet he was lonely. He could not see Me or touch Me. He could only feel Me. So everything I wanted Adam to share and experience with Me, I fashioned in you: My holiness, My strength, My purity, My love, My protection and support. You are special because you are an extension of Me. Man represents My image. Woman, My emotions. Together you represent the totality of God.

So, Man, treat Woman well. Love her, respect her, for she is fragile. In hurting her, you hurt Me. What you do to her, you do to Me. In crushing her, you damage your own heart, the heart of your Father and the heart of her Father.

Woman, support Man. In humility, show him the power of emotion I have given you. In gentle quietness, show your strength. In love, show him that you are the rib that protects his inner self.

⌒ Releasing the Word in Your Life ⌒

Father, in the name of Jesus, I repent of my ignorance of the Word of God. I ask You to forgive me of the foolish things I have prayed.

In Jesus' name I bind every word that has released Satan or drawn his weapons toward me. I bind every hindering force to which I have ever given strength by the words of my mouth. I break the power of those spiritual forces, in the name of Jesus.

Father, in the name of Your Son, I ask You to guide me in wisdom and understanding through scriptural methods to set in motion all that is good, pure, perfect, lovely, and of good report.

I make a covenant with You to pray accurately. I will watch my words. I will speak only what glorifies God. I will let no corrupt communication proceed out of my mouth, but what is good to edify and minister grace through me to the hearer. I will not grieve the Holy Spirit of God whereby I am sealed to the day of redemption, but I will give glory and honor and praise to the Lord Jesus Christ for all that shall be done.

I thank You, Father, that I am the body of Christ. The enemy has no power over me. I proclaim all that is good, all that is blessed of God, all that is in the perfect will of God, all that God has designed for me shall come to me, in Jesus' name.

All of the evil and the bad reports, all that the enemy has designed to deceive me, to lead me astray, to destroy me, my home, my marriage, my children, or my finances shall be stopped with the name of Jesus and the words of my mouth.

I am blessed in the city and blessed in the field. I am blessed in the baskets and blessed in the store. I am blessed coming in; I am blessed going out. God will provide houses I did not build, wells I did not dig, and vineyards I did not plant. I am the head and not the tail; I am above and not beneath. I am blessed of almighty God, strengthened with all might according to His glorious power. The Greater One is in me; He will lift me up above my enemies. The Spirit of truth is in me, He gives me divine wisdom, divine direction, divine understanding of every situation and every circumstance in life. I have the wisdom of God.

God's hand is upon me. He will increase my boundaries. He will keep me from evil and keep me from causing others pain.

I thank You, Father, that I am led by the Spirit of God. I have the mind of Christ, and the wisdom of God is within me. In Jesus' name. Amen.

♊ ACTION POINTS: MY VALUE IN GOD'S EYES

1. Recite again the "Releasing the Word in Your Life" prayer on pages 23–24 presented in this chapter. It is imperative that you keep the Word in your heart, mind, and soul in order to win the battle that Satan has designed for you.

> Your word I have hidden in my heart,
> That I might not sin against You.
> Blessed are You, O LORD!
> Teach me Your statutes.
> With my lips I have declared
> All the judgments of Your mouth. (Ps. 119:11–13)

2. List all the traits you feel are ugly about yourself. It is important to disarm Satan, the Accuser, and identify the self-esteem problems facing you on a daily basis.

Now remind yourself of this passage of Scripture, which shows the ultimate destiny of Satan, the Liar who uses these thoughts to interfere with all God has for you:

> Then I heard a loud voice saying in heaven, "Now salvation, and strength, and the kingdom of our God, and the power of His Christ have come, for the accuser of our brethren, who accused them before our God day and night, has been cast down." (Rev. 12:10)

3. List all the things you believe are beautiful about yourself. This is one of the hardest lists you will make, for many of us are reluctant to think that we are beautiful in any way. We need to confess with our mouths the attributes that God has given us to bless the people around us and to accomplish His purpose in our lives.

_____

_____

_____

_____

Now reaffirm these gifts by seeing yourself as God sees you:

> He has made everything beautiful in its time. Also He has put eternity in their hearts, except that no one can find out the work that God does from beginning to end. I know that nothing is better for them than to rejoice, and to do good in their lives. (Eccl. 3:11–12)

Then reread the "letter from God" on pages 21–22. This is another example of how God sees you.

Pray the following prayer:

> *Father, I praise You in the name of Your Son, Jesus Christ. I ask that You reveal to me everything that has brought me harm so that I may put it under the blood of Your Son. Show me, Father, how to see myself through Your eyes. I pledge only to speak those things about myself that would bring honor to Your creation. I acknowledge that I was fearfully and wonderfully made in Your image. Nothing that has happened in my past, nothing that has been said of me to cause me pain, will hinder my life again. I am beautiful. I am the King's daughter. Amen.*

4. Read chapter 1 in the book of Esther.

chapter three

I Am Not Ashamed of the Gospel

hat do you do when you find a new product that really does clean the soap scum off your shower door? Do you keep it to yourself, or do you call your mother and yell with the satisfaction of a gold miner, "Eureka! I've found it"?

What happens when you find a miracle cream that actually reduces wrinkles and does not just puff up your eyes until you can't see your lashes anymore? Do you keep this treasure to yourself, or do you call your best friend, who is aging with you, to share this incredible find?

If you see a fabulous movie that made you feel like a million bucks, don't you just tell everyone you know to go and see it?

In keeping with a more spiritual theme, what happens when you read a book by a renowned Bible scholar that has changed your attitude on life? Do you hide it under your pillow, or do you run to your Bible study with several copies in hand and give them to your friends?

You, like the rest of us, probably do all of the above. So why is it, then, when we accept Christ as our Savior, that we have such a difficult time witnessing to others about the saving power of our God? Do we not feel that He is worth sharing with others? Do we feel that He is a God who can be put into a file labeled "Sunday Only"? Are we intimidated about speaking of God in public? Are we afraid of looking foolish and being rejected by those to whom we witness?

In my life, the latter applied more than all other reasons. As Jesus' disciples, we represent Him the very instant we accept Him as our Savior, yet we don't take the opportunity to share our testimony when the moment lends itself. The apostle Paul described a life that had truly been changed by Christ:

> If indeed you have heard Him and have been taught by Him, as the truth is in Jesus: that you put off, concerning your former conduct, the old man which grows corrupt according to the deceitful lusts, and be renewed in the spirit of your mind, and that you put on the new man which was created according to God, in righteousness and true holiness. Therefore, putting away lying, each one speak truth with his neighbor, for we are members of one another. "Be angry, and do not sin": do not let the sun go down on your wrath, nor give place to the devil. (Eph. 4:21–27)

Yet we do not always reflect this image. Because of our fleshly nature, we are people pleasers. We want people to like us, and we want people to want to be around us. Sooner or later, the Lord will give you a choice. Will you be a people pleaser or a Father pleaser?

Several years ago I found myself in a very safe comfort zone in my journey with the Lord. I was content. I had been married for fifteen years, and the women of the church who wanted me to be a concert pianist or a singer of arias had long left. The people in our church knew I adored my husband and cherished my children. I'd had most of them to my home for dinner, rejoiced with them at baby dedications and weddings, or wept with them as they buried their loved ones. None questioned my love for them. I felt that I belonged. Wouldn't you know that God would choose that time to take me to another level, a level I did not want to acheive?

One beautiful spring morning I was in Saint Simons Island, Georgia, with my husband. I had accompanied him to a speaking engagement at the church of some of our dear friends, and we were staying in a lovely cottage on the Atlantic Ocean. Our time there was close to heaven, so close that God decided to communicate with me in a very direct way.

I was alone as my husband left to minister to someone in the church, and I was having an all-too-familiar conversation with Jesus. I could sense He wanted me to do more in the way of speaking in our church, but I was not cooperating.

In fact, I was listing all the reasons why I could not accomplish the task when I heard a knock at the door. It was the pastor's son. He was there to bid us good-bye as well as thank my husband for a prayer of blessing they had shared together. I explained to him that my husband was not available. Turning to leave, he said something to me that caused me to believe that God does not always play fair when dealing with His children.

"Mrs. Hagee, did you know that John Wesley lived in this area?"

"No, I didn't," I answered politely, wondering why he had returned to give me this bit of church history.

"Yes, ma'am. He was a great evangelist, and he wanted everyone to know about Jesus Christ."

I wondered, *Dear Lord, have You been talking to this poor young man about my stubbornness?*

The young man, oblivious to my stunned expression, went on. "He used to have a favorite saying that went something like this: 'I fuel myself with the enthusiasm of the Word every day and people come from far and near just to watch me burn.' I just thought you might want to know that . . . Have a safe flight home." With that, he turned and walked away.

I closed the door and began to weep. What reason could I give the Lord for not sharing with others what He had done in my life? That I wasn't trained in doctrinal exegesis? That excuse didn't seem to be enough.

The real reason was that I was afraid to embarrass God. The thought of making a mistake in expounding His Word was so overwhelming that I had not done what I could. How could He forgive me?

He did. He always does. I came to Him as David did, in the spirit of repentance. He knew my heart and my desire to please Him. He knew I now wanted to be a Father pleaser. I could feel His strong arms around me, letting me know that He would help me every step of the way.

I was exhausted! (You usually are when you wrestle with God.)

Yet at the same time I had a renewed spirit because I knew He and I were going places. Places I had never been before. Places He had chosen and paths that only He knew. All I had to do was to follow the Shepherd who had promised to never leave me or forsake me—even unto the end of the earth.

GOD'S SAVING GRACE

Before you can testify of God's salvation, you must know that you are saved and that your name is written in the Lamb's Book of Life. I can ask an individual the question, "Are you saved?" and nine times out of ten she will answer yes. Yet when I ask the same person, "Have you prayed the sinner's prayer? Are you absolutely certain that your name is written in the Lamb's Book of Life?" the answer is rarely in the affirmative.

Why is that? It's simply that she has never received Jesus Christ into her heart. Salvation is not a denominational doctrine or a family inheritance. It is a *personal* experience.

I give everyone in my class the opportunity to pray the sinner's prayer if she has any doubt about her salvation, and I give you, the reader, the same opportunity.

First, you must repent of your sin! Consider your life and anything in it that would grieve God. List those things.

_____

_____

_____

_____

_____

Now read the following Bible verses as you consider how God feels about those sins:

> When he saw many of the Pharisees and Sadducees coming to his baptism, he said to them, "Brood of vipers! Who warned you to flee from the wrath to come? Therefore bear fruits worthy of repentance, and do not think to say to yourselves, 'We have Abraham as our father.' For I say to you that God is able to raise up children to Abraham from these stones. And even now the ax is laid to the root of the trees. Therefore every tree which does not bear good fruit is cut down and thrown into the fire." (Matt. 3:7–10)

> Repent therefore and be converted, that your sins may be blotted out, so that times of refreshing may come from the presence of the Lord. (Acts 3:19)

Do you feel convicted to turn away from sin? If you do, you are ready to take the second step, which is to believe that Jesus Christ died for your sin. He has paid the price for those moments when you failed. If you ask for forgiveness, He will freely give it. The Bible makes that very clear:

> Much more then, having now been justified by His blood, we shall be saved from wrath through Him. For if when we were enemies we were reconciled to God through the death of His Son, much more, having been reconciled, we shall be saved by His life. (Rom. 5:9–10)

Hand those sins over to Him, and feel His love and forgiveness in your heart. Then you must ask Him to come into your life. He is the door to the Father. Jesus Himself said, "I am the door. If anyone enters by Me, he will be saved, and will go in and out and find pasture" (John 10:9). And the apostle John later told the early Christians, "Whoever denies the Son does not have the Father either; he who acknowledges the Son has the Father also" (1 John 2:23).

Take a moment to ask the Lord Jesus to be a part of each day of your life. At a time when you are ready, recite the following prayer of salvation:

> *Lord, I ask that You forgive me of all my sins, both known and unknown. I ask that You accept me as Your own and write my name in the Lamb's Book of Life. From this day forward I will read Your Word and obey it. Because of the blood of the Cross, I am now forgiven. My sins are buried in the sea of forgetfulness, never to be remembered against me anymore. I am now a child of God, and Jesus Christ is the Lord of my life. Amen.*

Now your name is written in the Lamb's Book of Life. No one can blot it out. You are His. You will spend eternity with the Father in heaven.

Once you have been redeemed you have the obligation to redeem others with your testimony, a testimony you are not afraid to give about a God of whom you are not ashamed. Before Jesus left this earth, He commanded His disciples:

"Go therefore and make disciples of all the nations, baptizing them in the name of the Father and of the Son and of the Holy Spirit, teaching them to observe all things that I have commanded you; and lo, I am with you always, even to the end of the age." Amen. (Matt. 28:19–20)

Jesus meant this commandment for all those who follow Him, then and now. It is important that you know your responsibility to be obedient and give your testimony with the purpose of bringing others to the saving knowledge of Jesus Christ. However, it is not your responsibility if the person hears your testimony and then refuses to receive the Lord Jesus as Savior. This person has chosen to reject Christ. God has given human beings that right. Since the Garden, women have been making choices for their good or for their detriment. Not all will choose Christ, but you may be surprised how many will do so.

A SURPRISING MOMENT

About five years ago God had another significant lesson for me. My husband was ministering in Bogotá, Colombia. The church services were held in an arena because the membership exceeded 125,000! When I saw those thousands of people worshiping God with such total abandonment, I was ashamed of the lukewarm manner in which American churches worshiped. The people didn't care who saw them! They didn't care who stood next to them! They were showing their heavenly Father their absolute love and adoration for Him in the purity of their praise.

At that instant I knew God was revealing something to me about myself. I had been so concerned with getting people's approval that I had failed to fully express the love I felt for Christ for fear that I would appear foolish. I was convicted for the praise and adoration I had withheld from my Father.

When we returned to San Antonio, my husband asked the leaders of our church, who had accompanied us to Bogotá, to share their experience with the congregation. I did something I had never done before. I asked my husband if I could sit on the platform and participate in the service.

"What do you want to say?" he asked me.

"I don't know. I really don't know!" I replied.

In blind faith he let me sit on the platform, not really knowing what I wanted. He isn't inclined to do that often because he is protective of what is said or done from his pulpit. Looking back, I now understand how sensitive my husband was to the Holy Spirit. He could sense God was dealing with me.

Twelve men were sitting on the platform with us. *What in the world am I doing here?* God had yet to tell me. *Maybe I can slip off the platform, and no one will notice,* I thought. No such luck. It was almost my time to speak. I tried to come up with some profound statement that would cause the congregation to be deeply moved. There was nothing. Absolute zero!

My heart was pounding as two thousand people looked my way. I thought the Lord had deserted me. As if in another body, I took the microphone and walked to the pulpit.

Suddenly the Lord spoke, but I soon realized I did not want to hear what He had to say. *I want you to shout "Hallelujah!" at the top of your voice* was the clear instruction.

Surely this was not the voice of the Lord. Why would He want me to look like a fool in front of my church? I looked back to my husband. Perhaps he would rescue me. Wrong! He motioned for me to say something.

I looked forward and said, "The Lord has told me to do this." I would put the full responsibility on Him for my actions. I took a deep breath and shouted with a thundering voice, "Hallelujah!"

The congregation was stunned. I was stunned. I looked back at my husband, and he was totally stunned. God gave me more words to say, which tumbled out of my mouth like living water. I looked back at the shocked congregation and spoke out of my heart.

"I have been afraid that if I fully expressed my love for Christ, I would make a fool of myself, and you would not approve of me. I was wrong. I ask the Lord to forgive me, and I ask you to forgive me. I need to obey the Lord in all He has for me to do. If I look foolish, then so be it. I am willing to be a fool for Christ's sake."

With that, I sat down.

The congregation stood and applauded, not so much for what I had said but for what I had done. I had obeyed Him. Jesus and I were on another journey. I was weak with emotion but confident that I had taken the next step on a path of spiritual growth.

That week I led six people to the saving knowledge of Jesus Christ. I spoke of the love of God to strangers in the hospital, on airplanes, and any place I found the slightest opportunity. As easily as I shared the gospel, just as easily they prayed the sinner's prayer. Isn't it just like God to kiss His child on the forehead with a confirmation that she is on the right path?

Our God is a good God. He wants us to prosper in all things. I call Him the God of two choices. He sets before us life and death and tells us to choose life. He sets before us blessings and curses and tells us to choose blessings. He wants the best for us. We receive His best when we are obedient. I ask you to obey His desire to make you a fisher of lost souls. Once you do, your life will take on a worth that is far greater than rubies. You will be a valued partner with Christ as together you bring the lost to the throne of a loving God. Choose to be a Father pleaser.

I pray for a passion to rise up in you that will draw the lost to you and give you the opportunity to make them jealous for what you have in Him. I pray that you fuel yourself daily with the enthusiasm of the Word of God so people will come from far and near just to watch you burn.

∽ ACTION POINTS: I AM NOT ASHAMED OF THE GOSPEL

This week you will write your testimony, which is the story of God's work in your life. You will be amazed at what the Holy Spirit will bring to your mind as you think of all the things God has done for you. Use the following steps to create a testimony that will be easy to give to others. Remember it need not be long; it may be short and to the point.

1. My life before Christ.
Before you begin, let me give you my testimony as an example:

> I was born into a Mexican-Catholic family. We attended mass regularly and performed all the required sacraments of the church. I was a "good girl" by the church's standards. My father ran a very strict home, and I was the oldest of

three girls and one baby brother. There was no opportunity to misbehave. I remember being so absolutely boring that I actually made up sins at confession to be able to qualify for Communion.

As I grew older, I never asked many questions about God. As far as I was concerned, I was saved, I was a good person, and I had nothing to worry about. When I was nineteen years old, I was asked a question that would change my life for eternity: "Have you ever prayed the sinner's prayer?"

It was a question I had never heard before. Suddenly a battle ensued in my mind. A voice was saying to me, *Don't pray this silly little prayer. You're already saved. You're only wasting your time.*

In the next instant I heard the opposite instruction: *Pray the prayer, Diana. You have nothing to lose. Once you pray this simple prayer you will never be the same.*

I decided to pray the sinner's prayer. Immediately an explosion occurred within me. I knew that I had been lost and without repentance. I had equated a good life with salvation. I had been wrong. God and His infinite grace sent someone to lead me through the sinner's prayer and to His Son's cross. From that day until now I have never been the same.

Now write your own testimony of your life before Christ.

_____

_____

_____

_____

_____

_____

_____

2. My life after Christ.

Again let me give you my testimony before you begin:

After my salvation, my outward life did not change significantly, but my attitude about myself changed dramatically. I had always had a poor opinion of myself. I was shy and extremely quiet in public for fear I would be noticed and rejected. After receiving Christ, I knew I was important to Him, so important that He chose to die on the cross for me. I began a journey that would take me to places I had never been before, a journey that would create in me a self-worth that came from the throne of a loving God.

One very important change in my life was the way I spoke to God. No longer was I reciting memorized phrases; I was actually talking with God. Through His Son, I had direct access to the throne. No matter what concerned me, He knew instantly. I was no longer afraid to ask Him to provide for my needs. He was no longer a distant God. He was the God of now. He was there for me in a way I never knew possible.

Now write your testimony of your life after Christ.

_____

_____

_____

_____

_____

_____

_____

_____

End your testimony with two questions: "Has this ever happened to you?" and "Have you ever prayed the sinner's prayer?"

3. Think of someone whom you would like to lead to Christ. Practice leading that person in the prayer described in this chapter. Trust me, you will need to

know it because once you have yielded to Christ, He will draw the lost to you. A woman of God is never ashamed of the gospel; a King's daughter is always ready to lead the lost to Christ.

Pray this prayer:

> *Lord, give me the confidence to share my testimony with others. Allow me to show the love You have unconditionally shown me. Give me the passion that will make the lost jealous for what I have in You. Begin with my family, Lord. Allow Your light to shine through all the broken places in my life. Use my testimony to lead others into everlasting life. Amen.*

4. Read chapter 2 in the book of Esther.

chapter four

The Holy Spirit and Me

Ephesians 5:18 instructs us to be "filled with the Spirit." There has always been a tremendous amount of controversy about when, how, and why this phenomenon occurs. I believe as long as the human race exists, there will always be conflict surrounding this subject. I have a simple solution. Go to the Word of God and ask the Father to reveal His Holy Spirit to you in a very intimate and personal way. The question you need to ask yourself in the privacy of your prayer closet is this: *Do I have all of God I want?*

My husband asked an Orthodox rabbi in our city a common, yet complex, question: "What do *you* believe about the Word of God?" His answer was simple but profound.

He began to speak out of his heart and out of something that is a rare gift— personal experience: "The Word of God is the protoplasm of all things living. It is the basis of all creation. The Word was spoken and life was.

"There is also a dynamic to the Word. It knows what you need at any given time. In Hebrew writing, the letters leap upward like cloven tongues of fire. This represents the dynamics of the Word. It is never stagnant. That is why you can read something one day and it means one thing to you, and you read the same passage of Scripture the next day and it means something totally different. It meets the needs of the individual at any given time. The Word has power. The Word has discernment. The Word of God is alive."

This description of God's Word has never left my heart. If God has all the power in heaven and on earth, then His Word, through the Holy Spirit, can direct me in all paths and provide all things for me.

I am a very practical person. I want to know what God wants me to know. I want to have what He wants me to have. I want to do what He wants me to do. If there is more of Him, then I want it. This one thing I know: the more I know Him, the more I can recognize His voice and do His will.

Derek Prince teaches that salvation is merely the foundation of the Christian walk. When someone builds a home, he prepares the ground for the foundation. Then he lays the foundation. But the builder does not stop there. Before he moves into his home, he adds the walls, the ceilings, and the roof. All are vital, individual parts of a home, yet they work together to make the home functional. Salvation is your foundation. The infilling of the Holy Spirit and the fruit of the Spirit build your spiritual house. You live in this house; all of these parts make your Christian walk functional.

Derek Prince has an excellent teaching on the Holy Spirit in his book *The Spirit-Filled Believer's Handbook*.[1] I will share some of his thoughts here to help equip you in your journey to becoming a woman of God.

The first question we will ask is this: Is there a difference between the primary results of salvation and the primary results of the baptism of the Holy Spirit? Let's compare these experiences to see if this is so.

THE RESULT OF SALVATION: AUTHORITY

The first result we see when we are born again is *authority*. John spoke of this authority in his gospel:

> But as many as received Him, to them He gave the right to become the chil-
> dren of God, to those who believe in His name: who were born, not of blood,
> nor of the will of the flesh, nor of the will of man, but of God. (John 1:12–13)

When we accept Christ as our Savior, we accept in Christ the nature of God Himself. This miracle is known as a new birth or being born again. In turn, the believer receives the authority of Christ. You are a daughter of the King; therefore, you have the authority of the King. You have the authority over sin and temptation. You are an overcomer. This is your destiny.

However, authority does not always give the believer the ability to do *all* things. That is accomplished with power.

THE RESULT OF THE BAPTISM OF THE HOLY SPIRIT: POWER

From the moment of Christ's resurrection the first disciples were overcomers. They possessed authority over sin and the temptations of everyday life. Yet few changes occurred in the lives of the people in Jerusalem after the resurrection of Christ.

That was changed instantly after the descent of the Holy Spirit on the day of pentecost. Within several hours from the moment the disciples were baptized with the Holy Spirit of God, more than three thousand unbelievers were converted and baptized.

Why was there such a change? Why did the disciples make such a dramatic impact on the people who heard their testimony? *Power was added to authority.* Paul spoke of this power in 1 Corinthians 4:20: "The kingdom of God is not in word but in power." This power made the authority the apostles possessed effective. This power made a forceful and explosive impact on the unbelievers around them.

Listen to Luke's description of this scene in the book of Acts:

> When they had prayed, the place where they were assembled together was shaken; and they were all filled with the Holy Spirit, and they spoke the word of God with boldness. (4:31)

> With great power the apostles gave witness to the resurrection of the Lord Jesus. (4:33)

We, as Christians, can easily see the characteristic of authority within our lives once we have been born again. We turn from our sinful nature, we attend church, and we avoid the temptations of this life. Yet we create no impact on the lives of others. We lack the power.

And one benefit of the baptism of the Holy Spirit is added power to witness to others.

1. THE POWER TO BE AN EFFECTIVE WITNESS

Each of us inherits this power through the baptism of the Holy Spirit. Therefore, one major difference between salvation and the infilling of the Spirit is power. If God knew we needed His authority when we accepted His Son to be overcomers, He also knew we needed additional strength to be effective witnesses.

One purpose for the baptism of the Holy Spirit is to be an effective witness for Christ. Another purpose concerns the prayer life of the believer.

2. THE POWER TO PRAY ACCORDING TO GOD'S WILL

Paul told the Roman Christians:

> Likewise the Spirit also helps in our weaknesses. For we do not know what we should pray for as we ought, but the Spirit Himself makes intercession for us with groanings which cannot be uttered. Now He who searches the hearts knows what the mind of the Spirit is, because He makes intercession for the saints according to the will of God. (Rom. 8:26–27)

For me, this is an integral part of my Christian walk. Many times I have come to crossroads where I did not know how to pray. Then my only direction has been the third person of the Trinity, the Holy Spirit. He lives inside me. I can pray only to a certain degree with my knowledge and ability; the supernatural moves me beyond this point. When I pray on a level empowered by the Holy Spirit, I can bypass my emotions, my opinions, and my desires to pray with discernment. Paul spoke of supernatural prayer several times in Scripture:

> Rejoicing in hope, patient in tribulation, continuing steadfastly in prayer. (Rom. 12:12)

> But you, beloved, building yourselves up on your most holy faith, praying in the Holy Spirit. (Jude 1:20)

> Praying always with all prayer and supplication in the Spirit. (Eph. 6:18)

> Pray without ceasing . . . Do not quench the Spirit. (1 Thess. 5:17, 19)

It is not possible for me to pray always or to pray without ceasing in my own strength, yet with the Spirit of God living inside me, I can do *all* things.

I often laugh when I tell the story of a church member who saw me in the grocery store one afternoon. As she approached me to say hello, she noticed that I was talking to myself. I was in such fervor, she felt uncomfortable about speaking to me, so she continued shopping. Later, in a Bible study, I explained to the women that I often pray in the Spirit when I do everyday chores, such as cleaning house or shopping for groceries, much to my friend's relief. She confessed to me that she thought I had a "little problem" with talking to myself in public places. I pray whenever I can, wherever I can, and I feel the peace of God within my heart when I do.

Both my husband and Brother Prince assert that the indwelling of the Holy Spirit in the believer is similar to the fire that was supernaturally kindled upon the altar of the tabernacle in the Old Testament. The book of Leviticus, a handbook for the priests and Levites that outlines their duties in worship, states, "The fire shall ever be burning upon the altar; it shall never go out" (6:13 KJV).

As that fire was kindled on the altar, so it has been kindled in our spirits. If we, as believers, do not quench the fire by our careless works, then it will burn within the temples of our bodies in the form of prayer and worship with such intensity that it will never go out.

My mother-in-law tells a story of a particular night when my husband was in Bible college. Shortly after he began his education there, he started to minister. Every Friday, after a week of classes and a full-time job, he would get in his car and travel to a nearby city and preach for a weekend revival. As always, his mother would pray for her four sons before she went to bed. This Sunday night was no different.

After being asleep for a long while, she was awakened with John's name on her mind. She sensed he was in grave danger. She began to pray in the Spirit of God and, after several minutes, could feel the urgency that had awakened her dissipate, so she went back to sleep. The following morning, she called my husband and asked him what he had done the previous night.

"I was returning to school from a revival," he stated quietly, not wanting to alarm her with all the facts.

"No, what were you doing at 2:30 in the morning?" she asked, searching for a more accurate account.

My husband knew it was time to "'fess up." As long as he could remember his mother had had a "sixth sense" about her. That "sense" was the Spirit of the living God within her.

"I was traveling back to school from preaching a revival. I was so tired, I fell asleep at the wheel. Suddenly I was awakened and was face-to-face with an eighteen-wheeler. While I was asleep I had wandered into the oncoming lane. Without thinking I turned my wheel and avoided the truck. I landed in a ditch. My car had some minor damage, but we are both fine."

"The Holy Spirit woke me up and let me know you were in trouble," Mom Hagee replied in a matter-of-fact tone. "I prayed until He released me and I had peace."

My mother-in-law came to know the Holy Spirit when she was a young child. (I will tell you her unique story later in the book.) She realizes that He operates in her life every hour, and she understands how to respond to His voice.

Since we have become parents, my husband and I have prayed that anything our five children do that would offend the Holy Spirit be revealed to us. The power of the Holy Spirit has done exactly that. You can imagine with five kids that we are always hearing something from the Holy Spirit. I dare not give you every account for fear my children would disown me, but it has helped us raise them in the "fear and the admonition of the Lord." Our son Chris could write a whole book on this subject. He is one of our most dynamic children, and his main question to us throughout his "exciting formative years" was, "Who told you?" He was so tired of hearing our answer—"The Holy Spirit did"—that he just stopped asking.

Brother Prince uses a beautiful example from the Song of Solomon to describe what happens when we, as mortals, come to the end of our natural ability and understanding and the Holy Spirit takes over our minds to conduct His own worship and prayer through us. He cites the verse, "I sleep, but my heart is awake" (5:2).

We all know that the bride must sleep to survive. Yet no matter how exhausted she may be, no matter how deeply she sleeps, within her innermost being is the

Holy Spirit Himself, who never slumbers or sleeps. Throughout the day and night, the passion of His fire burns upon the altar of her soul. It is a fire of worship and prayer. This prayer life is not possible without the supernatural indwelling of the Holy Spirit.

First, the infilling of the Holy Spirit gives us added power to be effective witnesses. Second, the Holy Spirit gives us the power to pray according to the will of God. And third, the Holy Spirit becomes our Guide and Teacher when we read the Word of God.

3. THE POWER TO UNDERSTAND GOD'S WORD

Jesus promised His disciples that after the Holy Spirit of God came to dwell in them, He would be their personal Teacher: "The Helper, the Holy Spirit, whom the Father will send in My name, He will teach you all things, and bring to your remembrance all things that I said to you" (John 14:26). The Holy Spirit would enable them to remember Jesus' teachings and correctly understand them.

This same benefit is afforded to all His children. His Word is powerful and sharper than any two-edged sword. It is the power that saves the lost and heals the sick. The Word parted the seas and turned water into wine. It is a miracle-working Word, and I want to understand it. I can't through my own power, but I can through the discernment of the Holy Spirit who dwells within me.

Another purpose of the infilling of the Holy Spirit in our lives is the pouring out of God's love in the believer's heart.

4. THE POWER TO EXPERIENCE THE POURING OUT OF GOD'S LOVE

Paul spoke of God's love for us when he said, "The love of God has been poured out in our hearts by the Holy Spirit who was given to us" (Rom. 5:5). The Word of God is not referring to human love for another person or our love for God; instead it is speaking of the love of God for His own.

The human race has experienced many forms of love. The so-called love of sexual passion that was displayed by David and Bathsheba. The love of a husband for a wife, like that of Boaz for Ruth. The love of parents for their children, such as Abraham for Isaac, and children's love for their parents, witnessed through

Shem and Japheth for their father, Noah. Outside family ties is the love of one friend for another, the love of David and Jonathan.

There are many forms and descriptions of love within the languages of the world, yet only one form describes the love that God, the Father, has for His children. This divine form of love is defined by the Greek word *agape.*

Agape love denotes the three kinds of love referred to in Scripture. First, the love that the Godhead—the Father, Son, and Holy Spirit—have for one another. Second, the love that God has for His children, which led Him to give His only Son to die on the cross so that you and I would be free from the bonds of sin and receive everlasting life. And third, the love that God imparts through His Holy Spirit to the hearts of His children. The apostle John taught the early Christians: "Beloved, let us love one another, for love is of God; and everyone who loves is born of God and knows God. He who does not love does not know God, for God is love" (1 John 4:7–8).

John was referring to agape love, the love imparted to a believer at the time of her new birth in Christ. If a person has not known or shown this kind of love, then she has never known the Source of this love. It can be said that the measure with which you come to know God is the same measure of love that will manifest within you, and in turn that you will manifest to others.

Peter added to the description of this incredible form of agape love in the Scriptures:

> Since you have purified your souls in obeying the truth through the Spirit
> in sincere love of the brethren, love one another fervently with a pure heart,
> having been born again, not of corruptible seed but incorruptible, through
> the word of God which lives and abides forever. (1 Peter 1:22–23)

In his book Brother Prince mentions that an initial measure—not the full measure—of divine love is imparted at the time of our salvation. That occurs with the infilling of the Holy Spirit within our hearts. He quotes Paul in Romans: "Now hope does not disappoint, because the love of God has been poured out in our hearts by the Holy Spirit who was given to us" (5:5).

In this very powerful verse Paul was stating that the love that has been poured into our hearts by the Holy Spirit is the maximum amount the Father can give His children. It's like standing in front of the Mississippi River and wondering when you will run out of water. It isn't possible. Spirit-baptized believers have the river of Living Water as an infinite source of divine grace and love, which will always be there to provide any need they have.

Divine love does not have a price. Divine love does not demand something in return. Divine love does not seek the worthy. Divine love is unconditional. This is the kind of love I want within me. It is partially imparted with the foundation of salvation. However, we have all experienced the additional thirst that tells us we need something more.

If I am His vessel, then I want to be filled with His presence, His power, and His Spirit. I want no corrupt thing to interfere with my walk with Jesus Christ. When I am faced with witnessing to unbelievers, I want the passion of the Holy Spirit to lead me into directing them to the Cross.

When my children are in trouble, I want to be able to get on my knees and call on the name of Jesus and have Him respond through the Holy Spirit to give me perfect direction in wisdom and prayer for their lives. When I need to make decisions in my life of which God the Father will approve, I want the Holy Spirit to reveal the meaning of the Word to me in a way that will cause me to walk in the path God has chosen for me. And I want the love of God in my heart, the kind of love that will draw men to the throne of the living God.

Let me end by answering the question, How much of God do I want?

I want as much of God as I can get!

℮ ACTION POINTS: THE HOLY SPIRIT AND ME

1. Reread "Releasing the Word in Your Life" on pages 23–24. Pray that prayer each day this week.

2. Look up the following verses and realize that these promises are available to you as a daughter of the King.

You are . . .

- the temple of the Holy Spirit (1 Cor. 6:19).
- sealed with the "Holy Spirit of promise" (Eph. 1:13).
- translated into God's kingdom (Col. 1:13).
- holy and without blame before God (Eph. 1:4; 1 Peter 1:16).
- a joint heir with Jesus (Rom. 8:17).

Write out the verse that means the most to you.

_____

_____

3. And as a daughter of the King, you are also . . .

- a fellow citizen with the saints (Eph. 2:19).
- the apple of your Father's eye (Deut. 32:10; Ps. 17:8).
- beloved of God (Rom. 1:7; Col. 3:12; 1 Thess. 1:4).
- blessed (Deut. 28:1–14; Gal. 3:9).
- qualified to share in Jesus' inheritance (Col. 1:12).

Read through these verses, and then write out the verse that means the most to you.

_____

_____

4. Read chapter 3 in the book of Esther. Then end with this prayer:

Father, I ask that You reveal Yourself to me in a way I have never known before. If there is something You have for me that I have not experienced, then show me now. I ask You to pour Your Holy Spirit into my heart. With this infilling, I ask You to impart in me the passion to witness as Your disciples did on the day of pentecost. I ask that You help me with my prayer life, lifting me to levels far beyond my natural strength and understanding. When I pray, I want the authority and the power of the living God. Guide me, through Your Holy Spirit, in the path You would have me go. Father, I ask that You pour into my heart a love so rich that it can be described only as agape love. A love that is so pure that its only source can be the throne of the living God. Lord, if there is more of You, then I want to have it. Amen.

chapter five

Dreams with a Happy Ending: Setting Goals

My paternal grandmother came to the United States when she was fifteen, but she never became an American citizen and never learned to speak English. In San Antonio that was very easy to do in the fifties—and in some parts of town it's still easy to do, believe it or not.

In the summer of 1957, when I was five and a half, my mom and dad and my younger sister, Rosie, and I moved to California where my dad had found a job. What an adjustment! Our family had been living with my grandmother for most of my life, and we didn't speak English at home, except an occasional "Good-bye" or "Hello."

That fall I entered first grade, and for the first time I encountered people who spoke only English. At the time when I should have been learning to read and write, I lost the ability to communicate. Consequently I was very shy and *very* silent.

My mom and dad realized that they had created a huge injustice by not having us speak English. So when I was a first grader, my parents set a goal: learn English quickly.

A rule was established in our home: no Spanish spoken here.

And that first goal had a reward: once I broke the language barrier, school was easy for me. If my parents hadn't set that goal, I'm not sure how I would have survived. I eventually became the first female on either side of my family to graduate from college.

Not all of us have an early experience like this, which teaches the rewards of goal setting. Unfortunately too many of us have no hope for the future, and no one can set goals without dreams. Yet the Word of God states, "For I know the thoughts that I think toward you, says the LORD, thoughts of peace and not of evil, to give you a future and a hope" (Jer. 29:11).

Even Christians who know this promise in God's Word still don't believe that a positive future belongs to them. They tend to allow the "fiery darts of the wicked one" to stifle their dreams. The analogy for this in Scripture comes from Roman warfare. In ancient wars, soldiers dipped arrows in poison. When a soldier was wounded, the injury from the arrow would not kill him. Instead he would return to camp where the wound would soon become infected by the poison. Then he would die. So goes the attack of Satan. When the "wicked one" attacks us with his darts, the poison of doubt, insecurity, fear, and worry festers in our minds. Soon we are discouraged about our circumstances, and the future is not even on the horizon. Hope eventually dies within us.

Satan has convinced us that it is a waste of time to dream. His fiery darts have taken our eyes off a vision for the future and made us focus on the past, which can sometimes be our worst enemy.

My dad could have easily felt that way. He was an only child whose father died when he was nine. To help provide for himself and my grandmother, he had to drop out of school in the ninth grade and go to the migration fields in California to pick peaches. But Dad had an incredible work ethic, and he was not going to allow his hope for the future to be displaced. He eventually moved back to San Antonio with his mother and worked as a truck driver, carrying produce throughout the Southwest seven days a week.

He married my mom in 1951, and by 1954 they had two small daughters, me and my sister, Rosie. He needed to make more money and spend more time with his family. Soon he heard about a job at Kelly Air Force Base in a skill that was very new at the time: computers. He knew nothing about computers, but was not afraid to hear the word *no,* so he took his chances for a better opportunity.

The morning of the interviews Daddy took his place in a very long line. After a while he noticed something strange. People would go into the interview room and then leave quickly thereafter.

He thought, *I know what they are asking these people. They want to know if the person has a high school diploma. The minute I get there, I'll tell them no, and they'll send me away just as quickly.*

Yet he stayed in line. He remembered his wife and two daughters and how much he needed this job; he would not allow his hope for the future to be displaced.

Finally he got to the head of the line, and he waited patiently for the interviewer to ask the dreaded question. Instead the man said, "Before I ask you any questions, are you willing to work nights?"

Work nights? Of course. Dad was used to staying awake through the night to make a truck run.

Hearing Dad's positive response, the man placed a paper before him, saying, "Sign here. We will train you in computers."

After two years at Kelly, Dad heard about a job in California working for someone called Howard Hughes. He applied for that job and became a part of Hughes Aircraft's Telstar team. Ten years later he was supervising more than four hundred employees, most of whom were college graduates, some of whom held master's degrees in technology. His work ethic never dwindled; he continued to work seven days a week.

If you have failed in the past, you may be afraid to set your hopes on your dream for fear you will fail again. Or if you have had great success in your past, you may be afraid you will never achieve that success again. I want to encourage you to break through Satan's lies, just as my dad did, so that you can set goals for your life, which you can achieve with God's direction and help.

What is a goal? The destination of a journey or the object of a person's desire or ambition. And where do we begin? We have already taken the first step by deciding to become daughters of the King. Now let's look at seven steps we can take toward setting dreams that have a happy ending.

I. HAVE A VISION FOR THE FUTURE

We learn from the Word of God that "where there is no vision, the people perish" (Prov. 29:18 KJV). My husband dreams with God. He is a visionary. I accuse him of having a vision, a new goal, every thirty minutes. I am more of a behind-the-scenes person who helps to orchestrate the world to achieve that goal. I wonder how his dream will be accomplished, but John sees much farther than I can see, so I trust his judgment.

A friend once described the partnership between my husband and me like this: "Diana, in my mind's eye I see Pastor Hagee jumping into an empty swimming pool, and you are yelling at the top of your voice, 'Wait a minute, Honey!' as you're holding a water hose in your hand, trying to fill the pool before he dives in headfirst."

Seems an apt description to me. My mother-in-law says that for every crooked pot in this world, there is a crooked lid. I believe without a shadow of a doubt that my husband and I were ordained by the Master to be together. I need goals in my life to keep me focused on accomplishments and not on circumstances. My husband is a goal setter, and together we strive toward meeting goals the Lord has set before us.

What happens if you are not married to such a man? Maybe you are the visionary in your household. That's okay as long as the two of you agree on your dreams and work together to complete them. Or what happens if you don't have a partner in this life, by choice, divorce, or death? And even if you are married to a wonderful man, should you have personal goals?

Of course, no matter what state your life is in—whether in fair weather or a storm—goals will help you through a trying time so you can finally see a dream come true. No matter what adversity life sets before you, you must decide that God has a plan, a destiny, for your life. (As unbelievable as it now seems, your present difficulties may just be part of your journey to the goal God has set before you.)

To learn His plan for our lives, we must make time to be with Him.

2. Make Time to Be with God

When I first married my husband, I would go to women's meetings and hear them talk about the amount of time they spent with God. Some would wake at four in the morning and spend two to three hours in prayer. Others said they would make sure they were in the Word or in prayer four to five hours a day. I would be overwhelmed by their accounts. I would also be embarrassed about the little time I spent in formal prayer because of my duties at the church and in my home. By the time my children arrived, I felt certain God had forgotten my name, I spent so little time with Him. I was letting the fiery darts of the evil one enter my mind and fester with the infection of inadequacy and failure.

I remember sharing those feelings with my mother-in-law. By that time she had served the Lord in ministry for more than fifty-three years, and there was little she had not experienced. She is a no-nonsense individual, so I knew she would honestly share her feelings about any issue.

Her first response to my concern was: "Ask yourself if you are giving Him all the time you can." She told me God would reveal the answer to that question, and He would let me know where I could rearrange my schedule to create a time when He and I could talk.

She added, "He misses His time with you much more than you miss your time with Him." What a revelation! I couldn't imagine that God knew my name, much less that He actually missed time with me. That knowledge in itself gave me a desire to be with Him even more.

She told me to stop comparing myself to other people. "God doesn't do so," she said, "so why should you?" She challenged me to go to the Word of God to see how God felt about comparisons. She hinted that I should look in Paul's second letter to the Corinthians:

> For we dare not make ourselves of the number, or compare ourselves with
> some that commend themselves: but they measuring themselves by them-
> selves, and comparing themselves among themselves, are not wise. (10:12 KJV)

Every time we compare ourselves to others we react in one of two ways. If someone is doing something better than we are, we immediately feel inadequate. This is not pleasing to God because His Word promises that we "can do all things through Christ who strengthens" us (Phil. 4:13).

Or if we are doing something so much better than someone else, we become puffed up in our attitude, relying too much on our own talents and accomplishments instead of rejoicing in what God has done through us. Either way, we lose our focus on God and replace it with a focus on ourselves or someone else. Our God is a jealous God, and He shares the glory with no one!

Mom Hagee also helped me learn to pray. "Prayer is a constant," she said, "something that should be done at all times . . . We rise in the morning with praise on our lips for God. We ask Him to guide our paths throughout the day."

Vada Hagee is a prayer warrior. When she intercedes in prayer, the demons tremble and the heavens part. She is not timid about the power she has in prayer. At age eighty-eight, she still weeps for the wonderful things God has done, and continues to do, through prayer. Yet there was a season when she felt that God was not hearing her prayers. Learning of that was a shock to me. How could such a servant of God feel distant from Him?

During that time she asked God why He was so far from her. He quickly informed her that she had distanced herself from Him by relying on her own words in prayer more than on His instruction of what prayer should be. The Lord referred her to Matthew 6:5–13, where Jesus gave His disciples a Bible study on prayer. He told them not to be like the hypocrites who prayed in visible places for recognition or prayed vain and repetitious prayers, but to pray in private. He instructed them to pray from the heart.

God, our Father, knows the things we need before we pray for them, Jesus said. He wants us to ask. He even gave us a manner in which to pray. Mom Hagee heard the Lord telling her to go back to the Lord's Prayer in Matthew 6 and use these familiar phrases as a blueprint for her prayers.

"Our Father in heaven," she began. Then she reasserted to herself and to the Lord, "You are the only God. You are the Father of Abraham, Isaac, and Jacob. You are my only God. Not Allah or Buddha. Not materialism. Not my husband or my children. You, Lord, alone are God."

"Hallowed be Your name." Mom Hagee heard the Lord saying, *Before you go into prayer, no matter what your desire, you should praise Me because I inhabit the praises of My people.* She found that when she began to praise Him before she mentioned her petitions, she lost sight of the problem, she lost sight of the world, and she put her focus on Him. She remembered that He alone was responsible for helping her to nurture the good in herself and overcome the evil. Without Him, her life would have been aimless.

"Your kingdom come. Your will be done." These phrases led Mom Hagee to reaffirm that God's will was the only will she wanted for her life. "Only Your purpose," she would say and mean it in her heart before she mentioned any needs or petitions. "I trust You, Lord, with my goals and my future."

"Give us this day our daily bread." Now, and not before now, was the time for petition. But she began by remembering that whatever she needed for the day, God would bring her. "It's beyond the food for our table. It's beyond the money for our mortgage. It is all our needs," Mom Hagee said. "God knows all our needs, and He will provide for His children."

"And forgive us our debts, as we forgive our debtors." We cannot go to the throne of God without a repentant heart. With all of David's sin, he was a man who had the heart of God because of a repentant spirit. This is the time to mention where we have failed to accept responsibility for our actions in the last twenty-four hours and to repent! Scripture clearly states that our prayers will be hindered if we have anything against a brother or sister. It is not sufficient to repent of our own sins; we must have a pure heart for others as well.

"And do not lead us into temptation." We forget that temptation is around all of us every day in one form or another. Christians are not spared from temptation. We need to ask God to keep us from temptation (to place a protective hedge around us) and, if we are tempted, to help us to say no.

"For Yours is the kingdom and the power and the glory forever." Mom Hagee always ends her prayers with praise, just as she begins them, knowing that her glorious God will help her get through the day.

After this lesson from my mother-in-law, my prayer life changed dramatically. Instead of praying the repetitious prayers I had learned as a child, I began using the outline of the Lord's Prayer, talking to Him as a daughter to a loving Father. I did not lock myself in a closet and stay away from my daily chores, but I took my prayer closet with me. I prayed in the shower. I prayed on my way to work. I prayed while I shopped for groceries. Sometimes my prayers were long conversations or simply two or three words. One of the most powerful prayers I prayed was, "Lord, intervene!"

As you look for God's destiny for your life, ask Him to show you what He wants for you, and then examine yourself to see if you are ready within your heart to accomplish that goal.

3. Seek God's Will for Your Life

Who has God created you to be? What has He commissioned you to do? A well-known saying sums it up this way: "What we are is God's gift to us. What we become is our gift to God."

As you ask God to direct you, think about your particular skills. What do you enjoy doing? What seems to come naturally to you? Read through the parable of the talents in Matthew 25:14–30. God has given you a gift, and He expects you to use it.

Don't be too humble here. Recognize the talents God has given you (whether they are intellectual abilities in math or science or service abilities in hospitality, evangelism, or helps), and list your talents and skills.

_____

_____

Once you have identified God's gifts to you, you are ready to put your gifts before Him—your goals—in writing.

4. Write Down Your Vision and Make It Plain

How do you begin to write your goals?

First, begin with the small things. My husband's mother taught him that to be diligent in the large things of life, he needed first to succeed in the smaller ones. So with goal setting, you will begin with everyday events before you take on the larger plans for your future.

What do you have planned for tomorrow?

Goals for Tomorrow

Think about a list of goals for your tomorrow. Train yourself to be successful in the smaller things first. The book of Habakkuk urges us to "write the vision and make it plain" (2:2).

Remember, there is always time to do God's work. Your agenda usually bogs down your day. When preparing your list, make sure that you prioritize your commitment to your home and family, especially if you have a husband and children.

Next, if you work outside the home, meet your obligations to your employer. You must not forget that you are a representative of Christ, and His kingdom is seen in all you do and say.

Then, is there a service that you can donate to the work of the Lord in your church or your community? This is very important in your journey to becoming a King's daughter. The more you give of yourself (as long as these activities have been ordained of God), the more time He will provide for you to do the things you need to do.

I recall the time a woman asked me to pray for her marriage. "What's the problem?" I asked so I could be specific in my prayers.

"My husband is complaining that I'm not keeping our home well or caring for our children as I should."

When I asked her what she did with her day, she answered in a very self-justified manner, listing all the Bible studies and intercession meetings of which she was a member and all the volunteer hours she was giving at a local shelter. She was about to join my volunteer force at the church when her husband finally objected.

After listening to her, I said, "Do you really think such a schedule is wise? You should go to your husband and ask his forgiveness. Then ask him to pray with you and help you choose the commitments you should keep and the ones you should release, no matter how noble they are."

She was not pleased by my response, but I hope she did as I suggested. Our God is a God of priorities. He comes first; our families and church follow. He will be faithful to reward us when we follow His priorities.

I have also seen the opposite situation. I ask for volunteers and some women reject the request, using their families as an excuse for not working in the kingdom of God. I really don't understand why we bother with such alibis. God knows the desires of our hearts, which are either pure or impure. Often I find that when someone says, "I can't," she is really saying, "I don't want to!"

Some mothers so wrap themselves in the lives of their children—enrolling them in gymnastics, ballet, karate, music, and sports, you name it—that they don't have time for the things of God. The schedules they keep to maintain these commitments are horrendous. As mothers, we must not make our children our idols and put them before God. There is no greater testimony that you can give your children than to serve God.

My husband tells me he is going to preach a sermon one day titled "We All Have Buts." This idea was inspired one afternoon when he was visiting with a rabbi. They were discussing the Hebrew origin of certain words in Scripture, and he was amazed to learn that one of the Hebrew origins of the word *but* is "zero," as in numerical or accounting terminology. When *but* is used in speech, it automatically cancels all that was said before, and the speaker is destined to live with what he says after that.

For example, when Moses sent the spies into the promised land that God had specifically given to the children of Israel, they came back with two reports. Caleb and Joshua saw a land filled with milk and honey. One that was inhabited by giants, yes, yet still a land that could be taken—with God's help. "Let us go up at once and take possession, for we are well able to overcome it," Caleb said.

The other men who had gone up with Caleb and Joshua saw all the *buts*: "We are not able to go up against the people, for they are stronger than we . . . The land through which we have gone as spies is a land that devours its inhabitants, and all the people whom we saw in it are men of great stature" (Num. 13:26–32).

Forty years later Joshua and Caleb did take the land, yet the rest of the spies were destined to live by the words of their mouths. They were not allowed to enter the land of milk and honey. Instead they died in the desert!

We are guilty of the same sin. We say things such as these:

- "I would love to join the choir, *but* I am just not good enough."
- "I wish I could finish school, *but* I don't know how it is possible."
- "I would love to get out of debt, *but* I am too far gone to see that happen."

We must learn to get the *buts* out of our thoughts and speech. They have dictated our lives much too long. When we make an effort to be available to the Lord, He will make sure that we have time to be the women we need to be.

Ask God what He would have you to do tomorrow. He is faithful to let you know what He wants of you. Write these goals in the space provided, and make them plain and specific.

MY GOALS FOR TOMORROW

Spiritual Goals:

_____

_____

Personal Goals:

_____

_____

Career Goals:

_____

_____

Educational Goals:

_____

_____

Now pray over your list to make sure that it is realistic.

GOALS FOR THE FUTURE

Once we become accustomed to meeting daily goals, long-range goals become more realistic. Many women feel that certain opportunities for their lives have passed; it is too late to attain them. These feelings come from allowing the fiery darts of the Evil One to infect their minds and take their hope.

Joyce Landorf Heatherly, a dear friend of mine, wrote a book about the "balcony and basement" people in our lives. These people can be parents or husbands, friends or loved ones. A balcony person is someone who is always telling you, "You can do anything you want to do in life." This person encourages you and stands with you through tough times. A basement person is someone who is always dragging you down. This person gives you reasons why you should settle for the status quo.

If you have only basement people in your life, you must learn to distance your-self from them. If you are related to them—and therefore can't maintain a safe dis-tance—you need to turn your head upward and look to the ultimate balcony person of your life: your heavenly Father. He loves you. You can hear His voice say to you, *You can do it! . . . I love you! I made you! You can accomplish anything! . . . And I will be with you every step of the way. I will protect you. I will keep your foot on the right path and keep you from stumbling. Go on. Try! You are My daughter! I want the best for you. Together we can do it!*

Have you never attained your high school degree? Are you discouraged because you never went to college? Has it been a disappointment to you, and has Satan used that to keep you from attaining other goals? Look to the Word of God, which says, "The heart of the prudent acquires knowledge, and the ear of the wise seeks knowledge" (Prov. 18:15). Set your mind on getting your degree, whether it is a high school diploma or a bachelor's, master's, or doctorate. Write it down and make it plain.

My Goals for the Future

Spiritual Goals:

_____

_____

Personal Goals:

_____

_____

Career Goals:

_____

_____

Educational Goals:

_____

_____

Now commit your goals to the Lord in prayer. Make your needs and desires plain to Him.

Do you need finances to accomplish one of your goals? Know that the Lord owns the riches of the world and He promises to supply all of your needs.

Do you need time to accomplish a goal? Remember that the Lord stopped the sun for Joshua; He can make time for you to accomplish your goal. As the King's daughter, you have access to all His resources to accomplish the dreams He put in your heart.

5. CHECK YOUR GOALS WITH THE WORD OF GOD

Church members often ask me, "How do you know when God is talking to you?" or "When do you know the difference between God's correction and Satan's condemnation?"

The Word of God is always at the core of any question you may have for your life. Is what you are hearing in accordance with the Word of God or contrary to its teaching? Test your goals against these scriptural injunctions:

We are commanded to do all to the glory of God. "Therefore, whether you eat or drink, or whatever you do, do all to the glory of God. Give no offense, either to the Jews or to the Greeks or to the church of God, just as I also please all men in all things, not seeking my own profit, but the profit of many, that they may be saved" (1 Cor. 10:31–33). Does your goal glorify God?

We are to seek peace. "Where envy and self-seeking exist, confusion and every evil thing are there. But the wisdom that is from above is first pure, then peaceable, gentle, willing to yield, full of mercy and good fruits, without partiality and without hypocrisy. Now the fruit of righteousness is sown in peace by those who make peace" (James 3:16–18). Does your goal bring personal peace?

We are not to offend anyone in the body of Christ. "Whoever causes one of these little ones who believe in Me to sin, it would be better for him if a millstone were hung around his neck, and he were drowned in the depth of the sea. Woe to the world because of offenses! For offenses must come, but woe to that man by whom the offense comes!" (Matt. 18:6–7). Does your goal offend anyone in the body of Christ?

We are not to violate the Word of God. Deuteronomy 28 lists twenty-eight blessings and sixty-four curses that come to you if you obey or disobey God's Word. Does your goal violate the Word of God?

Use these scriptures and others that might be important to you as checkpoints for your goal.

6. Stay Focused on Your Vision; Don't Give Way to a Defeated Attitude

As a mother, I am amazed when I hear my son Matthew preach the Word of God. He comes by it honestly. He is the sixth generation of Hagees to preach the gospel. He is the forty-eighth descendant of the original John Hagee family to be in the ministry since they came from Europe to America on a ship called *Spirit* for the purpose of religious freedom. He has had a passion for the Word of God since he was a child. He set his course early in life, and he has not wavered from that goal. I call him my "man-child."

When he calls me "Momma," I feel warm inside, just as I did when he sat on my lap as a baby with his arms around my neck. He could ask for the world, and I would figure out how to get it for him. However, I often forget he is twenty-two, and I watch over him a little too closely, something he's very aware of.

The other day he asked me a question as I was preparing dinner. "Momma, do you know what I want for my twenty-third birthday?"

There was that *Momma* word again. I answered as any self-respecting Mexican mother would: "Whatever it is, Baby Boy, Momma will get it for you!"

He stood close to me, put his massive loving arms around my shoulder, and said, "I would like you to stop ordering for me at restaurants and stop asking me if I have washed my hands after I have gone to a public rest room."

Of course, I agreed to grant his desire. I did remind him that I had three months before his birthday, so I still had some time before I had to comply with his wishes. As you can tell, I am very protective of my children. My husband says I have never cut my umbilical cord, only stretched it to its maximum capacity.

However, when I sit in the pew and hear Matthew preach, he is no longer my little child; he becomes a man of God who was sent to this earth to minister the Lord's gospel to our church—and one day to the nations. Each time he has enriched my life with the Word of God.

One particular Sunday Matthew preached a sermon about a great dreamer in the Scripture who kept on dreaming whenever adversity came his way. His name was Joseph. His brothers were naturally jealous of him—he was obviously his father's favorite son. And they despised him even more when he revealed a dream to them, a long-term goal for his life, ordained of God. "All of you will one day bow down before me," Joseph had said.

Can you imagine how enraged his brothers were? But Joseph never let go of his dream. His brothers sold him into slavery. Yet he held on to his dream.

He was enslaved in Potiphar's house. Yet he held on to his dream.

Potiphar's wife wrongly accused him of rape, and he was thrown into prison. Yet he held on to his dream.

Later, when the Egyptian king had a disturbing dream, the royal butler remembered Joseph as someone who had interpreted the butler's dream while they were in prison together. Joseph used the gift of interpretation that God had given him, and he was finally promoted to the palace. The path to the palace was a difficult one, filled with many obstacles, yet Joseph never lost sight of the goal God had set before him.

When Joseph was finally reunited with his brothers, he could have reminded them of their hatred and jealousy. He could have reminded them of their betrayal. He could have flaunted his position over them. Yet he said nothing of the kind. Instead he declared, "It was not you who sent me here, but God." (See Gen. 37–45.)

Once you have written down your goal and committed it to God, determine not to lose sight of your goal and give up. Remember Joseph; he stayed on the path to the palace even though adversity came from every direction.

7. BE WILLING TO CHANGE IF GOD DESIRES IT

You must also learn to be flexible when attaining your goal. I have learned this the hard way. If I am inflexible, I will break. So I have added my own beatitude to the Lord's list: "Blessed are the flexible, for they can bend without breaking."

Again, think of Joseph. He waited on God, and he learned to be flexible wherever he was—in Potiphar's house as a slave, as a prisoner in a dreary jail for at least two full years. We must remember that God's ways are not always our ways; His time frame is not always our time frame. However, His ways are always right, and He is always an on-time God.

Often when I have seen a delay in reaching a goal, I finally realize that God wants me to make a change in the way I am doing things. Change is hard because it takes us out of our comfort zone and into uncharted territory. Yet my husband always says, "If you hear the voice of the Shepherd behind you when you are on a journey, it is because you have gone down your own path. The voice of the Great Shepherd should always be in front of you saying, 'Follow Me.'"

When you have attained your goal, do two things. First, give praise to the One who helped you attain the goal. He is well pleased with your thanksgiving offering. Second, set a new one. Never be without a goal in your life. Whether it is having a special time with your family, pursuing further education, getting out of debt, buying a home, or entering retirement, never lose sight of your dreams. Remember, dreams are golden ladders that take you to heavenly places. Dreams are mountaintops where you can see your destiny.

ᶜↁ ACTION POINTS:
DREAMS WITH A HAPPY ENDING: SETTING GOALS

1. Take two of your short-term goals from page 58 and work through the exercise on page 65 to formulate a realistic game plan for success.

2. Now take two of your long-term goals from pages 59–60 and work them through the process on page 66 to formulate a realistic game plan for success.

3. As you think about these goals in the days to come, remember these scriptures, and claim your position as a daughter of the King:

- A daughter who walks in Christ Jesus (Col. 2:6)
- A daughter who can do all things through Christ Jesus (Phil. 4:13)
- A daughter who shall do even greater works than Christ Jesus (John 14:12)
- A daughter who presses toward the high calling of God (Phil. 3:14)

Now pray this prayer:

Father, You know the plans You have for me, plans to prosper me and not harm me, plans for my future. I was created in Your image for a purpose. You have given me gifts and talents to accomplish Your purpose. Show me these gifts and talents, that I may develop them. Bind my mind to the mind of Christ Jesus, renewing me daily, that I will be conformed to the image of Christ Jesus. According to Your Word, whoever lacks wisdom needs only to ask, and I am asking for wisdom, understanding, and knowledge. Establish my feet on the path You have set before me. Direct my goals as You direct my feet. Father, Your Word is a lamp to my feet and a light to my path. Set my heart and mind on You. Amen.

4. Read chapter 4 in the book of Esther.

GOAL SETTING

1. Have a vision for the future.
2. Make time to be with God.
3. Seek God's will for your life.
4. Write down your vision and make it plain.
5. Check your goals with the Word of God.
6. Stay focused on your vision; don't give way to a defeated attitude.
7. Be willing to change if God desires it.

Be ready for success!

REACHING YOUR GOAL

Short-Term Goal Setting
Goal:

_____

_____

Obstacle:

_____

_____

Game Plan:

_____

_____

Success!

_____

_____

Long-Term Goal Setting
Goal:

_____

_____

Obstacle:

_____

_____

Game Plan:

_____

_____

_____

Success!

_____

_____

_____

To God Be the Glory!

chapter six

Ten Commandments for Women in the Workplace

*L*et me make this point very clear: every woman is a workingwoman. No matter what the circumstances, her work is never done. Now, however, the majority of women also work outside of the home. We must deal with many facets of the workplace and still remain proper representatives of a never-changing, never-compromising God.

One aspect of working in what is known as a "man's world" is creating balance between sharing your knowledge and not coming across as an overbearing female. When a man is aggressive in the workplace, he is described as someone who is driven to succeed. When a woman is aggressive, she is known as an obstinate, mulish, infuriating, bothersome, unbearable, cruel, impossible, dictatorial, scheming, calculating, loud-mouthed, hard, rigid, domineering, manipulative, irritating, pushy, inflexible, rebellious, stubborn, bossy, intolerable, harsh, tyrannical, hot-tempered, premenstrual, menopausal, queen of mean, Jezebel-like control freak.

Often I tell my husband, "Look into my eyes. Do you realize that even though I am supposed to be submissive, I still have a brain? The brain that God gave me works. It has bright ideas. It can solve problems and create new concepts!" Since the Lord came into my life and freed me of my insecurities, I must tell you, I have lost my timidity. Therefore, the Lord now has to deal with me in a whole new way. Bless His heart!

I am the chief of staff at John Hagee Television Ministries. The way in which I came to this position is another part of my growth as a daughter of the King.

Life was good. I was in my comfort zone. I had adjusted to being a pastor's wife. Unique as I was (since I didn't possess the traditional gifts of singing and/or teaching), I was content. I worked behind the scenes at the church, organizing volunteers and special events.

Suddenly the chief of staff of our television ministry resigned to run his own television station, and the search was on to fill his position. I agreed with my husband in prayer that God would bring the perfect person to be chief of staff.

Time passed—but no answer came.

I began to go to the television ministry building every day to see if there was anything I could do in the interim.

More time passed—but still no answer.

One day my husband told me that the Lord had given him the answer to the person who should take the position.

"Who?" I asked excitedly, for I had received no answer about a person for the job.

"You," he answered cautiously. As the pastor, he knew he had heard from God. As my husband, he also knew I would not receive that answer with joy.

He was right. I rebelled for quite some time. I was enjoying my comfort zone. I was safe there. And I didn't even know how to program a VCR, much less run a television ministry! My husband explained that I would be his eyes and ears for that department of our ministry. He told me he wanted the television outreach to be run as our church, with compassion and concern for a lost and dying world.

Finally I realized that I would find no peace until I submitted to my husband's authority and the Lord's plan and purpose for my life. I cautiously began a new chapter, and I have grown to love it. I work with wonderful people who have a vision for evangelism. I have made new friends through this special outreach, and I am blessed every day as we see souls come to the cross of Christ through the airwaves. It was not my desire to be here, but I believe it was God's plan for me. Pure obedience allowed me to be in His divine purpose.

In the capacity as the chief of staff of such a large corporation, I have had to go head-to-head with some very powerful men, both in the Christian world and in the secular world. It has truly been a challenge to present my point of view tactfully without appearing overbearing. Often I cried out to the Lord, *How can I do this? What are my guidelines?* And He answered, *Look to My Word.*

GOD'S GUIDELINES

As I mentioned in the previous chapter, our Lord presents His Word and His teachings to us in a simple manner, so we can all understand the concepts of Scripture. The scholar spends his life studying the Word, yet a young child can learn to live by its dictates.

My mother-in-law had four sons. Needless to say, it was a challenge to keep all of the aggressive young boys in check. Early in their lives she told them, "You will obey me and the Word of God while you live in my home. There are two ways to live: under the law or under grace. Since you are too young to understand grace, you will live under the law!"

The law is introduced to us in Scripture by the word *covenant,* an agreement or a contract made between two parties. We, as believers, can humbly say that our contracts are made with God. The beauty of the covenants of God is that they are unconditional; these covenant promises will be kept despite our success or failure to meet the conditions of the covenants. Although enjoyment of the blessings of the covenants may be conditioned upon obedience, the fulfillment of the promises depends not on man, but on God.

To me, one of the most important covenants in Scripture is the covenant of grace, which may be described as the "gracious" agreement between the offended God and the offending sinner. Here God promises salvation through faith in Christ, and the sinner accepts this agreement, promising a life of faith and obedience.

Another covenant of God is the Mosaic covenant, or the Law. Our society has strayed so far from the covenant that God made with Moses on Mount Sinai that we forget the Law is the Ten Commandments, not the Ten Suggestions. To the best of my ability I try to live under these mandates for my life. When I fail, I depend on the grace of God to forgive my shortcomings and set my feet on the right path. How does this happen? I don't know. How can God show such infinite mercy? I don't know.

Some define *grace* as "the goodness of God at Christ's expense." The price that

Christ paid at the cross is incomprehensible to me, yet I have faith that His death was exchanged for my everlasting life. However, I still must have some guidelines to help me live day to day.

The first purpose of the Law is to reveal the standard of righteousness that God expects of His children. The apostle Paul wrote that the "law is holy, and the commandment holy and just and good" (Rom. 7:12). The Law reveals the holiness of God.

Second, the Law is meant to set God's people apart from a sinful world. The Law is not meant to help us attain salvation; only the blood of Jesus can provide that gift.

Third, the Law is present to reveal sin to God's people. Paul made it quite clear that there is no justification in the Law: "Therefore by the deeds of the law no flesh will be justified in His sight, for by the law is the knowledge of sin" (Rom. 3:20).

In two other verses, Paul emphasized that the Law was given so that sin might be made known to the people of God:

> The law entered that the offense might abound. But where sin abounded, grace abounded much more. (Rom. 5:20)

> What shall we say then? Is the law sin? Certainly not! On the contrary, I would not have known sin except through the law. For I would not have known covetousness unless the law had said, "You shall not covet." (Rom. 7:7)

Rabbi Yechiel Eckstein offers a beautiful perspective of the Law in his book *What You Should Know About Jews and Judaism.* Many see the Law as a burden; however, observant Jews regard it quite differently:

> Judaism understands the love of God as the willingness to accept upon oneself the "yoke of the kingdom of God." For when seen from within, this yoke or burden is one that the observant Jew accepts willingly, out of abiding love and immeasurable joy. He regards the Torah and its laws as God's precious gift to Israel, as the concrete manifestation of His goodness and love

for His people. It gives form to his quest for moral living. The observant Jew regards the Law as a way of life linking him with the Divine, a vehicle enabling him to fulfill God's will, and a means of bringing him ever closer to the spiritual realm. Instead of bondage the Law represents true freedom. Rather than a burden, it is the Jew's greatest delight.[1]

Christians have an immeasurable gift because we live under the guidelines of the Law of Moses and also have the covering of the blood of Jesus. My heavenly Father knew that I would need these laws to help me make decisions and to represent Him and His image in the best way I can. Our ultimate goal is to be more like Christ, not to separate ourselves from our King by our actions. Allow me to apply these ten powerful laws to the Christian woman in the workplace.

THE FIRST COMMANDMENT:

You shall have no other gods before Me

Our God is a God who cares very much for His children. He altered history so that His chosen people would be delivered from the bondage of Egypt. He allowed His only Son to be sacrificed on the cross so that we might be freed from the bondage of sin. In return, we are to have no other influence in our lives but Him.

Some women have the second job of the family in order to provide additional income for the household. Others' careers are integral parts of their lives and futures. In either case, under no circumstances should we make our jobs our gods. The true holy God will not take second place to anything or anyone! In Exodus 34:10, the Lord renewed the covenant with Moses and the Jewish people after they disobeyed Him by creating the golden calf. He asserted in no uncertain terms that He is a jealous God:

> Behold, I am driving out from before you the Amorite and the Canaanite and the Hittite and the Perizzite and the Hivite and the Jebusite. Take heed to yourself, lest you make a covenant with the inhabitants of the land where you are going, lest it be a snare in your midst. But you shall destroy their

altars, break their sacred pillars, and cut down their wooden images (for you shall worship no other god, for the LORD, whose name is Jealous, is a jealous God). (Ex. 34:11–14)

God will never allow anything in our lives to come before Him. I firmly believe that once we have made the Lord the Savior of our lives, we all work for Him, no matter what our "tent-making" job may be. Keeping this fact in focus will help us to represent Him in all facets of life, including the workplace. A job is not the most important thing in life. Jesus is. If we are married, a job is not the second most important thing in life. Our husbands are. If we have children, then a job takes its place after them.

We must maintain the priorities that God has set before us in His Word. Remember, a job is not the source of our prosperity; God is. The apostle John warned the early Christians about falling into the entrapment of the world:

> Do not love the world or the things in the world. If anyone loves the world, the love of the Father is not in him. For all that is in the world—the lust of the flesh, the lust of the eyes, and the pride of life—is not of the Father but is of the world. And the world is passing away, and the lust of it; but he who does the will of God abides forever. (1 John 2:15–17)

Like these early Christians, we sometimes see our Lord as a God of last resort and not the God who is our first and only Source for every good and perfect thing. Today God is still saying to His people, "Thou shall put Me first, and the business second." Once we have set these priorities in place, our lives will be freed from stress and responsibilities that the Lord never intended for us.

What about women who have decided to stay at home to raise their children? They live under the same law. The home is supposed to give us shelter, to be a haven from the world around us, and to be a place where we, as well as our families, find refuge and joy. It is not supposed to control our lives and the lives of our family members.

Unfortunately too many women I know have made their homes a showplace that becomes their god. The family cannot live in some of the rooms. Their children's friends are not allowed to come over for fear they will mess things up. I admit that on some days when my children were young, I prayed no one would come to the door and see the disarray in our house. Then I would hear their laughter, and everything would come into balance. They were happy; it was their haven, and the sound of their joy made all the mess bearable.

If you have not given your home to the Lord, do it now. Let the Lord know how thankful you are to have it, and make sure all that happens within the walls of your home is dedicated to Him and His glory.

THE SECOND COMMANDMENT:

You shall not make for yourself a carved image—any likeness of anything that is in heaven above, or that is in the earth beneath, or that is in the water under the earth; you shall not bow down to them nor serve them.

Often we feel this commandment applies only to people in biblical times or in developing countries and not to us because we do not need any image to help us worship the God of Abraham, Isaac, and Jacob.

However, sometimes the people we work with—or for—can become our heroes. When this happens, we take our eyes off the Lord as our example and look to others for guidance. Instead we need to keep our eyes focused on Him and no other. As we reflect His image, others will look to the God within us for direction and not to the world around them for answers.

As for the women who maintain the home, there should be no images that take away from their families' walk with Christ. From Genesis to Revelation, God's Word warns us of idols and how they separate us from God. The children of Israel made a golden calf while their leader was conversing with God. Rachel took the idols of her father's house and did not tell her husband she had them. When her father, Laban, came searching for the idols, Jacob said, "Let the one who has taken your idols die." Because Rachel deceived her husband, he spoke a curse of death over her, and the next year she died in childbirth. All because of other gods (Gen. 31:26–32).

Idols create delusions and pollute our souls. The apostle John warned the early Christians:

> We know that we are of God, and the whole world lies under the sway of the wicked one. And we know that the Son of God has come and has given us an understanding, that we may know Him who is true; and we are in Him who is true, in His Son Jesus Christ. This is the true God and eternal life. Little children, keep yourselves from idols. Amen. (1 John 5:19–21)

Consider these questions to determine whether you have idols within your home:

- What kinds of statues or pictures do you have in your home? Do they depict the occult gods of Eastern religions? (You may consider them artwork, but the Lord doesn't. Neither does the kingdom of darkness.)
- Do the games that your children play bring dishonor to the kingdom of God?
- Are the soap opera characters you have been watching for years your idols? Have the lives of these fictitious characters become so real to you that you cannot miss an episode?
- Do Hollywood celebrities direct your life more than the Word of God?
- Do you worship nature?
- Are Christian authors or preachers more important to you than the God who created you?

Remember what happened to King Saul. He decreed that while he was king, no one should consult mediums or sorcerers at punishment of death. Yet later he disguised himself and went to the witch of Endor to ask her to call up the prophet Samuel who had died so Saul would know the outcome of a battle with the Philistines. In doing so, he was basically telling God that he could rely on another source for help, not God Himself. Samuel then told Saul, "The LORD has departed from you and has become your enemy" (1 Sam. 28:16).

The thought that God would depart from me and not answer me anymore is something I cannot bear. I know that today women are calling psychic hot lines and consulting horoscopes and tarot cards for the future. Yet God is the same yesterday, today, and forever. He has not changed His mind or His attitude. He is a jealous God, and we risk the terrible outcome of God's Spirit departing from us, His turning His back on us, if we betray Him.

Any attempt to put something between your soul and God is idolatry. It is imperative to remember that when Jesus died on the cross, His death made it possible to worship Him face-to-face. You can approach the throne of God without a priest or a prophet or a preacher.

Remember, the Lord's very name is Jealous. And don't forget the latter half of this commandment: "For I, the LORD your God, am a jealous God, visiting the iniquity of the fathers upon the children to the third and fourth generations of those who hate Me, but showing mercy to thousands, to those who love Me and keep My commandments" (Ex. 20:5–6).

As I said, I come from a Mexican heritage, a culture that is polytheistic, worshiping many gods through Indian influence. My husband and I wanted nothing to do with any influence other than the God of Abraham, Isaac, and Jacob, so our family had a time of prayer together, asking the Lord to rid our family lineage of any generational curse.

THE THIRD COMMANDMENT:

You shall not take the name of the LORD your God in vain, for
the LORD will not hold him guiltless who takes His name in vain.

In the Scripture the name of God is always a revelation of His divine character. *Jehovah-nissi,* the Lord our Banner; *Jehovah-rohi,* the Lord our Shepherd; *Jehovah-shalom,* the Lord our Peace; *Jehovah-shammah,* the Lord who is there; *Jehovah-rophe,* the Lord our Healer; *Jehovah-jireh,* the Lord our Provider; *Jehovah-m'Kaddesh,* the Lord who sanctifies; and *Jehovah-tsidkenu,* the Lord our Righteousness—all are names and attributes of God.

For more than forty-three years my husband has said from the pulpit, "God's last name does not begin with a *D!*" His name is good; His name is pure; His name is powerful; His name is all we will ever need. We must treat it with reverence.

Several years ago I was sitting with a rabbi at a banquet. As we spoke about each other's faith, he asked me a question that would affect the rest of my life: "Diana, I have always wanted to ask a Christian this question. Why is it that you abbreviate Christmas, which is the celebration of the birth of your God, with an *X*?"

The only answer I could give him was "disrespect for the name of God." Righteous Jews will not write the name of God for fear it will be offensive. Even within personal letters, they symbolize the name of the Creator in this fashion: *G_D*. And a praying Jew bows every time the name of God is mentioned in Scripture as a gesture of respect.

We also violate the third commandment anytime we use the name of God in a way that does not reveal His divine nature. This goes beyond profanity. Once we confess to take the name of God as our Savior, He expects us to be true to our profession of faith. We are to act like Christians in everything we do. Not just to "talk the talk," but "walk the walk." Sometimes people join a large church, such as Cornerstone, more for business purposes than for spiritual growth. These people "talk the talk," but when they interact with our members in their businesses, they don't have the same integrity that the Lord and other Christians expect. The prophet Isaiah warned Israel:

> Hear this, O house of Jacob,
> Who are called by the name of Israel,
> And have come forth from the wellsprings of Judah;
> Who swear by the name of the LORD,
> And make mention of the God of Israel,
> But not in truth or in righteousness. (Isa. 48:1)

As representatives of Christ, we should show respect for Him and His name at all times. His name has power, for the Word of God states that the mere mention of the name of Jesus causes the demons to tremble. And the name of God is said to be healing, provision, salvation, peace, and deliverance. It is no ordinary name.

If your coworkers make derogatory remarks about your God, don't participate. If you are offended by lurid speech, make them aware, with kindness and conviction, that you would appreciate respect for God. The Word of God says that we live in the world, but we are not of it. We must take a stand for what we believe and the God we serve.

What about the language spoken in our homes? What do our children hear coming from our mouths? Do we have one vocabulary at church and another at home? What kind of language do we allow to enter our homes through television, music, and videos? Are we teaching our children to take the name of the Lord our God in vain—and we do not even know it? Have we become so accustomed to the darkness that we can't see the disrespect we have developed for our Lord? I have posed many questions, and if the answers to any of them point to a violation of this law of God, we must ask our Father to forgive us.

I *must* call on the name of God when I want forgiveness and salvation. I *need* to call on the name of God when I want healing, provision, or deliverance. I *want* to call on the name of God when I have praises on my lips for Him. I *must* learn to keep my heart and mouth pure before Him and His powerful name.

THE FOURTH COMMANDMENT:

Remember the Sabbath day, to keep it holy.

Don't you just love the simplicity of this commandment? Set God's day aside and keep it sacred. I have many Jewish friends who observe the Sabbath and make it very clear that nothing will interfere with this sacred day, which begins at sundown Friday and lasts until sundown Saturday. During this twenty-four-hour period, they attend synagogue and share the Sabbath meal with their family. They refrain from any form of work, as the Lord instructs.

The Hebrew root of the word *Sabbath* means "to cease or stop," "to rest," and "to desist." There is no record of the Sabbath being introduced to God's children before its mention in Exodus 16:23–30:

> Then he said to them, "This is what the LORD has said: 'Tomorrow is a Sabbath rest, a holy Sabbath to the LORD. Bake what you will bake today, and boil what you will boil; and lay up for yourselves all that remains, to be kept

until morning.'" So they laid it up till morning, as Moses commanded . . . For the LORD has given you the Sabbath; therefore He gives you on the sixth day bread for two days. Let every man remain in his place; let no man go out of his place on the seventh day." So the people rested on the seventh day.

Certain Hebrew scholars state that just as the rainbow is the sign of the Noachian covenant and circumcision the sign of the Abrahamic covenant, the Sabbath is the sign of the Mosaic covenant.[2] In fact, some rabbis believe that the Sabbath is equal to all the rest of the commandments put together. The Sabbath is referred to as the "majestic queen," a radiant bride, and a heavenly jewel. Keeping this day holy is the only act in the Old Testament that was sanctified and hallowed by God: "Then God blessed the seventh day and sanctified it, because in it He rested from all His work which God had created and made" (Gen. 2:3). The instruction is plain: we are to remember the Sabbath, and we are to keep it holy.

When I was a child, all businesses were closed on Sunday for the purpose of worship. That has changed dramatically. Sunday is now used as a shopping day, a "catch-up" day, or a day at the lake. But it is not our day; it is God's day. He told the Israelites: "Six days shall work be done, but the seventh day is a Sabbath of solemn rest, a holy convocation. You shall do no work on it; it is the Sabbath of the LORD in all your dwellings" (Lev. 23:3).

Women at our church often request prayer for a change of work schedule so they can attend services. I always ask them if they have tried to make arrangements with their employers for Sunday off; nine out of ten tell me they are afraid they will lose their jobs by bringing it up. I understand that many families dearly need a second income, yet I urge them to speak to their employers about this issue.

"The king's heart is in the hand of the LORD, like the rivers of water; He turns it wherever He wishes" (Prov. 21:1). We know He has the power. Surely He can turn the heart of your boss. Give God the opportunity to move mountains on your behalf. Make your petition known with respect and kindness, then step back and watch Him work. If your employer is unwilling to change your schedule, God might be telling you to look for another job. However, God sees your desire to be obedient to His Word, and He will honor your obedience.

When we work six days and give God His day, He will allow us to do more things and do them more effectively in six days than in seven. All of us want abundance and prosperity, and to attain that desire, we must obey Him in all things.

THE FIFTH COMMANDMENT:

Honor your father and your mother, that your days may be long
upon the land which the Lord your God is giving you.

Some Bible scholars believe that the first four commandments deal with man's relationship with God and the latter commandments deal with man's relationship to man. The fifth commandment is considered to be a link between the two categories; it symbolizes the relationship of the parent (the authority of God) to the child (man). Honor your mother and father, who represent the authority of the home.

Unfortunately the spirit of rebellion that drove Adam and Eve out of the Garden still exists in our lives today. As outside influences have more contact with our children through television, music, and child care centers, parents' authority has declined dramatically. If we do not return to respecting authority, our children will lose sight of its importance. The Scripture tells us to honor our parents so that we will have long life, a blessing we all want to receive.

We have also lost respect for authority outside the home. As a child, I remember that we youngsters always had to address an adult as "sir" or "ma'am" and reply to an adult's inquiry with a "Yes, sir" or a "Yes, ma'am." Showing any form of disrespect for any elder was out of the question. I am forty-nine years old, and I address any authority figure with the proper salutation. Sometimes doing this seems to make younger people uncomfortable, yet what my parents taught me remains ingrained in me.

If we work outside the home, our supervisors or bosses are our authorities. We may not agree with their views or philosophies, but we should never undermine their authority. If we cannot respect their leadership, we should simply respect their position.

If you find yourself in a group of people who begin to speak badly of the authority figures in your place of employment, separate yourself from them. God will honor your decision. If someone speaks badly of others to you, it is only a matter of time before this person begins to speak badly of you to others. Wrongdoing is often popular, but ultimately it separates us from God.

Within the home it is without question that the woman should maintain respect for authority. First of all, the wife should be submitted to her husband as Paul stated in Colossians 3:18: "Wives, submit to your own husbands, as is fitting in the Lord." The first time I announced that I would be teaching a class on submission in my church, very few women attended the course. Many told me they would rather have a root canal! Then I renamed the class "Submission and How I Conquered It!" and the class was full. Contrary to popular belief, submission is not man's idea, but God's mandate.

When I asked the Lord, "Why do I have to do this?" a phrase in 1 Peter 3:1–2 sealed the purpose of submission to me: "Wives, likewise, be submissive to your own husbands, that even if some do not obey the word, they, without a word, may be won by the conduct of their wives, when they observe your chaste conduct accompanied by fear." The thought that my conduct could lead an unsaved person to the saving knowledge of Jesus Christ was awe-inspiring to me.

Submission also entails making sure that your children respect their father as the authority of the home. For this reason, the mother who spends most of the time with the children should never speak badly of the father because doing that will eventually wear down any respect the children have for him. I cringe to think of the turmoil we can cause within the household and within the lives of our children when we allow rebellion to enter.

I have told many single mothers in our church not to speak badly of their ex-husbands to their children. They may have little respect for the man, but they must honor the position. "Even if you and your husband cannot stand to be in the same room with each other," I say, "remember, your children love their daddy. If they lose respect for him because of your insults and comments, you will have to answer to the Lord for your actions."

Now I know that this can present a problem for the single mom whose husband has chosen an ungodly lifestyle of alcohol or drug abuse or promiscuous living. Then the mom has to say, "We do not agree with Dad's lifestyle, but you still need to honor your father for the position he has as your dad."

As a mother, I want the best for my children. I want them to be blessed coming in and going out. I want them to have long life. I want them to honor the Word of God and obey their parents. I want them to love their future spouses and raise their children in the fear and admonition of the Lord. As they learn authority in the home, they will find it easier to respond to authority outside the home, whether in school or in the workplace.

THE SIXTH COMMANDMENT:

You shall not murder.

This is the first commandment that deals directly with the relation of man to man. God's Word emphasizes that human life is sacred. The simple fact that God created man is the validity of its sacredness. God has a purpose for every individual, and to take a person's life is to intervene with God's purpose for that life. It is to say that man is superior to God. This will never be.

We are also capable of killing people's reputations with our tongues. Lives that have been justly lived can be destroyed by rumors and innuendos. As small as the tongue is in the body, it commands much space in Scripture, particularly in the book of Psalms:

> I said, "I will guard my ways,
> Lest I sin with my tongue;
> I will restrain my mouth with a muzzle,
> While the wicked are before me."
> I was mute with silence,
> I held my peace even from good;
> And my sorrow was stirred up. (Ps. 39:1–2)

> When you saw a thief, you consented with him,
> And have been a partaker with adulterers.
> You give your mouth to evil,
> And your tongue frames deceit.

You sit and speak against your brother;
You slander your own mother's son. (Ps. 50:18–20)

Hide me from the secret plots of the wicked,
From the rebellion of the workers of iniquity,
Who sharpen their tongue like a sword,
And bend their bows to shoot their arrows—bitter words,
That they may shoot in secret at the blameless;
Suddenly they shoot at him and do not fear. (Ps. 64:2–4)

And there are many other references in Scripture to the tongue's destructive ability (for example, Prov. 18:20–22; James 3:1–2, 4–9).

Do you gossip? If something that you say did not happen to you personally, or it does not edify another person or glorify God, then it is gossip. There is no big hell for murderers and a little hell for gossips. There is only one lake of fire. With one lie or exaggeration you can kill a reputation that took years to build.

Every day choices face us. We can choose to obey God and bless others, or we can choose to disobey Him and curse others with our words. Both choices have consequences. One choice brings God's blessings into our lives, and the other brings Satan's curses. My husband says that people take garbage to a garbage can. So do gossipers. If you are a receptacle for gossip, then people will bring gossip to you. If you reject gossip, then Satan will not include you in his plan to destroy others.

One of the best compliments that can be given a person is that she has never been heard to speak ill of anyone. This person is the image of Christ, and she will draw others to the Cross. When someone receives a promotion at the office, rejoice with him or her. Don't congregate by the coffee machine and gossip about this person in jealous fervor. When people excel, congratulate them, and let them know how proud you are. Be light in a dark world, and build up others with the words of your mouth.

What about the woman in the home? Do your children hear you speak badly about other people on the phone? Do you have friends over and defile your marriage by speaking ill of your husband?

The still voice in your mind that says, *Speak good and not evil,* is the voice of the Spirit left by God to guide His children in the path we should take. Don't ignore this voice. If you do, it will become so faint that one day you will no longer hear it, and you will feel separated from God.

Be like Jesus and look for opportunities to speak words of blessing and healing over the body, the soul, and the mind. Begin with your husband and your children, then the people around you. Soon you will feel the fulfillment that only the Spirit of the living God can give.

THE SEVENTH COMMANDMENT:

You shall not commit adultery.

The union of husband and wife is the relationship within the family on which all other relationships are based. When God created man, He knew that it was not enough, so He created woman. Both are necessary to give full expression of the divine image.

Because of the supernatural importance of marriage, promiscuity is also a direct violation of the seventh commandment. Marriage is so sacred that unchaste conduct before marriage will desecrate the consecration of an eventual marriage. Therefore, unfaithfulness before marriage is as much adultery as after marriage.

Adultery is a sin of devastation. It is a sin against the individual. When a man and a woman consummate their marriage on their wedding night, a blood covenant takes place. Through the sexual act, the husband has broken the hymen of his virgin wife, whereby blood is spilled. This act, consecrated by God as a blood covenant, should never be violated. When adultery occurs, the perfect unity and balance of the spirit, soul, and body between two people are destroyed. Only God is capable of restoring this devastation.

Adultery is a sin against the family. The sacredness of the marriage covenant encompasses fatherhood, motherhood, and childhood. When adultery occurs, this divine circle is broken. The children of the union suffer incalculable harm when they are awarded to one parent and separated from the other. Often a child's perspectives on marriage, the family, and future relationships are thwarted from this point forward.

Adultery is a sin against society. Society is a union of families. When divorce occurs through the sin of adultery, there is an economic upheaval in the family unit. Instantly both parties lose half of what they have acquired in their union together. The woman is often tossed into the workplace, and many times she is unqualified to compete in the business world until she receives new training since she devoted her life to rearing her family.

Our culture has adopted a phrase that did not exist when I was a child: "dead-beat dads," fathers who disappear from the family without taking responsibility for their children's well-being. As a consequence, welfare rolls are bulging. The numbers of youth gangs are at an all-time high because young people want to identify with some kind of authority.

Much of the adultery in today's society occurs in the workplace. A woman may become enamored with an individual whom she is around at least forty hours a week. Once the door is open to thoughts that there is someone else who can meet her needs better than her husband can, Satan has a foothold.

Society has led us to believe that marriage is only a civil contract, and civil contracts are often broken at the cost of a minimal fee. Why isn't marriage the same? Marriage is a divine contract; however, too many people enter marriage without any recognition of God. If you are considering marriage, it is essential that you and your fiancé receive formal Christian counseling to ensure you are secure with the commitment you are about to make. Taking this step will also guarantee that God is in the midst of your decision from the start.

I address the workingwoman in the home and in the workplace. Avoid the trap that the great deceiver has set before you. Remain true to the law of God. He will reward you in ways you cannot measure. If you are single, remember that violation of this commandment outside marriage will still make you as accountable to God and His law as if you were married. If you have already violated this law, know that a forgiving God is waiting to heal your wounds. It is also imperative that you turn from this sin forever.

When the woman was caught in the act of adultery in John 8:11, Jesus let her know that she was forgiven, but she must not go back to her sin. My husband often preaches about grace and forgiveness, but he always makes a statement that seals the act of recurring sin: "Extending forgiveness without demanding change makes the grace of God an accomplice to evil."

Several years ago he taught a series on the covenants in the Bible, which left such a lasting impression on our ministry that we adopted the "salt covenant" as the partnership symbol for our television supporters.

In biblical times men carried salt pouches on their belts as they worked or traveled long distances because they would have to take salt into their bodies to keep their muscles from cramping during the heat of the day. The pouches also provided another service. When two men made a pact or a contract between themselves, each would take a pinch of salt from his pouch and place it in the pouch of the other. Each man would then shake his pouch to seal their agreement since it was impossible to retrieve one's original salt grains from the other's pouch.

This same symbolism has become part of many of our young couples' marriage ceremonies. Once they have exchanged their vows, the young man and young woman exchange salt. Then they shake their pouches so the salt grains can never be retrieved and their vows can never be broken. (We ask them to put their pouches in a visible place in the home to remind them of the eternal vows they have made.)

THE EIGHTH COMMANDMENT:

You shall not steal.

We all acknowledge that taking another person's property without permission is considered theft, and we all agree that theft is wrong in the eyes of God and in the laws of society. But what about the "casual lapses" that occur in our lives?

If you are in the workplace and you take something from the office that does not belong to you, do you consider that theft? Do you keep your home stocked with pencils, pens, computer paper, and other items that you casually "borrowed" from your workplace? God calls this stealing.

Or do you take extra-long coffee breaks? Or sick days when you are not sick? Do you adjust your time card to meet your hourly quota? Or do you arrive late and leave early? Do you spend hours talking on the phone or sending personal e-mail messages to friends on company time? All of these actions point to the sin of stealing. When we become accustomed to the philosophy that "everybody does it!" we forget that a just God is recording each one of these acts.

If you are an employer, do you give your employees their just wages, or do you try to "save" a little and deny them what is rightly theirs? If you do not treat them as God would demand, you are stealing from them. The Lord's half brother James warned the early Christians, "Indeed the wages of the laborers who mowed your fields, which you kept back by fraud, cry out; and the cries of the reapers have reached the ears of the Lord" (James 5:4).

When you prepare your income tax return, do you list more deductions than you really have? As much as I dislike paying taxes, I know that when Jesus was asked about Roman taxes, He directed the people to "give unto Caesar what is Caesar's."

In the home we sometimes borrow someone else's possessions and don't return them, for example, books, cameras, videos, or tools that were to be on loan for a season. We might assume that a friend has forgotten that we have his property so we'll just leave well enough alone. Whether we realize it or not, we have stolen property in our homes.

I have stood at the grocery store checkout counter and watched the clerk make an error on what she has charged me. Instantly a heated debate takes place in my mind:

> *Wow, you just saved two dollars and fifteen cents on that box of laundry soap!*
>
> *No, you didn't. That money is not yours!* another voice says.
>
> *This store will never know the error happened. I have spent thousands of dollars with this company over the years.*
>
> *Tell the woman she made a mistake, Diana.*
>
> *For goodness' sake, think of all the times they overcharged me and I never noticed!*
>
> *Give the money back, Diana!*

Does this conversation sound familiar? I have gone as far as the parking lot and then finally returned to the store to give back the money. Sooner or later I come to the realization that it is not worth two dollars and fifteen cents—or any other amount of money—to displease God.

When I have returned to the store, the clerk has been astonished that I would come back. Why is that? Why does every retail store in America have to install hidden cameras to catch thieves in their business? Stores spend millions of dollars on theft insurance every year, anticipating stealing to occur since many of America's children have become addicted to shoplifting. They consider it a fun pastime. We have turned our backs on a very simple instruction from a God who desires only the best for His children: You shall not steal.

Honesty is the best policy. To be known in the home and out of the home as a woman of truth and integrity is in itself a great reward. To know that you are pleasing to the Father, the King of kings, is an even greater reward.

THE NINTH COMMANDMENT:

You shall not bear false witness.

The ninth commandment deals with two aspects of a person's character: reputation and false witness. God is very familiar with the second aspect of this commandment: false witness. He was killed because He was "despised and rejected by men" (Isa. 53:3). False witnesses maligned His reputation as a "healing rabbi."

This commandment asks God's followers to tell the truth in any statement that directly or indirectly involves our fellowman. For instance, if an error occurs at the office and you are to blame, God calls you to tell the truth and not to come up with an alibi or point an accusing finger at someone else. In essence God demands the truth made by man, to man, concerning man.

Every day men and women are asked to give an oath of truth in a court of law as they put a hand on a Bible. Yet many of these same men and women commit perjury afterward; they assume no one will ever know the truth about their lies. The judge and the jury in that courtroom may not know the truth, but the Supreme Judge in heaven knows.

My husband tells the story of a woman going to a wise older priest to ask forgiveness for talebearing. "God will forgive your sin," the priest told the woman, "but you must do something for me."

She agreed.

"Put a feather on the doorstep of every person you gave false witness to. And the next morning collect every feather from every doorstep."

The following day the woman returned to the priest more repentant than ever. She was not able to recover any of the feathers, she confessed, because the wind had carried them away. "That is exactly what happened to the lies I told," she admitted. "They will never be recovered."

We live in a society where our word is no longer our bond. Contracts must be signed for every transaction between two people, and even then there is no guarantee that a contract will be fulfilled. Truth does not stand on its own merits; the best lawyer often redefines truth to his client's liking. Our schools are teaching that is it all right to lie if it means not hurting another person's feelings.

A friend took my husband and me through a tour of the Jewish diamond district in New York City. There we went into the prestigious Diamond Club where millions of dollars' worth of diamonds are bought and sold by men from all over the world. My eyes widened as I saw men pull small brown leather pouches from under their belts and pour the contents on the table in front of them. Mounds and mounds of glistening diamonds sparkled with the radiance of tiny stars. Potential buyers carefully took these clear, shiny stones with long tweezers and held them up to the sunlight for close examination before selecting the perfect specimen.

Once a man chose one, he simply put the diamond in his pouch and shook the hand of the seller.

We asked our friend what they were doing. He told us they were sealing their transaction.

"When will the contracts be written and signed?" my husband asked our friend.

"There will be no contracts," he responded. "Their word to one another is sufficient."

We could not believe this, so John asked how often a man went back on his word.

"Never!" our friend replied. In the forty-plus years he had traded in the diamond business he had not once encountered such a default.

I marveled as I realized that these Jewish men were wearing their prayer shawls under their clothing. As they shook hands with one another, the twisted coils that hung from underneath their coats dangled beside them. I watched the coils move back and forth, and I remembered a teaching my husband had given to our church. According to Hebrew numerology, these coils spell the name of God, and the knots within the coils symbolize the 613 laws given to the Jews by God. Among these laws was the law that demanded they not lie or bear false witness against their fellowman. From one generation to another, all the way down to the twenty-first century, Jews have remained true to the Law and the God of Abraham, Isaac, and Jacob.

We, too, can be true to the Law and our God. We can be women of truth and purity of heart. Peter advised the early Christians to do just that:

> He who would love life
> And see good days,
> Let him refrain his tongue from evil,
> And his lips from speaking deceit.
> Let him turn away from evil and do good;
> Let him seek peace and pursue it. (1 Peter 3:10–11)

We are also required to teach this gift to our children, for the Bible promises if we teach them the law of God when they are young, they will not depart from it when they become old (Prov. 22:6). As we interact with the world around us, we can be beacons of light that bring the lost ships into a safe harbor.

THE TENTH COMMANDMENT:

You shall not covet your neighbor's house.

The tenth commandment is unique because it deals with the inner and hidden life. The word *covet* means "to desire to possess," "to set the heart on," or "to pant for." The sin, as suggested by the word *covet*, means to desire to possess something that belongs to another. You may break this commandment, and at first no one will ever know. Sooner or later, however, it will reveal itself in some overt act. Yet God knows of its violation from the beginning.

The commandment in itself refers to someone else's possessions seven times: "You shall not covet your neighbor's house; you shall not covet your neighbor's wife, nor his male servant, nor his female servant, nor his ox, nor his donkey, nor anything that is your neighbor's." It is not wrong to desire any of these things unless they belong to someone else. When a man asked Jesus to compel his brother to divide the inheritance with him, the Lord answered, "Take heed and beware of covetousness, for one's life does not consist in the abundance of the things he possesses" (Luke 12:15).

Paul ranked the "covetous man" with the fornicator, the unclean person, and the idolater: "This you know, that no fornicator, unclean person, nor covetous man, who is an idolater, has any inheritance in the kingdom of Christ and God" (Eph. 5:5).

As women of God, we are to look at the material, social, and spiritual things that God has provided and give thanks for His goodness and mercy. Instead too many of us look at someone else's car or home or clothes or job—or even husband—and want what she has. I have been guilty of looking at someone else's beauty and inwardly desiring it. What I was telling God was that He made a mistake when He created me. Once I realized that, I asked Him to forgive me and to help me see myself as He sees all His daughters—through the majesty of His creation.

We must remember, even though the Ten Commandments are known as the Law of Moses, God gave these laws to His people through Moses. It is only at the mountain of Calvary that we can attain the strength to do what was given to us at the mountain of Sinai. It is only at the feet of Christ that we can find the strength and desire to fulfill the laws of God. Above all, it is only through our dependence on Him, who was and is the Eternal Love, that we, as His daughters, can do all things.

❧ ACTION POINTS:
TEN COMMANDMENTS FOR WOMEN IN THE WORKPLACE

1. Think about your attitude in the workplace, whether it is in the home or in the business world. Does it reflect your Christian walk? Judge that against Paul's words in his letter to the Philippians:

> Finally, brethren, whatever things are true, whatever things are noble,
> whatever things are just, whatever things are pure, whatever things are lovely,

whatever things are of good report, if there is any virtue and if there is anything praiseworthy—meditate on these things. (4:8)

Our attitude means everything to our daily walk with Christ. We should depend on the scripture that confirms that we are in this world but not of this world (John 15:19). This way we can determine to be happy in a very unhappy world.

List the vows you'd like to make for your conduct in your workplace at home and/or in business.

_____

_____

_____

2. Now look at another passage in Paul's letter:

Do all things without complaining and disputing, that you may become blameless and harmless, children of God without fault in the midst of a crooked and perverse generation, among whom you shine as lights in the world. (Phil. 2:14–15)

The word *disputing* is important in this scripture. I don't believe that Paul expected us to remain silent when someone is making a mistake, at home or in business. Remember I told John, "Look into my eyes. Do you realize that even though I am supposed to be submissive, I still have a brain?"

I believe that as good employees, as wives, as mothers, we are supposed to point out errors if we see them. But the way we do this makes a difference: with humility, with gentleness, and above all with integrity.

Is something amiss in your home or workplace? Anyone can point out a problem. Instead be a problem solver. Write how you might solve this with the proper attitude.

_____

_____

_____

3. My husband often talks about "an attitude of gratitude." We are to live every day with thanksgiving in our hearts for all God has provided for us.

There is no better way than to quote Paul from a letter he wrote to the Colossians while he was in prison. Needless to say, it was natural for him to complain about his circumstances. However, Paul learned to live above his circumstances in a realm where the peace of God directed his very thoughts:

> Therefore, as God's chosen people, holy and dearly loved, clothe yourselves with compassion, kindness, humility, gentleness and patience. Bear with each other and forgive whatever grievances you may have against one another. Forgive as the Lord forgave you. And over all these virtues put on love, which binds them all together in perfect unity.
>
> Let the peace of Christ rule in your hearts, since as members of one body you were called to peace. And be thankful. Let the word of Christ dwell in you richly as you teach and admonish one another with all wisdom, and as you sing psalms, hymns and spiritual songs with gratitude in your hearts to God. And whatever you do, whether in word or deed, do it all in the name of the Lord Jesus, giving thanks to God the Father through him. (Col. 3:12–17 NIV)

Note the provisions God has made for you and how you can maintain an attitude of gratitude.

_____

_____

_____

4. Read chapter 5 in the Book of Esther. End with the following prayer:

Father, I pray that You will write Your law on my heart. I will meditate on Your law day and night and try to do all that is written there, because then You will make my way prosperous and will give me good success. I desire to live a life of integrity; because of Christ Jesus I am a woman of integrity. I am the head, not the tail. I am above, not beneath. Whatever I set my hands to do You will bless and cause it to prosper. My desire is to become a woman of excellence, that everything I do will testify to Your grace and faithfulness and glorify my Father. In Jesus' name I pray. Amen.

chapter seven

Women and Courtship

*A*s the oldest girl in my family, I always watched out for my younger sisters. At one point I was particularly concerned about my sister Sandy. She had been dating a good-looking young man for several years (we'll call him Peter), but none of the family really liked him. In fact, we were actually pleased when they broke up.

Sandy, on the other hand, was absolutely miserable. She was still living at home, so my mom was getting the brunt of Sandy's unhappiness. One day Mom called and confessed, "I don't know what to do with Sandy anymore."

I said, "Momma, we're going to pray that God brings a godly man into her life."

"Okay," she said, "I can do that."

Now everyone knows that God needs just a little bit of help, so every Sunday I looked around the church for qualified young men. Nothing. No one.

And each Sunday as I was listening to the choir sing, which I call the first sermon we hear at Cornerstone Church, I prayed for each member. I visually moved down the rows and blessed each man or woman in the name of the Lord. I also prayed for their families and their lives.

All of a sudden, one Sunday, I saw a new, very nice-looking masculine face. I couldn't help thinking, *Hmmmmm!*

That Sunday I went home and immediately called Mom. "I think I found him," I said.

She said, "*Gracias al Señor!*" (Thank You, God!)

I went to my husband and told him of the young man. Without a moment's hesitation, he said, "You stay out of it!"

Reluctantly I agreed to do as he said, but I still prayed—and prayed. During that time I was planning a trip to Israel for the choir and the orchestra. At one meeting with the choir, I was taking reservations—people telling me, "Yes, I will be going," or "No, I can't"—when someone tapped me on the shoulder.

I turned around, and there was the handsome young man. "Excuse me," he said, "I want to know how long I have before I must give you a final answer. You see, I'm in medical school, and I don't know when my finals will be."

Now I had prayed for a godly man who could bring my sister closer to the Lord and also for a man who could support her and their children. All the items a mom and an older sister pray for.

Medical school! I thought. And then I asked, "And your wife, will she be coming?"

"I'm not married."

"Oh, I see!" That evening I went home and told John, "You told me to stay out of it, but I can't."

"Stay out of it," he repeated.

Again I resorted to the best biblical action of all: prayer.

Several weeks later my sister came to me and said, "I think I'm going to go out with someone this weekend." She sounded doubtful, and I knew why. She had not dated anyone since she broke up with Peter.

I was hesitant because I was waiting for her to meet my dream man for her. "You are?"

"Yes, but I don't know if I want to."

"Who is it?" I asked.

"Oh, a young man in the choir." Instantly I knew it was him!

God didn't need my help after all, I thought. *And He does answer my prayers.*

Four months later, the Lord proved it to me. Sandy and the young man, Dr. Scott Farhart, knocked on our door to tell us they were getting married. Scott is everything I'd ever want for my sister, for my niece, Jordan, and for my nephew, Jared. He is an elder in the church and one of my husband's Government of Twelve Leaders, a concept begun by the Lord when He commissioned His disciples, pouring His training into them so they could go out and train others.

John and I have directly discipled twelve men in our congregation and their wives, and they in turn are discipling twelve other men and women, who in turn are discipling twelve others—and so on. All in all five thousand people are involved in one of the families of the twelve (which are named after the twelve tribes of Israel) or in more than seven hundred cell groups developed as part of the Government of Twelve.

It seemed appropriate for my sister Sandy to conduct the session on dating with me since I had never dated anyone except John. My father was a very strict Mexican dad, and I grew up in the seventies when many guys in high school had long hair. Trying to convince my dad that a long-haired young man would treat me like a lady just wasn't worth the fight. I was sixteen when my younger sister Rosie, who was fourteen at the time, became ill with cancer. For the next four years I concentrated on my family and my education. Once I got to college I majored in pre-med, and the tough course load gave me little time for dating.

I began dating John in the late fall of my twenty-third year, and we married soon after my twenty-fourth birthday. That was twenty-five years ago, and I praise the Lord Jesus Christ for sending me the man He desired for me. He is the only man I ever held hands with and the only man I ever kissed.

My sister Sandy was the Bee County college queen, after she was bat girl for the baseball team. In the late eighties her dating roster was very full. Yet when I asked her to speak about dating, her first reaction was: "I didn't do very well in that area myself. I'm not good at choosing men. Scott's great, but the other guys I picked were not so good, as you know."

"That's exactly why I wanted you to talk about dating," I said. "Tell them how you went wrong. They'll listen to you because you've been there and experienced some of the pain."

Unfortunately dating has become difficult for Christian women since society has redefined the word *romance*. In our Woman of God conference I asked the women, "How many of you remember a really romantic movie when you were young?"

Most of the women raised their hands.

"Was there any nudity?"

I could hear loud murmurs of "No" throughout the sanctuary.

"Was there any bad language?"

Again the women responded with loud outcries of "No!"

"Instead the actors would look at each other in longing ways, and women in the audience would respond, 'Ohhhhhhh.' That's all it took. Or maybe a door closed and you imagined what was happening behind that door."

Today you can hardly watch a romantic movie without seeing nudity or hearing bad language. (My husband and I have walked out of some movies because of the images on the screen.) And this is all done in the name of romance, in the name of the dating game. No wonder so many women have difficulty dating as a Christian. But we shouldn't give up just because some people have distorted a romantic relationship. In this chapter Sandy is going to discuss dating as a single woman or dating again as a widow or divorcée, and I will discuss married women dating their husbands.

Dating or Dating Again

That evening Sandy asked the ladies to remember the story of Queen Esther. The women who were brought to Susa were from throughout the Persian Empire—from different countries, different cultures, and different religions. And they were not presented to the king as potential successors to Queen Vashti until they were purified for a year. For six months they were cleansed in myrrh. Then they used perfumes, aloes, and various healing oils for another six months. The waiting period was expected then.

Not now. Many women who are dating look for God to provide a man quickly. "We want to control the timetable," Sandy said that night. "But maybe God hasn't brought us the right man because He isn't satisfied with our relationship with Him. Maybe it's not because Mr. Right hasn't flown in from New York City. Or you haven't met the right guy in the singles class. Maybe the focus right now needs to be on your relationship with Christ. God is a jealous God. If we are not willing to be wholeheartedly sold out to Him, He's not going to be quick to give us someone else. He knows He's going to lose us for good if that person is going to take His place in our lives.

"I was the poster child for how to live in the church and in the world. I looked for men outside the church and thought it was okay because I was going to church. There were plenty of guys out there, plenty of wranglers, plenty of two-steppers.

But God was saying to me, 'No, come back here'. . . If finding a mate is the most important thing in our lives, we probably need to ask the Lord whether we are in idolatry. This pursuit can't supersede our relationship with God. He must be first."

Sandy said, "I found a wonderful husband, not by looking, but by focusing my eyes on Christ."

And Sandy reminded the women that God has His own timetable. His message to Habakkuk, when the prophet was questioning God about His slow response, is also meant for us today:

> For the vision is yet for an appointed time;
> But at the end it will speak, and it will not lie.
> Though it tarries, wait for it;
> Because it will surely come. (Hab. 2:3)

When we think of the single woman, we may think of loneliness, but a single woman who is committed to Christ is never alone. She has made a covenant with God, and He promises never to leave her or forsake her. She is committed to develop the talents and gifts God has provided for her to minister to those the Lord brings her way. Her single state may be for a season or for a lifetime, but either way her love for God allows her the strength needed to maintain a pure heart, mind, and body.

"What do we look for in a mate?" Sandy asked the women, and then she gave them a tentative list of seven criteria, which were adapted from the book *If Men Are Like Buses, Then How Do I Catch One?* by Michelle McKinney Hammond.[1]

A CHECKLIST

1. *Is he saved?* Does he have a relationship with God? Paul left no doubt about this requirement when he was advising members of the Corinthian church: "Do not be unequally yoked with unbelievers [do not make mismated alliances with them or come under a different yoke with them, inconsistent with your faith]. For what partnership have right living and right standing with God with iniquity and lawlessness? Or how can light have fellowship with darkness?" (2 Cor. 6:14 AMPLIFIED).

If the man you are dating is saved, does he care what God thinks about his behavior? Does he care if he takes the Lord's name in vain? Or if he sees a movie God wouldn't approve of? Is he accountable to God and spiritual authority?

Sandy told the women, "I had not dated any young man steadily before I met Peter, and I really had a problem with self-esteem, even though Diana thought I was so poised and self-composed. Peter was very nice-looking. He was athletic and played football. His ego was huge.

"In fact, his ego was so large that my personality became who he was. It was as if Peter said, 'Hang on to my arm, Honey, and we'll take off together.' I thought, *If he likes me, I must be okay.* I looked at the outward appearance, but never looked at his heart. He went to church, he 'talked the talk,' but he wasn't born again.

"Scott and I were so different from this. Scott always said, 'God's first, you're second.' And that's how I felt when I met him. No man would ever again become god to me."

2. *Does he want to be married?* If he doesn't, run. Find somebody who does. You aren't going to change this man. If he doesn't think the covenant of marriage is worth having, he's not worth having.

Ask yourself, *Is he pursuing me, or am I pursuing him?* You may be thinking, *If I don't call this guy, he won't call me. You don't know how shy he is, God.* Don't do God's work. Don't pursue him. Let this man recognize you as a pearl, or ask God to send somebody who does.

"Unfortunately," Sandy said, "I became pregnant when I was dating Peter. We were engaged, and I made the mistake of thinking a sexual relationship was okay because we were going to be married.

"My father was willing to go with us to a justice of the peace. He was even willing to help support us while Peter was still in college and I was finishing dental hygiene school. We would have been okay financially.

"Yet Peter didn't want any part of marriage and a family. In desperation I chose abortion. Later, after my dad said, 'You are not to see this man anymore; he did not want you,' I still saw him without anyone knowing.

"Peter said, 'We're meant to be together. Now that this is over, everything's the same as always.' He wanted to renew the physical relationship, and when I wouldn't, he went looking for someone else."

3. *Does he have goals and visions, both in the workplace and in ministry?* Can he provide for you? Does he keep a job? Does he have a ministry in the church or a desire to help other people?

"You would think that Peter's status at college as a fourth-year sophomore would have told me something," Sandy said, "but it didn't."

4. *Does he support your goals and visions?* If you are in a ministry, is he insecure about it? If you are in the music ministry or you are a cell leader or a Bible study leader, does he respect the time you spend doing this? Make sure he is comfortable with your goals, your visions, your successes in life.

Don't ever reinvent yourself for a man, only for God. Your mate must love you for who you are in Christ. He should totally support you in the workplace and in your spiritual ministry.

Sandy says, "I allowed Peter to mold who I was. When I was with him, I never was my own person, and he was brilliant at enabling me do that.

"Whereas Scott says, 'You go out there and do what you need to do, and I'll support you.' Instead I hung on to Peter's belt loop and let him pull me wherever he wanted to go.

"I never thought, *What do* I *want for* my *life?*"

5. *What's his relationship with his mom and his family?* How does he treat his mom? Does he visit her? Call her? Does he speak highly of her? If he treats his mom poorly, he may also treat you badly. How does he treat his family? That's how he may someday treat you and your children.

6. *What about his commitments?* Does he keep his word? If he says he's going to do something, does he do it? If he breaks his bond to someone you know, he might also break his commitment to you. Does he change jobs often or blame others for the mistakes he makes?

Don't think any of these warning signs are little personality quirks that you can change. Chances are, you can't—and if you can, you will probably go through a lot of hardship before that happens. Some people are too quick to settle into a relationship.

7. *Who are his friends?* If you dislike his friends because they curse or go out drinking, you need to realize that's probably the way he acts when he is with them. Remember that when you are dating, he is probably on his best behavior.

My husband often says, "Anybody can act nice for three to four hours on a date. The real man is at home, locked in a cage."

That evening Sandy gave an example of how misleading early dates can be. "When Scott called and asked me out for the first time, he said, 'I wonder if you'd like to go to the symphony.'

"'Sure,' I said, even though I'm not a symphony fan. On our second date we went to a foreign film with subtitles. Again, not necessarily something I'd like to do. For a while I wondered if I'd have anything in common with this man.

"Later I learned the explanation for this. Scott was on a limited budget as he worked his way through medical school. He told me, 'I had free tickets for the symphony, and I happened to win passes to this movie.' Our first dates really didn't represent his nature."

Sandy ended her discussion with a comparison of shopping for a mate and shopping for clothes. "If it doesn't fit, don't buy it," she said. Then she asked the women, "Have you ever gone into the dressing room to try on a dress you adore and had to tug the material to get it to fit without wrinkling or bunching up? The dress is exactly what you've been looking for—the perfect color and style—but it's a little too small. So you reason, *It's right after Christmas, and I've eaten lots of cookies and candy. I'm going to take it home, and I'll lose five pounds.* How many of you have given this same dress away several months later—with the tags still on?

"My advice is: if it doesn't fit, don't buy it. I know my God, and He supplies all our needs. He will bring you the desire of your heart if your first desire is for Him."

DATING GUIDELINES

Any discussion of dating would be incomplete without a frank look at dating guidelines. When we conducted the Woman of God seminar for teenagers, we gave them copies of "Preventative Measures" from Josh McDowell's book *Why Wait?*, which has recently been rewritten and retitled *Why True Love Waits.*[2] Quite a few of these measures are applicable to older women who are dating—or dating again. I will mention six here.

1. *Set your standards beforehand!* We all know that it's difficult to control sexual desires once we are in an intimate situation. Therefore, it is always wise to make a mental—and a written—list of what is acceptable dating behavior.

Ask yourself, *What is restricted to marriage, and what is acceptable in dating?* And then look to the Bible as you form an answer. The apostle Paul set standards for the Hebrew Christians that are still pertinent to us: "Marriage should be honored by all, and the marriage bed kept pure, for God will judge the adulterer and all the sexually immoral" (Heb. 13:4 NIV).

Establish a line that will not be crossed.

My sister Sandy admitted that she was not able to set that boundary as she should have because she was not putting God first.

2. *Be accountable to others.* I've noticed that when men or women begin to dismiss their marriage vows, they are often absent from church—not for days but weeks and months. I believe they are unable to face sitting in those pews where they feel their accountability to God and to the church's spiritual authority.

Single women need to be accountable to other people about their dating behavior. That may be to a cell group or a Bible study or an individual godly woman whom they admire.

3. *Let your lifestyle show.* It's not difficult to send a message about your standards and lifestyle. Your manner of dress, the topics of your conversation, your posture as you talk to someone—all communicate who you are.

A friend of mine told me of an experience when she was in her forties. As a professional woman, she traveled frequently throughout the country. One morning as she was getting ready to board a plane, she overheard a man who had been sitting near her in the gate area ask the clerk at the counter, "I'd like to have my seat moved so I can sit beside Ms. _____." My friend had been talking briefly to this man, and he knew her name. She also was sure he had seen the wedding ring on her finger.

Once they boarded the plane and the man began talking to her, my friend was quickly able to establish her standards. She asked the man about his work as an executive with a large airplane manufacturer. It was then natural for him to ask about her job.

That was my married friend's opening. "I work for a Christian publishing company," she replied.

After that, the man exchanged a few polite remarks and then settled into his seat to read papers from his briefcase.

4. *Keep your mind pure.* The saying, "You are what you hear and see," is all too

true. Early Christians struggled with the temptation to hear and see what would entice them, just as we do today. For that reason the apostle Paul warned the Corinthians to bring "every thought into captivity to the obedience of Christ" (2 Cor. 10:5).

Sandy knew the Lord at the time of her abortion. She admits that she'd love to use the excuse that she was lost. She knew better, but at the time peer pressure influenced her more than her Christian values. She felt she needed to do and be what everyone else wanted her to be, so she went to the bar where she met Peter and other places that led her to compromise her standards.

5. *Choose your companions carefully.* Those of us who are mothers know to watch our children's companions. Child psychologists have told us that our kids will probably be like the children they spend time with, but we don't always apply this concept to ourselves. We can have ten great friends, but it takes only one more who is misguided to influence us in the wrong direction.

6. *Set dating goals.* The following goals are prerequisites to maintaining a healthy dating relationship:

- Date only those who have the same values and convictions as you do.
  Do not be unequally yoked (2 Cor. 6:14).
- Communicate openly about sex. Set your standards early in your relationship.
- Avoid being totally alone. Go out in groups.

Some Christians talk about courtship (being with a man in a group or meeting him in a restaurant or at a movie) rather than dating.

"If you have a problem being alone with a man and you are attracted to him physically," Sandy said to the women during this session, "don't be alone with him. Go to the movies or places where you are among other people. It is not okay to have premarital sex. Believe me, I know. It is a sin. There is a severe price to pay. You can be forgiven, but don't put yourself in the situation again and again. When you give your body to a man, your desire for that man is now over your desire for God because you are not doing what God wants you to do."

After Sandy discussed dating from a single's perspective, I talked about dating our husbands.

COURTING OUR HUSBANDS

Why do we stop dating when we put on a wedding band? Why do we stop doing the things that attracted our husbands to us?

Certainly this is not scriptural. Peter advised the early Christians: "Wives, fit in with your husbands' plans; for then if they refuse to listen when you talk to them about the Lord, they will be won by your respectful, pure behavior. Your godly lives will speak to them better than any words . . . Be beautiful inside, in your hearts, with the lasting charm of a gentle and quiet spirit" (1 Peter 3:1–2, 4 TLB).

We have to know that Jesus Christ will hold both married men and women accountable to Him. It is not my job—nor is it yours—to be concerned with how your husband treats you, how he has treated you, or what he does or does not do (as long as there is no physical abuse in your relationship). Our only concern is what *we* can do to make our marriages better.

You're going to have a standoff if you start thinking, *Well, since my husband did this, I will do this.* Or *If my husband treated me better, I would do such and such.* You will soon create a quid pro quo relationship.

Do you want to be right, or do you want to be reconciled? If you want to be right, you will lose.

We are going to make a proclamation of what we want for our marriages, and then we are going to expect this to happen because of our commitment to the proclamation and because of God's promises to us.

A MARRIAGE PROCLAMATION

You might be wondering, *How does a proclamation relate to my marriage?* The dictionary defines *proclamation* as "an official public announcement." We sometimes make proclamations at Cornerstone Church when John has completed a teaching on healing or restoration. In this sense, a proclamation is a fact or a part of life. Spiritually, however, the words of a proclamation do not have to be operative in our lives at the time we speak them. Instead a proclamation may be an action that I hope and pray will be part of my life in the future. Paul told the early Christians that God "gives life to the dead and calls those things which do not exist as though they did" (Rom. 4:17). Some proclamations at Cornerstone Church invoke God's promise to call what we hope for into being.

That evening I read my proclamation to the women, one I hoped they would also make their own or modify in their own words.

"Lord, I thank You for my husband," I said, "and I cherish the years that we have had together. Bless his life abundantly. Bless the work of his hands, his labor for us and his children. I thank You for all his good qualities . . ."

After this first paragraph, I stopped and addressed the women directly, "Now, you may not believe all of this . . ."

I was stopped by the laughter that filled the sanctuary.

"You may not see all of this right now," I said, "but God wants this for your husband."

Then I went on reading my proclamation. "I thank You for all his good qualities. He has been a good husband, a good father, and a good provider . . ."

Again, I stopped and admitted to the women, "He may not have been any of those three, but that is what we want. *That* is what we're looking for."

"Yes," the women answered enthusiastically.

Then I continued. "Show me ways to let him know how much I appreciate him," I said. "Father, bless our marriage. May my husband treat me with respect, loving me as Christ loved the church. As a wife, may I have more worth than rubies to my husband, bringing him good and not harm all the days of our lives. Thank You for this man who is my life partner. Help me to express how much I revere and trust him.

"Father, teach me how to pray more efficiently for him. May he walk in health, having his strength renewed as an eagle. May You, Father, pour out Your blessing on him and our relationship together. May we together bless Your name, and may You always come first in our lives. I proclaim this in the name of the Father and the Son and the Holy Spirit. Amen."

I suggested that the women think of their husbands in this way. "Then see what happens," I said. A renewed relationship, a new romantic spark, is always possible.

HINDRANCES TO ROMANCE IN MARRIAGE

Women seem to think that men don't want romance as much as we do. When you're thinking that way, ask yourself, *Why will a man have an affair outside marriage and make romantic gestures to that woman that he doesn't make to his wife?*

I cringe when I see a woman come into church whom I've known for years, and I notice that she's had her hair done, she's bought new clothes, and she looks much more attractive. I immediately think, *Is there something wrong with her marriage?* Unfortunately we have a tendency to improve ourselves inside and out *after* our relationships begin to fall apart.

Sometimes I say to my husband, "I saw the most charming response from Mr. So-and-so or Mrs. So-and-so, but it wasn't to his wife or her husband; it was to someone else." Why can't we treat our spouses as nicely as we do the people around us?

People may reply to that question in this way: "That's one of the things about being married. We can still be ourselves." Wrong! A husband and a wife make a covenant between them and the Lord to cherish each other, not ignore or belittle each other.

Could it be one of Satan's plans to destroy our marriages and our lives through our passivity? Definitely. But there may be even more involved. In this session I mentioned several reasons that women aren't as romantic as they should be in marriage. For instance, some of us have never had a clear definition of romance in any relationship. We never saw our moms and dads kiss or hug, so we don't know how to reproduce that relationship in marriage. Our only point of reference may be a movie or what our friends said when they were talking about their romantic encounters. Other women's idea of romance is warped by the sexual molestation they suffered in childhood. Still others have experienced a divorce and don't want to get near a man again. The scars are too deep. They must receive God's healing before they can desire a relationship with a man again.

Another reason women aren't as romantic in marriage as they should be is that they long for approval. So many times a woman looks for approval from her husband, and not from the Lord, which is where she needs to go. If she doesn't feel her husband's approval, she doesn't feel romantic later in the day. *He has rejected me,* she thinks. But if we have approval from the Lord Jesus Christ, who can reject us? No one. And if we are not relying on approval from our husbands, we certainly can be romantic in the evening because they have not disappointed us. Our mighty God does not know the word *rejection* when it comes to His daughters.

We also have difficulty with romance because we long for relief from our daily duties. I'll never forget one day when my youngest children were all under three and a half years of age. I was talking on the phone to my friend Anne when Sandy, who was two, came to me, crying and screaming with her usual bellowing voice. She was frustrated because she had just learned to brush her teeth, but she had brushed so long that her gums had begun to bleed. Then all of a sudden I heard *boom, boom, boom, clang,* "whaaa," *boom, boom, boom, clang,* "whaaaa," and then a final *clang.*

I knew Matthew, at the age of three, was having difficulty getting up and down stairs, so I made a natural assumption.

"Anne, I think Matthew just fell down the stairs! I've got to go," I said. Before I could even hang up the phone, Tina came into the room with her comb twisted in her waist-length hair, "Look, Momma, I teased my hair like Tina Turner, but I can't get the comb out of my hair."

When my husband came home that night and said, "Hey, Babe," I replied, "Take the kids! And tonight—no way."

We are overwhelmed by our daily duties. But if you have little babies, you need to know that this time will pass. Enjoy the good moments while you can. And laugh at the hectic ones—if you can. Be sure to cherish these precious times.

We need to prioritize our lives, always putting Jesus Christ first. My prayer for my unmarried children is: "Lord, bring them spouses who will love them second only to You." Then everything else will line up in good order.

I cannot overstate how important it is to let our husbands know that we love them second only to Christ. Unfortunately some women put their children before their husbands. But how logical is that? They end up losing their husbands, and then they have a fragmented home. Keep the proper order: God first, husband second, children third.

ROMANCE IN MARRIAGE

That night I asked the women, "How many of you are married?"

About three-quarters of the five hundred women raised their hands.

"How many of you have all the romance you can stand?"

Four raised their hands as the rest of the women laughed. "Four out of five hundred. That's more than I thought I'd get!"

Every year my prayer for our marriage is that my husband will love me more passionately than ever before.

Some women tell me they don't know how to express their love for their husbands. "If I tell him, he'll reject me," they say. Or they protest, "We don't have the money for a weekend getaway." At one time in our lives my husband and I realized that we were losing the romance in our relationship. We knew we loved each other, so maybe we didn't need to express it so often. Let me tell you, that doesn't work.

John came up with an acronym: O.W.E.—One Way Everyday.

O.W.E.

In One Way Everyday John and I show each other how much we love each other. For instance, some mornings John will leave a rose from the bushes that border our driveway on my car seat so it is the first object I see when I open the car door. No matter how overwhelmed I may be by my schedule for the day, I'm instantly lifted up.

Sometimes I'll call him, and I'll say, "I love you and I bless you in the name of the Lord. May everything you put your hand to this day prosper. Bye." *Click.* Or before he was on a diet I would put a chocolate bar on his desk after lunch.

We have gone to restaurants where the tablecloth is paper, and John has drawn a heart with an arrow through it on the cloth with the inscription: J loves D. After we finish dinner I've torn his drawing off the paper table covering, folded it, and taken it home so I could remember the moment. It's amazing what you can think of when you program yourself with O.W.E.: What can I do today to show my husband that I love him?

I encourage you to begin to think in romantic terms. And be sure to communicate with your husband. If not, you may be missing each other's thoughts entirely. Or talking about entirely different situations. John and I had this type of experience when we were going to be married. Neither of us had much furniture: I had a rocking chair; John owned an easy chair and a gun cabinet. We obviously needed a bed, so that object became the center of one evening's conversation. Since we were still courting, it went something like this:

"Honey, what kind of bed do you want?" I asked him.

"Oh, I don't care. Whatever kind of bed you want."

"Well, I want to get the kind of bed you want."

"I'm sure whatever you like, I'll like."

With those nebulous thoughts, I went to Karotkins, a furniture store at North Star Mall. There I saw the most incredible bed I had ever seen: a dark cherry four-poster that just happened to be on sale for $600. We had saved $699, so it was right in our budget.

Still I didn't want to make the decision without John. So I called him and said, "Whenever you have a chance this afternoon, I want you to go into Karotkins, walk to the credit counter, make a 180-degree turn, and there you will see *the bed.*"

I could hardly wait for him to call back. At 5:00 P.M., when I hadn't heard a word from him, I called John. "Did you see the bed?" I asked.

He very quietly answered, "Yes."

"Well, what did you think?"

"That is the ugliest bed I've ever seen. I would not be caught dead in it."

I thought, *Oh, my. As much as I loved it, he hated it.*

"I kind of thought you liked wood," I said.

"I do."

"Well, the whole bed is wood."

"What do you mean wood?" he asked. "I went to the credit counter, I made a 180-degree turn, and there was this green velvet bed with a mirror on the canopy."

"That's not my bed!" I said. But I never would have known this if I hadn't continued to question him. Later we learned that my bed, which was on sale, had been moved to the storeroom after I saw it, and the new display bed with green velvet *and gold spangles* was put in its place. You can imagine what he thought when he saw the distasteful piece of furniture. He later told me his exact response: "What kind of woman am I marrying?"

Communicate with him. If you don't, you may not know that he's talking about a green velvet bed with gold spangles!

You can also create a mood.

CREATE A MOOD

At this moment I showed the ladies two nightgowns, saying, "Both of these gowns belong to me." One was my white high-necked, long-sleeved, hemline-down-to-the-floor nightgown. A Puritan woman could have worn it in a bundling bed. The white cotton gown, which my mother-in-law made for me, has pearl buttons that go to the top of my neck. If I'm wearing this gown, there might as well be a padlock on my neckline!

"Anyone have something similar to this?" I asked.

The ladies laughed. Many obviously did.

"I have worn this many times," I said.

Then I showed them my red silk negligee, hemline to my thighs, spaghetti straps, low neckline. "This also belongs to me. I have worn this many times . . .

"What response do you think I get from each gown?"

Their loud laughter told me they had identified with my question.

"Yes," I said, "you're right. I can create a mood. A man is very visual."

Again their laughter told me they agreed.

Next I turned behind me to a table on which we had placed a coverlet and pillow. "Assume this is your bed," I said. "This is the pillow . . . And I have done this." I began scattering rose petals over the bed. "That, girls, works!"

Again laughter.

"Some of you are thinking, *When a husband sees something like this, he's probably thinking he is in the wrong house.*"

Later, my sister Sandy told the women, "If I put these petals on my bed, Scott would worry that I messed up his rosebushes."

Obviously whatever each woman does must be unique to her husband's personality. John could care less about the rosebushes.

Finally I went over to a card table behind me. It was set for a lovely dinner, with candles and flowers and napkins folded in pyramid fashion.

"I've also done this," and I gestured toward the lovely table. "When my husband arrives home, he realizes that our dining room table is not set for dinner. 'I have a surprise for you,' I say. Then I serve a special dinner in our bedroom while I'm wearing my nightgown . . .

"I've done this for Valentine's Day because it is better than spending money on a present. It shows him that I love him and I desire him."

You need to express your love verbally and every other way. Have a date night.

Mark it on the calendar, just as if you were single. You might be on a tight budget, but you can do a lot without money. When we were first married, we had dinner in bed. I would make nachos with all the extras—beans and meat and tomatoes and avocados. We would watch a romantic movie and eat in bed. We gained quite a few pounds those first years, but it was worth it!

As women, we often make the mistake of loving our husbands the way we want to be loved. Our husbands, in turn, love us the way they want to be loved. Consequently we often miss the mark of meeting our spouses' needs and desires, and they in turn don't meet our needs and desires.

Our husbands have tremendous responsibilities. They must care for the financial needs of their families, and they must be the spiritual authorities and coverings for their wives and children. It is important for them to be our heroes, our champions.

Romance is a method you must employ to redeem your marriage. It is not God's plan for you to settle for a stagnated relationship. He wants the fire to keep burning, and the only way a fire will continue to burn is for someone to put fuel on it. As wives, we must make a conscious choice to fuel our marriages with romance and passion.

At the end of this session I told the ladies, "I pray that there will be a breakthrough in our marriages. To me, nothing is more beautiful than to see a couple who have been married fifty or sixty years and still hold hands and kiss each other on the cheek in public."

At the end of this session Sandy read a proclamation for the single women, and I reread my proclamation for the married women. We then had the women who wanted to renew their marriages and the single women who wanted to renew their commitment to purity in their dating relationships come forward to be anointed with oil.

Sandy reminded the women that Esther was purified for a year, yet we can be purified in one night from our past sins and weaknesses. "For years I felt real guilt over my abortion," she said, "even though I had received forgiveness from the church, from God, and from our family."

Sandy then told the women about her experience at that time. Consciously she had thought, *It's over. My abortion is in the past.* But unconsciously she never let it go. She thought, *This is so horrendous that I will probably deal with it for the rest of my life.*

She even thought, *I'll never find a husband. That's going to be my punishment for what I've done.* Little did she realize that Jesus would send Scott Farhart. After their first date she knew he was the man God wanted her to marry.

But Sandy did not share her past with him. *I've been forgiven under the blood of Christ,* she thought, *and I don't need to bring it up anymore.* But she continued to be hounded by depression and irrational thoughts.

When Sandy and Scott got married, he was in his third year of medical school, the year students do their rotations to different specialties so they can decide their area of expertise.

One evening when Scott and Sandy were sitting at the dinner table, Scott said, "I've made a decision about my specialty." He looked at her and said, "I want to be an OB-GYN."

Sandy wondered, *Where did that come from?* Scott had always talked about anesthesiology.

As if answering her silent question, Scott continued, "It's just so awesome to deliver a baby. I want to do that for the rest of my life."

"Well, Honey, I think that's great," Sandy replied.

"But I need to tell you something . . . We may need to leave San Antonio so I can do this." He paused to see how Sandy would respond to the idea; he knew how much she loved our family, and leaving would not be easy for her. Then he added, "If I don't agree to go through a rotation in an abortion clinic, the school told me they won't accept me to an ob/gyn internship and residency."

Sandy dropped her fork and stopped eating. *Here he's made this stand against abortion, and he's sitting at the dinner table with someone who's had one—and he doesn't even know it.*

She began to cry. When she could finally speak, Sandy said, "Scott, I've got to tell you something."

Sandy didn't know it at the time but just by watching her reaction, Scott knew, *Sandy's had an abortion.*

That night they cried together about that part of her past, and Sandy felt such a cleansing. After that, she thought, *I haven't felt forgiven before because I hadn't confessed to my husband. Now I'm going to be okay.*

Still her thoughts were twisted: *One of these days we are going to try to have a baby, and I'm not going to be able to conceive. That will be my punishment.*

Later when Scott was doing his residency in Denver, they decided to have a family. She was amazed that she became pregnant right away. At the same time, however, many people she knew were having trouble conceiving. Loved ones on both sides of our families suffered miscarriages and infertility problems. Sandy and Scott's best friends seemed unable to conceive. Again she blamed herself: *Anybody who's close to me is going to receive my punishment . . .*

Her thoughts were obviously too self-focused, but that's how her guilt continued to surface. For the next few years she experienced terrible depression. Anytime John preached about abortion she thought, *That's me. I'm in that group. I'm going to pay for this later.*

She also thought, *I'm Pastor Hagee's sister-in-law. What would people think about me doing that under his nose? I had the abortion on a Friday and was in his church on Sunday.* Yet she had confessed her actions to John, and he had forgiven her and had more love for her repentant heart than ever.

Often after dinner Sandy would retreat into their bedroom and just lie there crying. One night Scott came into the room and said, "Sandy, have *you* ever forgiven *yourself?*"

That night Sandy realized he was right. She hadn't applied what Jesus did on the cross to her life. She knew that was good enough for everyone else, but Satan was holding her hostage. Being a martyr almost felt more spiritual. Yet that night Sandy was willing to forgive herself.

Once Sandy had fully accepted Christ's forgiveness for herself, she sensed that the Lord would one day call her to lead others out of bondage. She dreaded that day, however. She would have to reveal her hidden past, and she thought that rejection would once again come into her life. What she did not realize was that God would be her source of strength. He would stand by her side when she gave her testimony.

Since that time Sandy has led many to the saving knowledge of Christ through her powerful testimony. She has changed the lives of countless others by sharing her story of forgiveness. I will never forget one incident in particular.

A few years ago Sandy received a phone call from a minister in our church who was counseling a young woman and her mother regarding the daughter's pregnancy. The mother was distraught because her husband had given her an ultimatum: either their daughter would have an abortion, or he would leave the marriage. The mother and daughter felt abortion was the only answer.

Sandy immediately went to the church and spoke to the two women as honestly as she could. She told them that the actual abortion would be a relatively quick procedure that would terminate the life of the girl's baby—yet permanently affect her and all her family for the rest of their lives. She shared her personal story and prayed with them. She never knew their final decision, but she trusted God.

More than a year later Sandy and I were at a public gathering when a very exuberant young woman came over to my sister and hugged her tightly. I did not know who she was, but Sandy recognized her instantly.

When Sandy asked her how she was, the young woman proudly showed her a stroller with a beautiful baby girl. Pushing the stroller was a proud grandfather—the same man who had threatened to leave the family if his daughter did not have the abortion. After hearing about Sandy's testimony, he chose the blessing of life for her baby.

Once Sandy completely accepted Christ's forgiveness, her past of wrong choices was used to bring blessings and life to someone else. Our holy, loving Father is truly faithful.

At the end of this Woman of God session, Sandy told the women, "You, too, can be purified in one night from your past sins and weaknesses when you receive a touch of oil, which represents the healing balm of Gilead. The price has been paid at the cross.

"Don't go back and say, 'Well, here's the bill again.' No. That bill is stamped **PAID IN FULL**. Your sins are forgiven. You have God's forgiveness and the power to be victorious the next time someone wants you to do something that is against God's will.

"You are free!"

⌒◦ ACTION POINTS: WOMEN AND COURTSHIP

1. If you are a single woman, read through the Single Woman's Proclamation.

If you are married, read through the Married Woman's Proclamation.

❧ *The Single Woman's Proclamation* ❧

Dear heavenly Father, You are the Potter, and I am the clay. I submit myself to Your hands. Mold me into a vessel of blessing for the man that You have prepared for me. Help me to help him and not hinder him all the days of my life. Continue to complete the work that You have begun in me that I might be a good thing in his life.

Let my touch always be healing, my words always inspiring, my love always intoxicating. Help me to have a spirit of prayer that my discernment may be keen and my contributions always timely. Teach my hands to work diligently and eagerly. Grant me a giving heart. Let my lips be ruled by wisdom, discretion, and prudence. Touch my spirit, and make me sensitive to the needs of the man You place in my life. Have him love me second to You.

Most of all, dear Lord, while I'm waiting, help me to be a vessel of honor for You, a reflection of Your splendor and Your grace. Help me to walk in the liberty of being a woman by Your design. To embrace my femininity as a priceless gift and rejoice in it. Help me to remain pure. Let my joy be a blessing to others around me. May I remember at all times that I was first created for Your pleasure, Your glory, and Your love. Amen.[3]

❧ *The Married Woman's Proclamation* ❧

Lord, I thank You for my husband, and I cherish the years that we have had together. Bless his life abundantly. Bless the work of his hands, his labor for us and his children. I thank You for all his good qualities. He has been a good husband, a good father, and a good provider.

Show me the ways to let him know how much I appreciate him. Father, bless our marriage. May my husband treat me with respect, loving me as Christ loved the church. As a wife, may I have more worth than rubies to my husband, bringing him good and not harm all the days of our lives. Thank You for this man who is my life partner. Help me to express how much I revere and trust him.

Father, teach me how to pray more efficiently for him. May he walk in health, having his strength renewed as an eagle. May You, Father, pour out Your blessing on him and our relationship together. May we together bless Your name, and may You always come first in our lives. I proclaim this in the name of the Father and the Son and the Holy Spirit. Amen.

Now write your proclamation for your life.

_____

_____

_____

_____

_____

_____

_____

2. If you are married, make a list of the ways you might O.W.E. your husband in the next week in the form on pages 118–119. If you are single and have a steady boyfriend, you might want to make a list for that person.

3. Pray and listen. Devote five minutes to prayer and listening to God. Train your ear to hear God's voice. If you ask Him to help you renew your marriage, He'll do so. You'll hear a voice inside saying you need to do this or that. For instance, you might be convicted by this thought: *You're constantly criticizing your husband; he never hears praises from you.* Or *he always thinks he has to do more and more to please you.* Or *he doesn't think that you're pleased with what he's bringing home financially, and consequently his self-esteem is low.* Or *he never thinks you consider him your hero.* Or *you are constantly taking control. You're always doing everything that should be done by him because you don't feel he can do it right.* All of these thoughts will come in your quiet time. Listen with an open heart, and allow

God to change you into the woman He intended you to be.

If you are single, you might work through this action point, using your boyfriend or another person in your life.

4. Read chapter 6 in the book of Esther. End by praying one of the following prayers:

⌒ For Single Women ⌒

As a single woman I seek You to guide me and direct every step I take. I won't look at others to complete me, because I have You as my Companion, Friend, Brother, Father, and Lord. Help me to be complete in You, Lord. You created me with purpose, and I know Your desire is for me to wait for Your best. I do hereby commit myself to You, to remain pure and set apart until I marry. I ask You, Father, to prepare the man You created for my husband to receive me as You have received me. I want to have a heart after the Father, that the joy of the Lord is my strength. Amen.

⌒ For Married Women ⌒

As a married woman, Lord, I repent. I ask You to forgive me for the unkind and discouraging words I have spoken to my husband. Forgive me for expecting him to make me happy and placing unbearable expectations upon him. You are my joy and source. Help me, Lord, to lift up my husband daily in prayer, for he who hungers and thirsts after righteousness will be satisfied. Thank You, Father, that You would bless him, enlarge his territory, keep Your hand upon him, and keep him from evil that he will cause no harm.

Father, I thank You for the gift of my husband. Help me to show respect and honor to him. He is the priest of my home. I praise You, that he seeks first the kingdom of God and Your righteousness, and that everything will be added to him. I am being conformed daily to the image of Christ Jesus.

Let every word I speak honor my husband, that his whole household will be blessed. In Jesus' name I pray. Amen.

⟶ For Single-and-Content Women ⟶

Father, as a single woman I acknowledge my place in You and Your role in my life. I know You as my Savior, and I believe in You and Your Word. The spiritual strength I receive from You enables me to be happy and fulfilled regardless of my marital status. Protect my thought life, and give me the discipline to cast down every vain imagination and take captive every idle thought. I desire a passion for Your holiness so that I may experience Your fullness in my life as I seek to know You, love You, and follow Your Word. Amen.

ONE WAY EVERYDAY
O.W.E.

1. _____

_____

2. _____

_____

3. _____

_____

4. _____

_____

5. _____
_____

6. _____
_____

7. _____
_____

8. _____
_____

9. _____
_____

10. _____
_____

chapter eight

And God Said . . . "Let There Be Sex"

My husband often says, "Sex is God's idea; all of us are here because of it. I know some of you have made other arrangements, but it is still God's idea."

If it is God's idea, why don't we, as women of God, know more about it? How many of you, before you got married, sat with your mom and dad in the living room and asked them every question you wanted to know about sex—and they answered?

Few, I imagine. When I asked the women at our Woman of God conference this question, they just laughed. Not one solitary hand was raised.

Then I asked, "How many of you thought you knew everything about sex when you were getting married?"

Only three raised their hands.

The rest of us learned by trial and error. The Lord Jesus Christ created sex. It has a purpose and a supernatural definition of what it is (a bonding between husband and wife during which the two become one), what it is for (procreation and pleasure for a husband and a wife), and what God intended it to be (which is clearly expressed in the Song of Solomon).

Yet, as in every walk of life, Satan takes what God created and tries to substitute a mirror image of what it should be. This is usually presented by the world's beliefs.

God does give tests, as I mentioned earlier: the choice of life and death, blessing and cursing, His way or the world's way. He says, "I put before you a Book, My Book, a Book of instructions. If you walk in the path of those instructions, you will not suffer the consequences. If you walk outside that Instruction Book, you will."

As my husband has said many times, it is *not* the truth that sets you free, but the knowledge of the truth. One of the purposes of this book is to bring you knowledge so you can combine this knowledge with the Word and make good choices for your lives and the lives of your children. How can we teach the younger women when we ourselves have never been taught?

Too many of us have a wrong impression of sex because of the way the world defined it to us at a young age. Consequently what we have perceived about sex and our bodies is wrong. And this is as true of women who are virgins or who were virgins until they were married and those who have been sexually active from an early age.

For this reason I asked Dr. Scott Farhart to speak to the women about sex during one session. He's also my brother-in-law, but that's not why I asked him. His credentials speak for themselves. He has been an obstetrician in San Antonio for more than twelve years and was elected chairman of the Department of Obstetrics and Gynecology at Northeast Methodist Hospital in 1991 and elected chief of staff of that hospital in 1995 at the age of thirty-five, the youngest chief of staff in San Antonio history. He has been an elder at Cornerstone Church since 1991.

In this chapter I would like Dr. Farhart to talk directly to you, just as he spoke to the women at our conference. Dr. Farhart adapted his presentation from *Sexual Health Today,* from the Medical Institute for Sexual Health in Austin, Texas.

A CONVERSATION WITH DR. FARHART

Every week in my office I see people who have made the wrong choices. Sex can be either beautiful or destructive. It can be an important act of love and intimacy between a husband and a wife. Or it can be very damaging, just like fire can keep us warm and cook our food, but can scar us permanently and even kill us when it's out of control.

There's a lot of misunderstanding about sex and sexually transmitted diseases (STDs) today. One reason is that many people think of AIDS when they think about sexually transmitted diseases. We hear about AIDS activists, AIDS fund-raising, but there are many other sexually transmitted diseases. In fact, in the last fifteen years or so, STDs have reached epidemic proportions in the United States. Yet most of us don't realize how many people around us are infected because the people who have the infections are embarrassed and don't want to discuss it, even with their boyfriends or girlfriends. Others don't have any symptoms of infection, and they don't know they're infecting other people.

Prior to the 1970s, the two most common sexually transmitted diseases were gonorrhea and syphilis, diseases that soldiers brought back from Korea or Vietnam. Both of them were easily treated by penicillin. In 1976, chlamydial infections began, and in 1981, AIDS was first identified. At the time it was said that only a few hundred people in the United States were infected with AIDS. Now there are more than one million. So from 1981 to now, we've gone from a few hundred to a million.

By the 1980s herpes was so common it was a front-cover story in *Time* magazine. And by 1992, pelvic inflammatory disease (PID), where the infection spreads from outside the body into the internal organs, had become so common that more than one million women were diagnosed with it every year. Of those one million, 200,000 were teenagers.

The human papilloma virus (HPV), which is transmitted through sexual intercourse, became rampant in the 1990s; this virus causes more than 90 percent of all cervical cancers. And the peak age in which people contract it is between twenty-two and twenty-five. It is so easy to catch this virus that you have a 50 percent chance every time you have intercourse with an infected person.

Right now there are more than twenty-five different sexually transmitted diseases, and two-thirds of all STDs are contracted by people under the age of twenty. Every year 15 million Americans will contract a sexually transmitted disease, and one-fourth of them are teenagers.

One of the questions people frequently ask me is: "Why are there so many STDs, and why are so many more people being infected with them now than in the past?" The answer: When somebody has intercourse with another person, she is actually having sex with all of that person's previous sexual partners. The chart on page 123 (illus. 8.1) illustrates the risk of exposure.[1]

There are basically two ways you can contract sexually transmitted diseases.

Illustration 8.1

Number of Sexual Partners	SEXUAL EXPOSURE CHART (if every person has only the same number of partners as you)	Number of People Exposed to
1		1
2		3
3		7
4		15
5		31
6		63
7		127
8		255
9		511
10		1023
11		2047
12		4095

© 2001 AAA Women's Services, Inc.

One is through contact with body fluids, such as semen, vaginal fluids, and blood. The other way is through direct contact, skin to skin, with a person. The ones that are contracted through body fluids are HIV, hepatitis, chlamydia, trichomonas (caused by a kind of parasite), and gonorrhea. Those that are direct skin-to-skin contact are herpes and the HPV virus that causes warts, syphilis, lice, and scabies. Some sexually transmitted diseases are bacteria, and some are viruses.

THE BACTERIAL DISEASES

CHLAMYDIA

The most damaging of all venereal diseases to women is chlamydia, which causes infections that spread inside the body and damage the uterus, the fallopian tubes, and the ovaries. One effect is infertility, which is a common reason that young women are not able to have babies. Another effect is that chlamydia so harms the woman's tubes that she can have a tubal pregnancy, where the fetus is stuck in her tube and the tube ruptures and she bleeds internally. This is the most common cause of death due to pregnancy in the United States.

Teenage females are much more susceptible to chlamydia and gonorrhea than adult women because the cells that line the cervix to protect the skin are much thinner and more susceptible to infection. Chlamydia rates have been consistently higher in teenagers with up to 30 to 40 percent of teenagers who are sexually active having been infected by it.

If you were to compare a normal cervix to a cervix that's infected with chlamydia, you would notice that the infection has caused the cervix to become swollen and red, and this area bleeds easily when you touch it. You might wonder why a woman would have intercourse with a man infected with chlamydia. Forty percent of the men who have it, however, have no symptoms at all. They don't know they're carrying the infection, and they innocently pass it on to their partners.

If you were to see inside a woman, below her belly button you would see the uterus in the middle, the fallopian tubes (wormlike shapes that come off the sides of the uterus), and the ovaries (white, oval-shaped areas). This is a normal, healthy pelvis.

Let's contrast this description with the inside of a woman patient who was in her twenties. She had contracted chlamydia when she was eighteen, and it had spread from the outside of her body into the inside, becoming pelvic inflammatory disease (PID).

In tests blue dye was injected to see if the dye would come out of her fallopian tubes. Instead the dye became stuck because her fallopian tube was scarred shut. The sperm couldn't get out, and the eggs couldn't get in, and that was why she was unable to get pregnant. She has had three operations since she was eighteen to try to become pregnant, and she still is unable to conceive.

If you looked at this young woman's insides with the camera turned up toward her liver, you could see scar tissue between her liver and her diaphragm, where her lungs are, right behind where she breathed. (A condition like this occurs in 20 percent of the women who contract PID.) This woman suffered sudden and intense pain, which would often go up into her shoulders, causing her difficulty when she breathed, when she coughed, and when she laughed. Even though she took antibiotics to kill the infection, the scar tissue was permanent. PID causes devastating infections that can change the course of a woman's life.

GONORRHEA

Gonorrhea is the main cause of pelvic inflammatory disease. It also can cause arthritis, infertility, and severe pelvic pain. A higher percentage of fifteen- to nineteen-year-old women are infected with gonorrhea than any other age-group. One reason is a difference in their immunity. Teenagers don't have as many protective blood cells in their bloodstream to fight off infection as older women do. Also the lining of the cervix of women who have had children toughens up, and they can defend themselves more easily.

Approximately 30 million people in the United States are teenagers, half of whom have had intercourse at least once. That means there are currently 15 million teenagers who have had some sexual experience. More than 3 million of those 15 million will get a new sexually transmitted disease every year. Twenty percent of the sexually active teenagers in the United States will develop a sexually transmitted disease every year.

In men a gonorrheal infection causes an inflammation that produces pus and can burn when they urinate. A lot of men will not worry about a small amount of pus coming from the penis. However, if an infected man has intercourse, the woman has a 40 percent chance of getting this infection with just one act of intercourse. If the woman becomes infected, she can develop pelvic inflammatory disease with all its devastating complications.

These venereal diseases are caused by bacteria and can be cured; others are viruses and are incurable.

THE VIRUSES

HUMAN PAPILLOMA VIRUS (HPV)

The most common sexually transmitted disease caused by viruses is the human papilloma virus, which in turn causes genital warts. There are 5.5 million new cases every year. One study of female college students showed that they had a 46 percent chance of testing positive for the HPV virus, which means that almost half of female college students become infected with this virus by the time they graduate.

HPV can cause warts on a man's penis. Sometimes the warts can be small and not detectable or painful. In fact, the man may not even know he has the smaller ones, so he'll have sexual intercourse with someone and not realize he is passing on the disease. HPV is also a common cause of cancer of the penis.

The HPV warts on a woman's vulva, the outside of her genital organs, can be very large. They often grow during pregnancy, sometimes becoming so large that they fill the vagina and the baby can't pass through. This is a very difficult problem, which often has to be treated by a laser.

These warts can be burned off, but this procedure is painful and requires general anesthesia. This procedure is also very expensive and might not be successful the first time; it may need to be repeated several times. This condition could require thousands of dollars to treat, and obviously is very emotionally upsetting.

HERPES

One in five people age twelve or over is infected with herpes. Between 200,000 and 500,000 new cases occur every year. And currently in the United States, 31 million people have herpes. One out of every four women and one out of every five men will become infected sometime in their lifetimes. And many people will continue to have outbreaks on and off for the rest of their lives. There is no cure for this. It is a virus.

The herpes ulcers on a man's penis can become very sore because the skin peels off and leaves the organ exposed. Over the years new outbreaks can occur near the site of the original infection, and it can also be transmitted orally.

When a woman first contracts the disease, her infection tends to be worse than a man's because the vagina offers a safe place for the herpes to hide. And she tends to get many more lesions, which can cause so much pain it's difficult for her to urinate; many times she has to have a catheter to enable her to urinate until the swelling goes down. She often suffers fevers, chills, muscle pain, and nausea. And sometimes she has to be put into the hospital just for pain relief.

If a baby is born at the time that the mother has an outbreak of herpes, the child has a 40 to 50 percent chance of becoming infected. If the baby becomes infected, he has a 50 percent chance of death. Of those that survive, half will suffer severe brain damage. So something that happened to the woman when she was a teenager drastically affects her and the lives of her babies.

HIV AND AIDS

Right now approximately 1 out of every 300 Americans over the age of 13 is infected with HIV. By 1994, AIDS was the leading cause of death of people between the ages of 25 and 44. By 1998, more than 375,000 Americans had died of AIDS, almost as many as the 400,000 Americans who died in World War II.

In the beginning AIDS mostly occurred in gay men. But as they saw their friends dying, they realized how dangerous the disease was, so they became much more careful. However, heterosexual men and women did not realize that the danger had spread to them through tainted blood in transfusions, IV drug transmission, and an increase in casual sex between bisexuals and heterosexuals. Now AIDS is an epidemic among heterosexual men and women.

HIV, the virus that causes AIDS, is increasing among teenagers in the United States. Right now, 25 percent, or 1 out of 4, of new HIV cases is infecting someone between the ages of 13 and 20. Teenagers make up only 10 percent of the population, but they account for 25 percent of all sexually transmitted diseases.

HEPATITIS B AND C

Hepatitis B is a viral disease that causes hepatitis, sclerosis, and liver cancer. There are approximately 200,000 new cases every year in the United States, and half of them occur through sexual intercourse. Hepatitis B is the most common cause of liver cancer, which has a very poor cure rate.

A newborn baby of a mother infected with hepatitis B has more than a 90 percent chance of contracting the virus. Seventy to 90 percent of these infants will carry this infection for the rest of their lives and grow up to have a high chance of liver sclerosis and other problems.

Hepatitis C is the most common chronic viral infection in the United States. There are 35,000 to 40,000 new cases each year, and the highest incidence is between the ages of 20 and 39. These primarily come through blood, although 20 percent can come through intercourse.

PROTECTION FROM THE EFFECTS OF STDs

In our society people think, *We have technology, drugs, antibiotics. We should be able to cure everything.* Some of the diseases are bacterial (gonorrhea and chlamydia), and we do have some antibiotics that will cure them. But these diseases can cause scar tissue that never goes away. This tissue can obstruct the fallopian tubes so that the woman cannot get pregnant and she has terrible pain. Her poor choice will affect her the rest of her life.

But viral infections (HPV, herpes, AIDS, and hepatitis) have no cure. So what are the options for single people who are trying to avoid sexually transmitted diseases? Only three: condoms, serial monogamy, or abstinence.

OPTION ONE: CONDOMS

Some people advocate condoms, which became very popular to try to prevent AIDS. Advocates said that if you use a condom, you won't get an infection. In a study from two medical journals, researchers examined the reliability of condoms that were used to prevent pregnancy, not to prevent disease (see illus. 8.2). The researchers interviewed a hundred couples who said they were using condoms, and only 14 to 16 percent of them used the condom every time they had intercourse and used it correctly.

Illustration 8.2

Typical Use of Condoms
For Pregancy Prevention

Of 100 couples using condoms, how many typically become pregnant in the first year of use?

- 15.8% (Jones & Forrest, Family Planning Perspectives, Jan/Feb 1992)
- 14% (Hatcher et al., Contraceptive Technology, 17th edition, 1998)

One reason condoms fail is that they can break. Or they can slip off the penis. In this study 15 percent of the women were getting pregnant using condoms, and pregnancy can happen only a couple of days every month. Since intercourse usually occurs more frequently, you can see why condoms don't work very well for disease protection.

Researchers also did a study of couples where one of the partners was infected with the HIV virus. You would think that these people would be very careful, but the study showed that only 50 percent of the couples used the condom correctly—and that was when transmission was a matter of life and death. Illustration 8.3 shows that when the condom was used for disease protection, only 5 to 17 percent of the people used it every time and used it correctly.

Illustration 8.3

Percent Who Use Condoms Correctly

• Overall, 5% to 21% of individuals in national surveys, or other large studies, report that they "always" use condoms.

• The highest reported rates of perfect condom use are about 50%. This occurred with couples in which one partner was infected with HIV.**

* *American Journal of Public Health*, 1995

** *Journal of Acquired Immune Deficiency Syndromes*, 1993

The other problem with condoms is that they do not cover all of the genitals. Some infections are transmitted by fluids, others by skin-to-skin contact. And the parts of the skin that the condom does not reach can transmit diseases like herpes, syphilis, the human papilloma virus (HPV), and warts.

A man can wear a condom when he has intercourse with a woman who has syphilis, but the condom does not make him safe because it does not come up into the hairline of the pelvic area. At this point, if he has sex with someone else, even if he's wearing a condom, she will contract this disease.

OPTION TWO: SERIAL MONOGAMY

Some people think that serial monogamy, staying faithful to one boyfriend or girlfriend at a time, protects them from sexually transmitted diseases. A woman decides, "I won't date anyone else, just that one boy." And since she's not seeing anybody else and he's not seeing anybody else, she thinks she's safe. But the average person will move on to a new partner within six months to a year, and then he or she will stay faithful to that new partner for the same period of time. Then the couple break up, and each moves on to another partner. They will stay faithful until the cycle repeats itself again.

People call this serial monogamy, meaning they're being faithful while they're in that relationship; but over the course of their lifetimes, they may have five, six, seven, eight, or a dozen different boyfriends. And as you saw in Illustration 8.1, every time you sleep with a new person, somewhere down the road you sleep with all his other partners, even if he was faithful during the time he was with that one person.

The last option for a single woman is abstinence until the person enters a lifelong, mutually monogamous, faithful sexual relationship in marriage.

OPTION THREE: ABSTINENCE

What is true abstinence? True abstinence is avoiding genital contact until marriage, which involves any activity, not just intercourse, that would allow contact between the skin and the genitals. When individuals adopt sexual abstinence as their choice, they will not become infected with a sexually transmitted disease, and they will not become pregnant. Abstinence has a 0 percent failure rate.

Right now more than 50 percent of high school men and women are virgins, and that number has increased 11 percent since 1991. Currently 25 percent of teens who have had sex in the past have vowed to become abstinent for the rest of their lives. Some people ask me, "Is it normal or healthy not to have sex until marriage?" I always answer, "Yes. In fact, it is the only way to guarantee that you will stay healthy physically and happy emotionally."

❧ ACTION POINTS: AND GOD SAID . . . "LET THERE BE SEX"

1. Read the scripture, which describes Satan's influence and our protection:

> Now the body is not for sexual immorality but for the Lord, and the Lord
> for the body. And God both raised up the Lord and will also raise us up by
> His power. Do you not know that your bodies are members of Christ? Shall
> I then take the members of Christ and make them members of a harlot?
> Certainly not! Or do you not know that he who is joined to a harlot is one
> body with her? For "the two," He says, "shall become one flesh." But he who
> is joined to the Lord is one spirit with Him. (1 Cor. 6:13–17)

Now read through the scriptures listed, which give God's opinion on sexuality and perversion:

Adultery

Nevertheless, because of sexual immorality, let each man have his own wife, and let each woman have her own husband. Let the husband render to his wife the affection due her, and likewise also the wife to her husband. (1 Cor. 7:2–3)

Promiscuity and Fornication

Flee sexual immorality. Every sin that a man does is outside the body, but he who commits sexual immorality sins against his own body. Or do you not know that your body is the temple of the Holy Spirit who is in you, whom you have from God, and you are not your own? (1 Cor. 6:18–19)

Pornography and Lewd Talk

Let no one say when he is tempted, "I am tempted by God"; for God cannot be tempted by evil, nor does He Himself tempt anyone. But each one is tempted when he is drawn away by his own desires and enticed. Then, when desire has conceived, it gives birth to sin; and sin, when it is full-grown, brings forth death. (James 1:13–15)

2. If you have made some of these mistakes or been promiscuous before marriage, remember that Christ will forgive your sin as long as you confess and repent. Read through the scriptures noted here to realize your new position as a daughter of the King.

You are . . .

- forgiven (Eph. 1:7; Col. 1:14; Heb. 9:14; 1 John 2:12).
- set free (John 8:31–33).

- free from condemnation (Rom. 8:1).
- reconciled to God (2 Cor. 5:18).
- healed by the stripes of Jesus (1 Peter 2:24).

Write out the scripture that is most meaningful to you.

_____

_____

_____

3. Read the story of the prodigal son in Luke 15:11–32. Now pray this prayer:

Lord, I ask Your forgiveness for the mistakes that I have made and any immoral acts that I have committed. Please help me to have the strength to make the right choices in the future. Help me to say no to anything that does not honor You. Help me to choose life over death and blessings over curses. I ask this in the name of Your Son, my Savior, Jesus Christ. Amen.

4. Read chapter 7 in the book of Esther.

For more information about sexually transmitted diseases and abstinence-based education, please contact The Medical Institute for Sexual Health at (512) 328-6268. They have a number of resources including a workbook with slides that can be used at your local school or church.

chapter nine

Ten Questions You're Afraid to Ask Your Gynecologist

At the end of the session on sexuality, Dr. Farhart answered questions from the women in the audience who had submitted questions before the session. This format gave Dr. Farhart permission to talk about matters that are not usually discussed in churches, yet are important to a healthy husband-wife relationship. The questions that follow were the most frequently asked by the more than five hundred women who attended the Woman of God seminars. Again I will let Dr. Farhart speak directly to you, just as he did to the women that night.

DR. FARHART ANSWERS YOUR QUESTIONS

Most of the questions involved two general themes: What is God's view of sex, and what does God think about what my husband and I want to do?

GOD'S VIEW OF SEX

"It's His idea, according to Scripture," I told the women that night. Then I quoted Genesis 2:18: "And the LORD God said, 'It is not good that man should be alone; I will make him a helper comparable to him.'" And I also quoted Genesis 2:25: "And they were both naked, the man and his wife, and were not ashamed."

Unfortunately that situation didn't last long. By Genesis 3, the man and the woman hid from God, ashamed because of the sin they committed when they disobeyed and ate fruit from the Tree of the Knowledge of Good and Evil. Adam and Eve never returned to their perfect state—and neither will we.

The Bible asserts that some sexual activities are wrong. The entire chapter of Leviticus 18 lists these activities: sexual relationships with family members, with persons of the same sex, with animals—and at the time of a woman's menstrual period. In 1 Corinthians 6:13–16 Paul discussed not having sex with a prostitute (as did many passages in Proverbs). He reminded Christians that in sexual intercourse, the two become one. God sees us as one flesh. The apostle Paul rightly asked the Corinthians, "Do you not know that he who is joined to a harlot is one body with her?"

Some Christians wonder about masturbation. The Bible really doesn't talk about this; the word is not even mentioned there. Most masturbation, however, involves the person's thought life. Few people masturbate watching *20/20* or while reading a cookbook. For men the stimulus is pornography, which is not pleasing to God. Much of our fulfillment should come from God, and masturbation, which can be used to release tension or fulfill needs, deprives a person from seeing God as the true Source of stress relief, comfort, and peace.

Instead Paul described normal marital relations in 1 Corinthians 7:2–3, 5:

> Nevertheless, because of sexual immorality, let each man have his own wife, and let each woman have her own husband. Let the husband render to his wife the affection due her, and likewise also the wife to her husband . . . Do not deprive one another except with consent for a time.

It's eye-opening that the Bible portrays a passionate relationship for a man and a woman in the Song of Solomon. You can see from reading the book that it's really God's desire for us to have a passionate and fulfilling sexual relationship. The voice of love in the Song is, in fact, a woman's voice, and this feminine voice speaks profoundly of love. One version's introduction to the Song of Solomon notes, "She portrays its beauty and delights. She claims its exclusiveness. She says, 'My lover is mine and I am his.' And she insists on the necessity of its pure spontaneity." Throughout the Song of Solomon, the woman describes the preciousness of the experience and indirectly suggests that sex is a gift from God.

The second general theme of the participants' questions was: What does God think about what my husband and I want to do?

SPECIFIC QUESTIONS

1. **"I love my husband, but I have a very low sex drive, which I feel hurts our marriage. I want to know what is wrong."**

A low sex drive came up frequently in the questions asked. Some women asked, "When we get older, is the sex drive better or worse?" One woman asked, "Will my sex drive ever catch up with my husband's?" "Yes," I replied, "when he's about ninety-five years old!" And still another woman asked, "Why is a man's sex drive so much higher than a woman's?"

The hormone factor. One of the reasons for a low sex drive is hormonal. Both men and women possess testosterone and estrogen; the amounts just differ. In men the testosterone level is about 95 percent, the estrogen, 5 percent. In women it's just the opposite: estrogen, 95 percent; testosterone, 5 percent. With menopause the estrogen and the testosterone levels go down. And men's testosterone levels go down as they get older. If a man's testosterone level drops, it goes from 95 percent to 50 percent, still way above the woman's 5 percent.

A woman's hormones will also fluctuate with her cycle. One woman asked, "How come I feel more sexually aroused at certain times in my cycle and not others?" Your hormone levels are going up and down with ovulation. Sometimes a woman's body will be in control, because of the hormones, and her brain is just along for the ride. We can be prisoners to our hormones.

Energy and emotions. A woman's sex drive can be hampered by her energy and her emotions. One participant said, "I am too much involved with things going on with my kids. I am tired by bedtime. Many times this causes misunderstandings between me and my husband. What can I do to make this better?" Another woman wrote, "I am so tired from being a full-time student and working, I really lack sexual interest."

The questions speak for themselves. These women have too much to do. In biblical times a woman wasn't in the workplace. Now the majority of women work outside the home. Mothers, wives, housekeepers, employees, supervisors, and even vice presidents—women wear many hats.

I try to explain to women who come into my office, "You're trying to be super-woman when you work on the job and take kids to all their activities. Naturally, the last thing you want is for anyone to touch you by the end of the day."

Part, then, is energy, and part is anger. In some of these homes, the husband returns from work, plops down on the couch, and doesn't do much of anything else. The woman resents that and becomes angry, even though she may not always admit it to herself. The man goes to bed after watching five hours of TV, and he expects sex. That's just not going to happen.

Women need to voice this tension to their husbands: "Honey, if you will help take some of the stress off me, I will have energy for you at night." Dr. Kevin Leman's book *Sex Begins in the Kitchen* is oh, so true.[1]

Another question was related to these issues of sex drive.

2. "I used to enjoy sex, but now I hate it. I really hate the extra seventy pounds I carry."

Women have to feel good about themselves to want to be exposed to another human being. Men are different, I told the women at the Woman of God conference: "They can have a beer gut, no hair, no teeth, but they don't look at themselves and think, *My butt is sagging. I'm embarrassed.* Men walk around the house in their underwear and obviously do not care. But women want the lights out, and they resent every Victoria's Secret model. Their view of their bodies hampers their sex drive."

Women who exercise, lose weight, and feel better about the way they look will probably experience increased sex drive. However, medications, such as antidepressants or seizure or high blood pressure medicines, can decrease the sex drive. Sometimes a physician can help in this area; talk to him or her and see if there is another medication you could take in its place.

One woman asked, "Is sex supposed to hurt?" No, it's not. And if it hurts, your body is telling you something's not right. This woman needs to go to a doctor.

Wrong thinking. Sometimes wrong thinking affects a woman's sex drive. One woman asked, "How can I get over being embarrassed about my body so I can enjoy being with my husband without wondering what he's thinking about my flaws? Sometimes I do not feel good enough for him."

That's wrong thinking. That's listening to the devil, to voices that talked to you as a child and spoke lies to you about your body or your face.

3. "How do you block off bad things that happened in the past during sex and now enjoy it?"

That's a good question. If you were abused sexually, your sex drive can be decreased because you do not view relations between a man and a woman the way you would have if someone hadn't robbed you of that innocence and delight. This feeling is legitimate, yet not everyone views it as a barrier to her sex drive. Some women think, *That's in the past. It doesn't affect me anymore.*

Yes, it does! You must seek counseling and go to the Cross with your pain to receive God's inner healing. At the end of this chapter Diana will give victims of sexual abuse an opportunity to do just that.

4. "Ever since my second baby, I've never been able to tighten my vagina. I feel I don't satisfy my husband anymore."

That's a common complaint. A woman who has given birth to a nine- or ten-pound baby is not going to have a tight vagina. Ask your physician about Kegel exercises, which can often help remedy this problem.

If in the middle of intercourse a woman is thinking, *This doesn't feel good to my husband; it's not as good as it used to be,* sex isn't going to be as good for her. Yet she may be wrong about her husband's satisfaction. I guarantee he's just happy to be there!

5. "In God's eyes is it okay for me, at the age of fifty, to still feel sexual?"

Yes, it is. Sarah and Abraham had a baby when they were in their nineties. Nowhere in Scripture does it say that a person should cease to be sexually active. And from a medical standpoint you are actually healthier. Some studies indicate fewer heart attacks and strokes among people who are sexually active. You burn up calories, so it may make you thinner. And it's also healthy for your bladder and vagina.

Another older woman asked, "Is it necessary to have a sex life after menopause if I don't think I'm missing anything?"

That depends on your husband. If he and you do not feel you are missing this experience, it's okay. First Corinthians makes it very clear that God doesn't intend for a husband and a wife to be deprived sexually. One of them may go looking for this experience somewhere else. In fact, sexual sin is probably the number one problem in America. Women are designed to be a spiritual covering for their husbands, to make sure they stay within the home.

6. "I have a difficult time being in the mood. I have to really concentrate and can hardly wait to be left alone."

A woman who feels this way should communicate her feelings to her husband. This is not the way God intended sex to be. When it's all over, if it didn't edify you and make you feel closer to your husband, you are not experiencing sex as God intended. Sex should help erase the stresses of the day and heal some of the hurtful words that might have been spoken. It's supposed to be a sanctuary from what the outside world has done to you.

7. "If I am not in the mood to have sex with my husband, should I?"

The answer is yes. The Scripture makes it very clear that a woman has the responsibility to fulfill her husband's sexual needs. Paul warned the early Christians:

> The wife does not have authority over her own body, but the husband does. And likewise the husband does not have authority over his own body, but the wife does. Do not deprive one another except with consent for a time, that you may give yourselves to fasting and prayer; and come together again so that Satan does not tempt you because of your lack of self-control. (1 Cor. 7:4–5)

Another question was more unusual: "Why have I not had an orgasm after twenty-one years of marriage?" That is not the woman's fault; it's his. But there is a crucial lack of communication. Some Christians grew up in homes where people didn't talk about sex. They don't think that's a pure thing to do. These

Christians have a wrong way of thinking about sex, so they might not feel comfortable talking with their partners about the way they like to be touched. A lot of times the guy needs instruction on exactly what his partner likes. If a wife doesn't teach her husband, he might not accidentally discover that on his own.

8. "Is it normal for me to desire my husband at inappropriate times? What positions are biblical?"

If it's not mentioned as sin in Leviticus 18, you can do whatever you want to do, but both partners must be willing. A sexual activity is inappropriate if it causes pain or makes one partner feel degraded or demoralized.

Yet another woman asked, "Is it normal for me to have more sex drive than my husband?"

I really wish God matched up men and women with equal sex drives, but that almost never seems to happen. Obviously husbands older than forty are not going to perform as they did when they were younger. And often this affects their self-esteem since men feel it's masculine to perform well. There may be times when your husband does not seem to have much of a sex drive—not because he doesn't want to be with you, but because he doesn't feel he can be with you as well as he used to. Guys are not very good at talking about that with their wives or with their doctors. Husbands and wives need to do so and to seek medications if that will help the men.

9. "How can I reach satisfaction with my husband without me causing it? I would like our experiences to involve satisfaction almost every time."

From a physical standpoint up to 70 percent of women will not experience an orgasm with just vaginal penetration. Sometimes the clitoris will not get pulled into intercourse, especially after childbirth, since the labia or clitoris will not pull down and there may not be much contact. There's nothing wrong with adding stimulation during sex. You can show your husband what you want.

10. "As long as it is kept between me and my spouse, is it okay to use pornography as part of the married sexual relationship?"

Pornography can *never* benefit your sexual relationship with your spouse. Its very existence conflicts with God's plan for a man and a woman to be one. Pornography always brings other partners into the sexual relationship. The pornography industry understands that men are visually stimulated and therefore exploits them while enticing them to fantasize about a sexual experience they may never have. Viewing pornography plants thoughts of dissatisfaction with the natural, loving experience of a husband and a wife, which is created by God. Instead pornography breeds a self-centered attitude of temporary pleasure designed by Satan.

Pornography is first a visual experience followed by persistent thoughts that become desires and consummate with actions. Many studies have confirmed Dr. Victor Cline's research at the University of Utah. Dr. Cline has specialized in the treatment of sexual deviances and addictions for many years. He has concluded that the use of pornography has these distinctive effects:

- *It is addictive.* The user develops a need to view and consume the pornographic material.
- *It escalates.* What used to excite and arouse no longer satisfies. The user requires rougher visuals to achieve the same level of arousal.
- *It desensitizes.* The viewer no longer feels repulsed at certain images of deviant behavior, sexual violence, or rape. The victim is no longer an individual, but merely a vehicle for the user's gratification. Compassion and care no longer exist in the sexual relationship.
- *It incites acting out.* The user has fantasized for as long as he can manage it, and now he desires to "act it out"—to experience this fantasy.[2]

Our society has reaped the bitter fruit of pornography. Our children molested, women violently raped, our young men seduced into homosexuality, and our marriages destroyed. In the book of James, God cautioned His people to guard their minds against this evil:

> Each one is tempted when he is carried away and enticed by his own lust. Then when lust has conceived, it gives birth to sin; and when sin is accomplished, it brings forth death. Do not be deceived, my beloved brethren.

Every good thing bestowed and every perfect gift is from above, coming down from the Father of lights, with whom there is no variation, or shifting shadow. (James 1:14–17 NASB)

God's plan for our sexuality leaves no room for pornography!

At the end of the session I emphasized, "It doesn't do a lot of good if what I've said tonight just stays in this room. Sex is really between a man and a woman. If you don't communicate things you're learning, if you never share what's bothering you, you won't have a mutually beneficial sex life. And you'll be missing what God intended, since there's so much spiritual, emotional, and relational benefit to sex.

"If your husband asks you, 'What did you learn at Woman of God tonight?' don't be afraid to tell him, even if you have to say, 'Dr. Farhart said so.' Fortunately I have a secretary who screens my calls!"

I ended my discussion lightheartedly. Then Diana introduced the next person to speak that night, her assistant Teresa, who told a story that was all too familiar to some of the women present—and all too painful. Diana will retell that story here.

TERESA'S STORY

When Teresa was seventeen, she became sexually active, but she didn't think much about it since she learned about sex when she was five years old. At that time she was introduced to George (not the person's real name), a neighbor across the street. All the mothers in the neighborhood liked him because he was always more than willing to take care of the children if their mothers had to run an errand. He seemed to be a nice, jovial man who had a wonderful talent for making wooden toys.

Unfortunately Teresa learned the price you had to pay for one of his toys. And Teresa wasn't the only one; other children in the neighborhood received wooden toys from this man when he baby-sat them. They had a silent club, you might say, because all of them knew what had happened to you if you had a toy from George.

When Teresa was about nine years old, she finally decided that what George was doing to her wasn't right. So she confronted him.

Teresa never forgot what he told her. (She remembers it clearly, even though she is now in her forties.) "You let me do this to you," he said, "and you enjoyed it. You encouraged it because you didn't make me stop. If you tell, you will get into trouble because you wanted me to do it."

A nine- or ten-year-old finds it hard to debate that. Children are taught to do what adults tell them to do. One of the last things Teresa's mother said to her before she went over to George's house (just as all mothers do before their children are entrusted to someone else) was, "You'd better do what George tells you to do."

So for the rest of her life, Teresa had to deal with the responsibility that a five-year-old little girl had gotten an adult man sexually excited and allowed him to do things that never should have been done to her.

Teresa doesn't remember much about those early years, but when she was ten, she determined that she was old enough to stay by herself. She wasn't going over to George's house anymore.

A couple of years later Teresa learned that her mother sent her little sister to George's when Teresa was away from home. And the little girl came home with a wooden toy. Teresa was so furious, she decided to break her silence and let her mother know that she shouldn't trust this man.

She asked her mom, "Do you wonder why George likes having kids over to his house? Could he be after something?"

Teresa's mother responded in a stereotypical way. She got angry with her daughter. "How can you say such things when George has done so much for you?" she asked.

With those words her mother unknowingly affirmed what George had told her. For the next thirty years she believed she was responsible for sexually arousing an adult man and allowing him to fondle her. She was a dirty, nasty little girl.

And after that man, an uncle abused her. And then a cousin. Teresa was well-developed, and the boys at school made fun of her and tried to grab her. She learned to laugh about it and think that was supposed to happen.

When Teresa became sexually active, it seemed to be no big deal because she felt she was created to be bad. She got involved with a man, and sex was all they did. They didn't talk. They didn't share their dreams. She ended up pregnant, and since the man was honorable, he married her. Still they lived two separate lives as the parents of an adorable baby boy until she got pregnant again.

When she told her husband, he smiled and said, "What do you need another kid for? You can have that baby, or you can keep me. The choice is yours."

Even though Teresa had no marriage to speak of, she couldn't see herself having value without her husband. She had no feeling of self-worth because she had been used all her life, and long ago the neighbor had told her it was all her fault. Teresa still believed him.

The decision seemed easy. The baby was an accident. There was no room in their lives for another child, so she went to the hospital to have an abortion. As Teresa went into the operating room, a nurse kept asking her, "Are you sure you want to do this? Are you sure?"

"Sure," Teresa replied, "why not? I have a miserable marriage. I don't need any more problems."

Teresa could tell that the abortion bothered the nurse, but that's all the woman said to her.

After the abortion Teresa would laugh as she remembered a plaque in the hospital reception area that read: Honoring God by serving mankind.

She knew how dichotomous this was, since God had placed truth within her when she was created. As she walked through the days after that abortion, she became more and more depressed. Yet she didn't want to accept responsibility for what she had done. *It's my husband's fault*, she thought. Their marriage became more strained, and Teresa became more and more depressed.

One day she thought, *I can't go on living as a dirty, nasty girl who has no one to love me.* She was empty and hollow. She felt she had failed as a person, a wife, and a mother.

That night she decided she was going to kill herself because she was ugly, evil—a dirty, nasty little girl who could never make anyone happy and would never know the love she so desired. And she was going to kill her son because she didn't want him to grow up to be like his father.

Teresa fell on the floor and cried out to God, "I know You're there, God. But did You really send Your Son to die for a nasty girl like me?"

And that night the perfect, pure, holy God came to her in a very special way. He put His arms around her, and for the first time in her life she felt love. The next day she purchased a Bible and started reading, which led her to see Christ as a real person, as her personal Lord and Savior.

But for many years Teresa had a box locked up in her heart. Anytime she started praying and God began revealing something about her past, she shut the thoughts down. She couldn't let God know how nasty she'd been. If He knew all that she had let men do to her, He wouldn't love and accept her anymore.

Then one day she heard a lady at a women's ministry event speak about children who were sexually molested. As the woman began, Teresa started to leave because she didn't feel comfortable. Then all of a sudden she was drawn to what the woman was saying. "One of the worst things that happens out of it," the lady said, "is that Satan through the molester makes the child feel responsible for what someone else has done to her. He inspires a spirit of rejection and guilt."

Tears began forming in Teresa's eyes because she felt so guilty.

And then the woman started reading from the Word. She ended by saying, "He bore your sins, your iniquities, your transgressions, your hurts, to the cross, and they were so hideous, He was so deformed, you could not recognize Him." And when she said that, Teresa knew that He had taken all her experiences; only those things would cause the holy God to look so hideous.

For the first time Teresa was set free. The door to that box had been opened. She wasn't responsible for what that man had done to her. Instead the man had chosen to violate a trust and impart a spirit of guilt and rejection that Teresa had carried for thirty years.

In the next years the peace that these men had stolen from Teresa was redeemed. God gave her a marriage of thirty-one years to one man. He gave her four children who love the Lord, and most of all He gave her His mercy and grace.

And He gives that to all of us.

A HEALING EXPERIENCE

That night at the Woman of God conference I asked three different groups of women to come forward to the altar together, so there was no distinction among them. First, the unmarried women who wondered after hearing about sexually transmitted diseases, *Where is the husband for me? And how do I find him? And what kind of sexual baggage is he bringing to me?*

I told them, "You are fearful of the future. Yet there is a man who is praying the same prayer for you, and he is a godly man."

Second, the married women who were in an unhealthy, unhappy marriage sexually, which, as Dr. Farhart said, is a symptom of something else. "You are tired of it," I said. "And you want what God ordained for your relationship . . . If you render yourself to the Lord, He will orchestrate the rest."

I knew some of the women were thinking, *You don't know my husband.*

And I admitted that I didn't, certainly not in the way the wife knew him. "But the Lord Jesus Christ knows him better than you do," I said. "As long as you line your life up with Him, He will take care of the rest."

And finally I called those who had been sexually abused to the altar. Maybe as a child, maybe as an adult, maybe even by a husband. I knew that some of these women had to have been abused since one in four females is sexually molested before sixteen years of age. Many of these young women carry the guilt and pain for the rest of their lives.

That evening I spoke directly to these women: "The voice inside you has told you for years that you don't deserve happiness. I want to replace that liar's voice with another voice. This voice says, 'I love you. I care for you. I know what happened to you, for the good or the bad. I've been waiting for you to come for healing so I can give it' . . . This is the voice of Jesus Christ. For all of these years, He's been waiting for you to come forward to receive healing."

As these three groups of women came forward, we could hear intense sobbing and cries throughout the sanctuary.

After they joined the facilitators and counselors at the altar, Dr. Farhart stood in front of the women, looking directly into their eyes. "I am the man who rejected you," he said. "I am the man who molested you." Then he took a step forward and bowed his head as he said, "I want you to know I'm sorry."

At that moment he represented the men who inwardly felt sorry for what they had done—and still others who might never feel remorse. Yet that can't keep us as women from forgiving them. In fact, forgiveness is the first step to our healing. In the action points that close this chapter, I'd like you to think about the person who abused you. It might have been sexually. Or it might have been emotionally. Or verbally. Then work through the steps to forgive the person and heal your pain.

That night at the conference many women came forward to turn their lives and their pain over to their Lord and Savior. And they were healed, just as you can be.

∽ ACTION POINTS: TEN QUESTIONS YOU'RE AFRAID TO ASK YOUR GYNECOLOGIST

1. Mentally write the name of the person who abused you—either verbally or physically or sexually.

Now take a separate sheet of paper and write a letter to that man. Tell him how you felt at that moment and how you feel now.

Then hold that letter in your hand as you pray to your Savior. Give the situation to Him. Ask Him to take away the pain and help you forgive this man.

Put the letter in an ashtray or on a metal dish and burn it.

2. Think of the situations that make you, like Teresa, feel like a nasty little girl.

Now take a separate piece of paper, and list them briefly. Ask God to forgive you for those experiences. When Teresa watched me hold up that cracked vase the first day of our conference, she thought, *Those holes aren't big enough to represent my sins.*

You may feel the same way. But I reminded Teresa and the women at the conference that the bigger the holes and the bigger the cracks, the brighter the light can shine through.

Remember this as you write the following scripture at the bottom of your list:

> "Come now, and let us reason together,"
> Says the LORD,
> "Though your sins are like scarlet,
> They shall be as white as snow;

> Though they are red like crimson,
> They shall be as wool.
> If you are willing and obedient,
> You shall eat the good of the land." (Isa. 1:18–19)

Now draw a large black *X* through your list. These sins are canceled. The bill has been paid in full. Burn this paper as you did the last one.

3. Let the light of the Lord shine through your cracks to those around you. Remember that the Lord has promised, "Beloved, I pray that you may prosper in all things and be in health, just as your soul prospers" (3 John 2).

As you enjoy God's blessing, ask Him if He knows someone who has also been abused and would benefit by your new understanding of His love.

4. Read chapter 8 in the book of Esther. Choose and pray one of the following prayers:

⁓ *For Women Who Have Been Sexually Molested or Abused* ⁓

Father, I acknowledge the violation that was committed against me. I place it right now in Jesus Christ's nail-pierced hands. I ask You to give me grace to forgive _____, who violated me. I have been held hostage to this offense and will no longer be held captive.

Your Word says, "If you forgive men their trespasses, your heavenly Father will also forgive you" (Matt. 6:14). What the person did was not right; it was wrong. It was sin, but I choose no longer to be held in bondage. No weapon formed against me shall prosper, and You will quiet every tongue that rises up to accuse me, for that is my inheritance as a daughter of the King.

In the name of Jesus I choose to forgive _____ for what he/she did to me, and I ask You, Father, to forgive him/her. I pray that he/she will come to the saving knowledge of Jesus Christ and seek Your forgiveness and healing in his/her broken life.

Thank You for Your healing power working in my life right now; heal my memory, heal my emotions, and heal my body by the blood of Jesus Christ. I bind up the spirit of rejection that was imparted to me through this violation. I receive the spirit of adoption extended to me by the Cross of Jesus Christ. Restore to me the hope of my salvation and the blessings that come with that hope. Father, You see me with the robe of righteousness that Your Son purchased on my behalf. You see me as pure and whole. Father, I am completed in You in Jesus' name. Amen.

～ For Women Who Have Been Promiscuous ～

Father, forgive me, for I have sinned against You and Your temple. In Jesus' name I ask that You forgive me of all my sins and transgressions. I want to walk in Your fellowship and blessings. I repent of my sins and ask that You renew my mind daily. Create in me a pure heart, Lord. Change me; mold me into a woman of God. I desire Your righteousness. I conse-crate myself to You, Lord, for You are a holy God. In Jesus' name. Amen.

～ For Married Women Who Want Their Marriages ～ to Reflect God and His Glory

Father, bless my marriage bed. Let no impurity taint what You have joined together. I thank You for my husband and our sexual union. I pray that neither of us will ever look elsewhere to meet our needs. Help me to remember that it is my ministry as a wife to meet the sexual needs of my husband. I desire to make myself attractive to him as I would for the King.

Lord, show me each day a way to let my husband know he is special to me. My desire is that he will see Your love for him through me. In Jesus' name. Amen.

chapter ten

The Favor of God

When John and I were building our first church, Church of Castle Hills, I was pregnant with our first baby, Christina. Only two people besides John were on the staff at the time: an assistant pastor and my husband's secretary. His secretary needed to retire, and her replacement wouldn't be available for a couple of months so I was the natural person to fill her position.

We were a new congregation, and money was scarce. We existed from Sunday offering to Sunday offering. One Monday after all the church bills were paid and the contractors had taken their draw, there was no money left for our salary. We had no money left for food for the week. Usually I am very stoic and able to support my husband, but not that day. I was very emotional because of the pregnancy. I began to cry as I said, "Honey, we have no food. I'm pregnant. What's going to happen?"

I could see the compassion in my husband's eyes. As the leader of our home, he wanted to provide for his family. His answer was to pray: "I don't know how You will provide, Lord, but I know You have said that You have never seen Your righteous forsaken or their seed begging for bread. I ask You to send Your favor upon us." Then John assured me, "Honey, everything's going to be all right."

After going through my purse and John's wallet, I figured we had enough money for cereal and milk for breakfast and bologna or tuna and bread for lunches. I didn't know what we would do for dinner.

Shortly after that the phone rang. One of our church members said, "Hey, are you all busy for dinner? I know it's short notice, but would you like to come over tonight? The thought to have Pastor and you over for dinner just occurred to me." I instantly accepted the invitation. And that was the first of many other phone calls.

Before the end of the day we had spontaneous dinner invitations for the rest of the week. Consequently we ate like royalty every night because every hostess cooked very special dishes for her pastor and his wife.

I will never forget this experience of God's favor. His provision comes in so many ways, and He is always ready to provide His favor to us.

THE FAVOR OF GOD

All of us long for the *favor of God,* which is defined simply as "liking" or "approval." The favor of God comes in many forms. We sense His favor when we begin to mature spiritually. We feel His favor when we are emotionally fulfilled. We abide in God's favor when we live in divine health. We benefit from His favor when we experience financial prosperity.

This chapter deals with finances. Since the first class, I have added this subject to our seminar because so many of God's people are in financial bondage. Living in that way is not God's will for our lives. It is God's will for His children to prosper financially: "Beloved, I pray that you may prosper in all things and be in health, just as your soul prospers" (3 John 2).

I have found five steps to receiving God's abundant favor.

1. YOU MUST ASK AND BELIEVE

Many of us as God's children do not have our needs met because we simply do not believe we deserve them to be met; therefore, we do not ask God to meet them. Scripture verifies this problem: "Yet you do not have because you do not ask" (James 4:2).

Earlier in our journey as women of God, I mentioned that it is essential to believe all that God's Word says to us. In addition, it is imperative to believe that all of God's Word applies to us. In Philippians 4:19 the Word states, "My God shall supply all your need according to His riches in glory."

If God can provide anything for His children, why then are so many of us in debt? Why do we always seem to be lacking financially? We don't ask.

2. YOU MUST OBEY GOD'S WORD

Unfortunately we are sometimes in disobedience to His Word. The enemy has used financial lack as a tool to ruin many marriages. Second to adultery, financial problems are the most frequent reasons for divorce. And many single women are afraid of marriage or scare future husbands away because of their severe debt. We must learn to adhere to God's guidelines to qualify for His provision.

Some of us pray the prayer of Jabez in 1 Chronicles 4:10 ("Oh, that You would bless me indeed, and enlarge my territory, that Your hand would be with me, and that You would keep me from evil, that I may not cause pain!"), asking for God's blessing on our lives, but we fail to read or abide by the verse that comes before the prayer: "Now Jabez was more honorable than his brothers" (1 Chron. 4:9).

God has a plan for us, as I have said throughout these chapters. Oftentimes we hinder God's purpose for our lives by taking turns that we shouldn't be taking—by disobeying His Word, by committing acts that were not a part of His plan for us. Obeying the Word is vital to achieving our destiny.

3. YOU MUST TITHE

Malachi 3:8–12 gives God's position on tithing:

> "Will a man rob God?
> Yet you have robbed Me!
> But you say,
> 'In what way have we robbed You?'
> In tithes and offerings.
> You are cursed with a curse,
> For you have robbed Me,
> Even this whole nation.
> Bring all the tithes into the storehouse,
> That there may be food in My house,
> And try Me now in this,"
> Says the LORD of hosts,
> "If I will not open for you the windows of heaven
> And pour out for you such blessing

> That there will not be room enough to receive it.
> And I will rebuke the devourer for your sakes,
> So that he will not destroy the fruit of your ground,
> Nor shall the vine fail to bear fruit for you in the field,"
> Says the LORD of hosts;
> "And all nations will call you blessed,
> For you will be a delightful land,"
> Says the LORD of hosts.

In these verses the Lord is saying so much to us, yet too many of us are oblivious to His desire for us. First of all, God is having a personal conversation with His children. He cares for us so much that there is no intermediary when He's discussing the subject of giving.

The Lord is also informing us that He knows we have taken from Him. A tithe is 10 percent of our gross income. When we do not give God what He has asked of us, we are stealing from Him. Our tithe should go to the church we attend. This is the storehouse of God for us.

Next, the Lord is telling us that curses will come our way if we do not obey His Word in regard to the tithe. To rob from God is to rob ourselves. Everywhere we turn we can see this. We live on loans and credit cards. We pay horrendous amounts of interest and are truly enslaved by our lenders. The pressures of financial lack and debt grind on our peace of mind and self-esteem.

God, our Provider, then asks us personally to try Him. Can you believe this? God, the Creator of heaven and earth, is asking us to give Him a chance! He wants us to prosper in all of our ways. He knows His Word is true. He knows that if we trust His Word in our tithes and offerings, we will never lack again. He promises to pour out His blessing on our lives.

Then, He takes it a step farther and promises to rebuke our enemies. And God personally guarantees that everything we plant will bear fruit. Amazing! But even more amazing is that too many of today's Christians don't give to God.

Close your eyes for a moment, and think of all your debt. Imagine going to a bank and sitting in front of a loving banker. I know that is hard to imagine, but try. He tells you that he will guarantee you will be debt free and all you put your hand to will prosper. In addition, there is a limited-time offer. If you sign up right now, his bank officers will make sure that no one will destroy what you have built, whether it be your marriage, your home, your business, or your family.

Immediately you ask the banker what you need to do in return. The banker simply tells you that all he requires of you is 10 percent of your income. You think a moment. You are already spending 25 to 30 percent of your income on debt reduction, and you are still sinking deeper in debt every month because you keep spending more on credit, due to your continued lack.

Sold!

Why is it easier for us to accept the world's deals than the Lord's promises? Try Him. Allow Him to shower financial blessings on your life. All you need to do is to choose to obey.

You may be asking, "What about me? My husband is an unbeliever and won't allow me to tithe." Or you may be saying, "My husband is a believer who doesn't think that tithing is for today. What about me?"

Whenever someone asks such questions, I always answer, "It is your biblical mandate to submit to your husband's wishes. If he chooses to disobey God's Word, he will suffer the consequence. If you do not have access to any finances so that you can give a tenth of that amount, then tithe of your time and talents to God's work. The Lord will honor your desire to obey His Word."

Get out of debt. I also often hear this logic: "I can't tithe now because I'm in debt," or "As soon as I get out of debt, I will begin tithing." This thinking is totally contrary to God's plan. If you keep 100 percent of your income, you will accomplish less than if you give God His tithe and allow Him to prosper you with the remaining 90 percent. Don't tie God's hands; allow Him to bless you. I know this is difficult to understand, but our thoughts are not His thoughts and our ways are not His ways (Isa. 55:9).

The widow in 1 Kings 17:12–15 who had just enough oil and flour for one more loaf of bread for her son did not believe she could give anything to the prophet Elijah; she was expecting to die of hunger after the bread was eaten. How could she give away the little she had? Yet God provided for Elijah and the woman and her son; her household was fed for many days.

My friend Teresa shares a modern-day example of God's faithfulness during a very difficult time, such as this widow's situation. Her husband had lost his job at a company where he had been working for more than twenty-three years. He was depressed and discouraged, since the job market did not seem to offer anything for him. How would he be able to provide for his family? Yet in obedience to God the family continued to give to the church regularly.

There were times that the few dollars they gave in the offering were the very last they had in their pockets; they had no idea where their next dollar would come from. Her husband worked odd jobs, but they had no income they could depend upon.

To make matters worse, after two years of irregular employment they were shocked to receive a notice from the Internal Revenue Service. They were about to be audited. They had gone from an income of $50,000 a year to $8,000. How could this be happening?

One hot July day the IRS auditor came to their home and sat at Teresa's dining room table. There was no air-conditioning, and Teresa could offer the woman only a glass of water since there was nothing else to drink in the house. The auditor pulled out a form and asked Teresa to go through her budget. There was no clothing allowance, no entertainment allowance, no health insurance. There were water payments, electricity payments, and mortgage payments.

The auditor asked my friend what the family budgeted for food. Teresa laughed and said, "Whatever is left!"

The auditor was confused. She could not understand why Teresa had so much peace and joy amid a very dismal situation.

The next item on the list was contributions, donations, and gifts. The auditor dismissed this item, saying, "You couldn't possibly have anything in this category."

Teresa interrupted her: "Oh, sure we do." Then she presented the woman with statements from our church and three other ministries.

The auditor was shocked. The total amount of giving was more than $1,000. That was impossible. A family of six was living on an earned income of $8,000 without food stamps or welfare benefits—and giving away $1,000? The auditor could not believe it. Teresa had to get all her canceled checks and bank statements to prove to the auditor that she was not fabricating the amounts.

Then Teresa told the auditor how God had provided for her oldest son to go away to a private university that very year. The Lord had additionally provided a complete wardrobe, the bedspread and other items for the dormitory room, and even the way to move all his belongings to college since they did not have a car at the time.

The auditor continued to insist that was impossible: Teresa's family could not survive living in that manner.

"Oh, yes, we can," Teresa replied. She told the auditor her family had been following God's principles. They paid their tithe and planted seeds with their offerings. She knew their giving was the only reason they were able to survive on that income; God had multiplied every dollar and stretched it as far as it needed to stretch to take care of every need.

His outstretched hand will always go as far as is needed to help His daughters. No, my friend didn't want to be in that situation, yet she saw the mighty hand of God reach out to meet her household's every need.

Teresa knew the power of God's faithfulness and favor, just as the widow did in 1 Kings: "The bin of flour was not used up, nor did the jar of oil run dry, according to the word of the LORD which He spoke by Elijah" (17:16).

A few months after the audit, the auditor called Teresa. The woman's husband was in another state where he was in critical condition following a severe heart attack. The auditor asked for prayer. She told Teresa she was the first person who came to mind because she knew God heard Teresa's prayers.

If you are currently in debt, don't feel overwhelmed. Once you qualify for God's abundance, you will be amazed at what is possible.

First, pray. Ask for His help, stand on God's Word, and know that with His help you can accomplish anything.

Second, make a plan. Write it down, and make sure it is realistic. Include a target date for your goal so you can anticipate an end to your debt.

Third, stop spending. Don't buy anything you don't have to buy.

Fourth, destroy all credit cards, except one that is to be used only in case of urgent needs; make sure the interest rate on this card is as low as possible. If you must use it, pay the balance in full each month to avoid interest charges.

And last, once you pay your debt, do not fall into that trap again. When you become debt free, you will feel liberated from an anchor that doesn't allow you to soar to the heights God has for you.

The next step to receiving God's abundant favor is to work.

4. YOU MUST WORK

Whether we like it or not, work is a mandate that God has given us in order to receive His favor and blessing. Proverbs 13:4 tells us, "The soul of a lazy man desires, and has nothing; but the soul of the diligent shall be made rich." Second Thessalonians 3:10 comments on work as well: "If anyone will not work, neither shall he eat."

If you are single, you know you must work to meet your daily needs and wants. If you are married, you may have the luxury of choosing whether to stay at home and manage your household or work outside the home. In any case you must work to receive God's benefits.

Sad to say, I have met men and women who ignore this scripture and want God and His people to supply their needs while they do nothing. This is not going to happen, simply because it contradicts God's Word.

Whether we work inside or outside the home, we must live within our means. Many husbands trust their wives to use their paychecks to take care of the family's needs, and that is fine. Receiving that kind of trust is a wonderful compliment. It is doubly important, however, to be a good steward of your family's money.

The virtuous woman of Proverbs 31 was keenly aware of finances:

> She seeks wool and flax,
> And willingly works with her hands.
> She is like the merchant ships,
> She brings her food from afar.
> She also rises while it is yet night,
> And provides food for her household,
> And a portion for her maidservants.
> She considers a field and buys it;
> From her profits she plants a vineyard. (vv. 13–16)

This woman was not afraid to work. She sought good quality and price. She did not take her profits and go shopping; instead she invested them in a vineyard that would eventually supply more fruit for her family.

You must learn to live not just day by day, but also to look toward the future. Look at your life and decide what you want; with your obedience and God's provision you will be awed at what will happen.

One of my dear friends is a single woman. Since the death of her father, she and her mother had lived in an apartment. One day she came to my office and shared her desire to buy a home. She had been fearful because as a single woman, she knew this financial burden would be completely on her shoulders. Knowing fear was not of God, she told me she had written down her vision and made it plain. She prayed and went to the Word, searching for confirmation. The Lord was faithful and gave her Psalm 113:9 to stand on: "He grants the barren woman a home, like a joyful mother of children. Praise the LORD!"

We prayed together. We were very specific with her needs and desires. She had always wanted a pool and was almost too timid to ask God for one, but we did. (When you are specific with your petitions and God sends His provision, there is no confusion that God provided.) This woman and her mother found the perfect home. Yes, it even had a pool. We met at the home and had prayer, asking God to make a way for this home to be hers. She made an offer to the bank that was within her means, but the banker denied that offer, telling her "the chance for the price of this house to be reduced is nil."

One night I had a dream. Trust me; I don't do this often, but the Lord clearly told me to tell her that she was to put money away as if she already had the house. He said He would honor her act of obedience. The next day I shared my dream with her. She said she couldn't understand why God would ask her to put money away for a home she couldn't afford, but she would comply with His request.

She began to do what God asked her to do out of pure and faithful obedience—and she waited. She tithed. She gave her employer far beyond a standard day's work. Six weeks later, the very banker who laughed at her initial bid for the home called and told her the house was hers! God provided.

Together we went back to what was now her home, held hands, and gave God the glory for His provision and favor. We anointed the doors of the home with oil and asked the living God to make it a lighthouse of His love. Her home has become a gathering place for her extended family, and all who walk in the doors feel God's presence.

This can happen to you. Remember to write the vision down and make it plain. Then make sure you are in obedience to His Word, and trust His promises so you can watch Him work.

5. YOU MUST GIVE AN OFFERING

God also asks for an offering, which is above your tithe. Your offering can go to any of God's work inside or outside your church, whether a building fund or mission work. Your offering goes the second mile.

My husband teaches our congregation that there are two kinds of giving in this world: reason giving and revelation giving.

Reason givers will not pray and ask God what to give His kingdom; they ask their accountants, or they consult the IRS code. They usually feel they give too much to God's work already but want to make sure they qualify for the maximum amount of deductions.

Revelation givers are controlled by the Holy Spirit. They know that God is their supply. They give not according to what they have but according to what God can supply. My husband uses a beautiful story in Matthew 26:6–13 to illustrate this point.

Mary of Bethany was an unmarried woman who was living with her older sister, Martha, and their brother, Lazarus. She is characterized as a woman who sat at Jesus' feet to seek spiritual truth and understanding. Before His crucifixion, she anointed the Lord with spikenard, a costly ointment, ten and one-third ounces of which were worth a full year's wages. As He sat at the table in the house of Simon the leper, she poured a whole year's wages on His head.

Some who were present criticized Mary's actions: "Why this waste? For this fragrant oil might have been sold for much and given to the poor."

But Jesus said to them, "Why do you trouble the woman? For she has done a good work for Me . . . For in pouring this fragrant oil on My body, she did it for My burial. Assuredly, I say to you, wherever this gospel is preached in the whole world, what this woman has done will also be told as a memorial to her."

When He prayed in the Garden, agonizing over His impending death, the fragrance on His brow reminded Him of the love someone had for Him. When He was brought before His accusers and mocked as an insurrectionist, the aroma of her sacrifice reminded Him, He was not alone. When He carried the cross to Golgotha's hill, the sweet presence of the oil told Him someone cared for Him. When He labored for His last breath on this earth, the offering of worship that Mary of Bethany bestowed on Him comforted His spirit as death took Him away.

Mary was motivated to do what she did out of love for the Lord. She did not think of the cost or the sacrifice she made to earn the oil; she thought only of her love for Him. And Jesus stayed true to His word; her giving was memorialized for eternity in Mark 14:1–9 and John 11:1–6.

Not long ago our daughter felt God calling her to give an offering to Him above her tithe. She has always been the frugal one of our five children. When she turned eighteen, we asked her what she wanted for the very special occasion. She gave us her usual answer: "I have everything I need." We obviously insisted, and she later came to us with her unique request: "Mom and Dad, I would like a mutual fund. If I add to it, I will be able to put a down payment on my own house one day!" Delighted by her wise request, we gave her what she wanted.

Through the years she faithfully added to this fund. She put every dime that came her way, beyond her tithe to the church, into her fund. Christina graduated from college and began working her first job. Again all she could earn aside from her tithe was going into her savings.

One day she asked me if we could talk. We went to lunch, and she told me she felt the Lord was asking her to give her whole paycheck as an offering, above her tithe; therefore, nothing would go to her mutual fund.

I knew that was a huge step for her—or for anyone, for that matter. I asked her if she was sure she had heard from God, and she said yes. "Then it's done," I said. "God must have a plan for you." I knew that God was not asking her to do this unless He was going to supply her needs later. If you do something that radical, God is opening a door that may not be obvious now.

Later, after Christina became engaged to Nathan, we began to look for a lot for their future home. She knew what she wanted but could not find it. After a while she became very frustrated, and an otherwise pleasant experience was becoming very unpleasant. I stopped the car and asked her to pray with me: "Tina, you list the things that you want your lot to have, and God will provide."

Tina took me up on my request. Her prayer was very specific. She wanted a lot that had a view, and she didn't want telephone wires to be seen from anywhere on the lot. She wanted it to be in her price range. I smiled; the "telephone wire" request would be a tough one, but this was between Tina and the Lord. We continued to look.

Several days later my husband and I and Tina and her fiancé were looking once again, this time in an area we had not seen before. We went to the lot that was advertised in the newspaper, and we all agreed it was not the one. Nathan insisted the two of them walk farther down the block. With some resistance, he finally convinced Tina. My husband and I stayed in the car, waiting for them. Much to our pleasant surprise we soon saw them running back to the car.

The look on Tina's face made my eyes fill with tears. I knew God had provided. Quickly they took us to the lot. There it was, nestled in front of a beautiful, lush green hill. We live in Texas, but the view from the lot looked as if we were in Colorado. I looked in every direction. Not one telephone wire in sight. I knew the price would be no problem. It wasn't.

God had opened the windows of heaven and was showering blessings on our daughter. She beamed, and I could see the confidence in her face; the Lord had answered her prayer. When the Lord asked for her whole paycheck, He did not need her money. He wanted her trust and obedience—exactly what He asks of all of us. In church we sing a simple song filled with truth:

> Trust and obey,
> For there is no other way,
> To be happy in Jesus,
> But to trust and obey.

An offering of your time. Your offering can be time rather than money. One of the most valuable commodities in our lives is time. Time is precious. Time is a rarity. That is exactly why the Lord wants us to give of our time to His work. He knows it is a sacrifice of love. Among other ways, we can give time to Him in intercessory prayer or in serving others to enlarge His kingdom.

I am known as the "Volunteer Queen" of Cornerstone Church. With every breath in me I believe that we do the body of Christ a great disservice if we do not allow Christians to serve.

A while ago one of my friends came to me with tears flowing down her face. I knew God had "kissed her on the forehead," my expression for a special blessing or approval from God, our Father. She told me the Lord had been dealing with her about volunteering her time at the prayer line for our television outreach. She worked outside her home and was very active as a volunteer at her children's private schools, so she could not imagine where she could find more time in her already hectic schedule.

The Holy Spirit was relentless; she could not escape His voice. Finally she decided to volunteer for the prayer line. That day she prayed and asked the Lord to bless her time. Her first phone call was from a frantic father in California whose teenage daughter had just informed him she was pregnant and was going to get an abortion in two days. Father and daughter had debated whether she was about to kill a baby or remove lifeless tissue from her body. He had begged her to wait, but she would not budge from her decision. Finally she agreed to a compromise: if he could convince her that she was truly carrying a baby, she would not go through with the abortion. This dad wanted prayer and direction; his grandbaby's life depended on him.

My friend prayed with him. By the end of the prayer she remembered that John had a sermon series on the life of an unborn child. She told this dad she would send the tapes overnight and asked him to listen to them with his daughter.

Then she waited. And she prayed throughout the next day.

On the day the young woman was to have the abortion, the father called and jubilantly informed my friend that his daughter heard the Word of God. It did not return void. The baby was spared.

My friend gave of her time. She was used of the Holy Spirit to save an unborn life. She had been obedient to His call.

We are to give God our best. I often ask women of our leadership to bring a covered dish to our meetings. A particular friend of mine was having financial struggles because her husband had suddenly lost his job. I avoided calling her and asking for a covered dish for fear it would put additional strain on her budget. Then she called me to ask what she could bring to the event. Knowing the ingredients would not be too expensive, I suggested she bring enough Mexican rice to serve ten people.

That evening my friend walked into the fellowship hall with a beautiful smile and her sweet-smelling offering. She had brought more than enough. Her love offering served more than seventy-five people! Through the years God has provided richly for her and her family, and they have been loyal volunteers to God's work. I think of her often as a woman who did her very best by giving God what she could.

I have given you five steps to receiving God's abundant favor. You must *ask* and *believe* that you shall receive according to His riches and glory. You must *obey* God's Word. Just as you provide for your children who live by your guidelines, so your heavenly Father will provide for you who obey His Word. You must give God what is His and not rob Him of the *tithe*. You must *work* in accordance to His Word. And you should *give an offering* to the Lord's work and to others, and in return God will give to you in ways you cannot even think or imagine.

A PROCLAMATION OF FAVOR

From the beginning of our journey we have been making proclamations over our lives and the lives of our loved ones. We are about to embark on a new road in our journey to becoming daughters of the King, a path that will lead us into His favor. David, a king who received much favor from God, told us about his experience:

> Let all who take refuge in you be glad;
>> let them ever sing for joy.
> Spread your protection over them,
>> that those who love your name may rejoice in you.
> For surely, O LORD, you bless the righteous;
>> you surround them with your *favor* as with a shield.
> (Ps. 5:11–12 NIV, italics added)

David also assured us that the favor of God is a protective shield over our lives forever:

> His anger lasts only a moment,
>   but his *favor* lasts a lifetime;
> weeping may remain for a night,
>   but rejoicing comes in the morning . . .
> O LORD, when you *favored* me,
>   you made my mountain stand firm;
> but when you hid your face,
>   I was dismayed.
> (Ps. 30:5, 7 NIV, italics added)

And the book of Psalms confirms that we can be confident of God's favor:

> Remember me, O LORD, when you
>   show *favor* to your people,
>   come to my aid when you save them,
> that I may enjoy the prosperity of your chosen ones,
>   that I may share in the joy of your nation
>   and join your inheritance in giving praise.
> (Ps. 106:4–5 NIV, italics added)

Jerry Savelle lists some of the benefits of walking in God's favor in his sermon series The Favor of God.[1] I have listed them beginning on page 164. Look through these benefits and know that they are available to you as a daughter of the King.

We must believe the Word of the Lord for our lives. He wants His daughters to prosper in every way. He extends His favor to us; all we must do is ask, obey, and receive.

As we have in past chapters, let us proclaim the favor of the Lord over our lives.

In the name of Jesus, I am the righteousness of God; therefore, I am enti-tled to covenant kindness and favor. The favor of God is among the right-

eous. The favor surrounds the righteous; therefore, it surrounds me. Everywhere I go, everything I do, I expect the favor of God to be in manifestation. Never again will I be without the favor of God.

Satan, my days in Lodebar, a place of barrenness, cease today. I am leaving that place of lack and want. I am going from the pit to the palace because the favor of God is on me. It rests richly on me. It profusely abounds in me, and I am part of the generation that will experience the favor of God, immeasurable, limitless, and surpassing. Therefore, God's favor produces in my life supernatural increase, promotion, prominence, preferential treatment, restoration, honor, increased assets, great victories, recognition, petitions granted, policies and rules changed on my behalf, and battles won that I don't have to fight. The favor of God is upon me, and it goes before me; my life will never be the same. Amen.

THE BENEFITS OF WALKING IN GOD'S FAVOR

You, as a daughter of the King, will be blessed in the following ways:

Supernatural increase and promotion. The Lord did this for Joseph when he was unfairly convicted of a crime: "The LORD was with Joseph and showed him mercy, and He gave him favor in the sight of the keeper of the prison" (Gen. 39:21).

Restoration of everything the enemy has stolen from you. The Lord restored everything to the Israelites when they were finally released from Egyptian bondage: "I will give this people favor in the sight of the Egyptians; and it shall be, when you go, that you shall not go empty-handed" (Ex. 3:21).

Honor in the midst of your adversaries. "The LORD gave the people favor in the sight of the Egyptians. Moreover the man Moses was very great in the land of Egypt, in the sight of Pharaoh's servants and in the sight of the people" (Ex. 11:3).

Increased assets:

> O Naphtali, satisfied with favor,
> And full of the blessing of the LORD,
> Possess the west and the south. (Deut. 33:23)

Great victories in the midst of impossible odds.

> Listen, all you of Judah and you inhabitants of Jerusalem, and you, King Jehoshaphat! Thus says the LORD to you: "Do not be afraid nor dismayed because of this great multitude, for the battle is not yours, but God's" . . . And the fear of God was on all the kingdoms of those countries when they heard that the LORD had fought against the enemies of Israel. (2 Chron. 20:15, 29)

Recognition in the midst of many. "Then Saul sent to Jesse, saying, 'Please let David stand before me, for he has found favor in my sight'" (1 Sam. 16:22).

Prominence and preferential treatment: "The king loved Esther more than all the other women, and she obtained grace and favor in his sight more than all the virgins; so he set the royal crown upon her head and made her queen instead of Vashti" (Est. 2:17).

Petitions granted even by ungodly authority. "If I have found favor in the sight of the king, and if it pleases the king to grant my petition and fulfill my request, then let the king and Haman come to the banquet which I will prepare for them, and tomorrow I will do as the king has said" (Est. 5:8).

Policies, rules, regulations, and laws changed for your behalf.

> If it pleases the king, and if I have found favor in his sight and the thing seems right to the king and I am pleasing in his eyes, let it be written to revoke the letters devised by Haman, the son of Hammedatha the Agagite, which he wrote to annihilate the Jews who are in all the king's provinces . . . You yourselves write a decree concerning the Jews, as you please, in the king's name, and seal it with the king's signet ring; for whatever is written in the king's name and sealed with the king's signet ring no one can revoke. (Est. 8:5, 8)

Territory gained for your behalf through God's intervention.

> They did not gain possession of the land
> by their own sword,
> Nor did their own arm save them;

> But it was Your right hand, Your arm,
>   and the light of Your countenance,
> Because You favored them. (Ps. 44:3)

We have just proclaimed something we never thought possible. It is time we begin to live in the inheritance that our heavenly Father has so freely given us. The Word of God says that He has never seen the righteous forsaken or their seed begging for bread (Ps. 37:25). The Word tells us that we should not be borrowers, for we become servants to lenders (Prov. 22:7). The Word declares that God gives us the power to get wealth (Deut. 8:18). Yet we continue to live outside our inheritance.

We are the King's daughters. We must begin to believe that we are entitled to His provision and favor. We must begin to think like the King's daughters. And we must begin to live like the King's daughters.

⌒ ACTION POINTS: THE FAVOR OF GOD

1. More than a thousand scriptures in the Bible deal with money. That's no coincidence. Psychologists say that how we handle our money indicates what is important to us. This week pray that God would enlarge your perspective on how He wants you to handle your money.

First, look up some of the scriptures related to credit and borrowing:

- Deuteronomy 15:1–11
- Psalm 37:21
- Proverbs 22:7
- Romans 13:8
- 2 Kings 4:11

What do you feel God is telling you to do through these scriptures?

_____

_____

_____

List the steps you intend to take.

_____

_____

_____

_____

2. Now look at some of the scriptures related to giving:

- Proverbs 3:9
- Luke 6:38
- 2 Corinthians 8:14
- 2 Corinthians 9:13
- 1 John 3:17–18

What do you feel God is telling you to do through these scriptures?

_____

_____

_____

List the steps you intend to take.

_____

_____

_____

_____

3. Read the scriptures related to work:

- Proverbs 12:24
- Proverbs 16:26
- Proverbs 21:5
- 1 Timothy 5:8

What do you feel God is telling you to do through these scriptures?

_____

_____

_____

List the steps you intend to take as you fulfill God's call in 2 Kings 20:1: "Thus says the LORD, 'Set your house in order.'"

_____

_____

_____

_____

4. Read chapter 9 in the book of Esther. End by praying the following prayer:

Father, I praise You and thank You for Your faithfulness, mercy, and grace. Thank You for Your love. You care about every need that I have and You desire to bless me and my household. Father, Your Word says You desire that I prosper and am in good health even as my soul prospers. Let me hunger and thirst after You for I shall be satisfied. I choose to walk in blessing and obey Your law.

I give my tithe as an act of worship, because obedience is better than sacrifice. I plant seeds of offering to minister to Your saints and enlarge Your kingdom. Father, I ask that You bless me and supply all my needs according to Your riches and glory. I praise You that the treasures of heaven are opened and poured out upon me. According to Your Word, all these bless-

ings shall come upon me and overtake me because I obey the voice of the Lord, my God. I desire to be more honorable than my brothers, that You would bless me indeed, enlarge my territory, and keep Your hand upon me. Thank You, Father. I am a child of the King. I walk in abundance and my household shall never know lack. Amen.

chapter eleven

Hospitality—An Attitude of the Heart

$\mathcal{A}$re you a woman who wakes at 4:30 A.M. and spends one hour alone with God followed by preparing a warm breakfast for your family, which includes your great-grandmother's famous angel biscuits with fresh preserves that you canned yourself?

Once the breakfast dishes are done, you check your children's homework one more time and see your family off to work and school. You then clean the rest of your home and do at least two loads of laundry. You get yourself ready for work by deciding which of your personally designed and handmade dresses you want to wear. You leave the house by 7:30 A.M. with a batch of homemade chocolate chip cookies for the PTA meeting that afternoon because, after all, you are the president.

After a full day at work, you stop by the grocery store to purchase the foods necessary to prepare a beautiful banquet for your family and ten invited guests. Later that evening the dinner dishes are done, the invited guests have left (all with pretyped copies of your original recipes in their hands), the children have completed all their homework, and you prepare them for bed.

After you check the family's investments on the Internet, you pay all the bills that are due and then balance your checkbook. Now it's time for your one-hour exercise video. After that, you prepare yourself for bed by putting on your husband's favorite negligee. Finally you play his favorite love song as you summon him to the bedroom.

You do all this, I might add, with a fabulous attitude and a radiant smile on your face, never quite understanding why your friends complain of the side effects of premenstrual syndrome.

If this describes you, I hope, for your sake, I never meet you for fear that I and the women of my church would do you bodily harm.

The Proverbs 31 woman is the portrait of the perfect woman; she does not exist in one person. Neither does the woman I just described. The portrait of the woman of God in Proverbs 31 is a composite of many women with many wonderful attributes. I want to free you of the burden that you must be all things to all people. That is an impossible task. However, you can be a woman who desires to please the Lord and who wants more than anything to do His will for her life.

The longer I'm a pastor's wife, the more I realize that life is, as James described it, "a vapor that appears for a little time and then vanishes away" (James 4:14). It comes and goes so very quickly, and once we identify our gifts and are willing to use those gifts to bless others, the quality of our lives will be as sweet as God has intended it to be.

I have the gift of hospitality!

I love this gift. I am a people pleaser by nature, and this gift allows me to please people. I know it's impossible to please all the people all the time. Nevertheless, the times my gift has brought a smile to a sullen face have made up for all the times I have failed to meet other people's unreasonable expectations.

Although I cannot touch a person's soul with a beautiful song as my children do, I can be the vessel Jesus uses to heal a wounded heart. In the next few pages I want to share with you what God can do through you when you adopt an attitude of hospitality in your heart. The apostle Peter advised, "Be hospitable to one another without grumbling [a good attitude]. As each one has received a gift, minister it to one another, as good stewards of the manifold grace of God" (1 Peter 4:9–10).

As I share my gift with you, I hope that I can break the myth that being hospitable and being a good hostess mean that you need to make Martha Stewart look like a slouch. Your gift does not spontaneously appear; it's developed through obedience and the willingness to make yourself a vessel of God's love as you adopt His attitude toward His people.

HOSPITALITY IN THE HOME

After the Lord, your family is your foremost priority, and you should always treat each family member as a blessing in your life. One rule in our home is that we will eat our evening meal together since some of our most precious memories have occurred around the dinner table. I find it very sad that this practice does not occur in all homes. Because of hectic schedules, some families find it more convenient to fend for themselves with their favorite fast food on their own schedules.

Your house is not a home until love and joy fill its walls. We, as the women of the homes, must try our best to make them places where the love of God abides.

Obviously the most ideal situation is to make a very special dinner every night, but this is not a perfect world and accomplishing this goal is not always possible. Still our desire to please the family is just as important as our success. We put forth the effort and the love, and the Lord, who is sensitive to our desire to do our best, will help us accomplish our mission.

I have found several ways to show my family hospitality, which I will share with you.

1. HOME COOKING AND A PLEASING ENVIRONMENT

At every meal I set the table with place mats and china or pottery plates, even though we may be having delivery pizza. For years my daughters complained because they knew it would mean more dishes to wash, but Mom insisted because this touch emphasized that our time together was always a special occasion. What difference does it make if it takes a little more time to clean up?

I love to see my daughters set the table with place mats and "real plates" as they call them because I know they are setting traditions for their families in the future. Even our sons go for the "mats" when I ask them to help with the table setting.

I can hear your question now: "What happens when I have a bad day?" When the children were small, it was a lot easier to have dinner ready because I was home more. I must explain that this was a choice I made for the benefit of my family. My husband has been very supportive of me through the years and has always helped me by bringing home ready-made food when I was caring for a sick child or by taking me out for burgers when I had a "Calgon" day. God promises to gently lead those who are with young (Isa. 40:11).

After all the children started school, I was working at the church most of the day and found it more difficult to accomplish my goal. I began to organize a bit more, and creativity became an absolute necessity. I would create a week's worth of menus and buy all the ingredients I needed for those menus. Then I would set aside a day for cooking. Once I had prepared the main dishes, I listed them on the bulletin board and put them in the freezer.

When I had an especially long day, I would set the table before I left in the morning and take my spaghetti sauce out of the freezer. When I got home, I would heat the sauce, boil the pasta, make a simple salad, and warm the bread. Dinner was on.

What about take-out food or leftovers? Not to worry. If I bring in ready-made food, I make sure that I serve it in serving dishes and not the cardboard containers it comes in. One of my trade secrets, which I don't want you to repeat, especially to my family, is using rotisserie chicken from the deli of my local supermarket. I ask the deli manager to cut the ready-made chickens in quarters (this saves time for me at home) while I complete my shopping.

When I arrive home, I put the chicken quarters in a large baking pan and top them with drained mushroom slices and store-bought chicken gravy. I cover the pan with foil and heat for thirty minutes. While the chicken is baking, I boil miniature carrots and season them with butter, cinnamon, and sugar. While the carrots are cooking, I make brown rice according to the package. (I like Uncle Ben's brown rice because it takes only thirty minutes to cook.) For a dinner salad I add tomatoes, cucumbers, and sliced avocados to a bag of salad greens. In the last five minutes I put store-bought wheat rolls into the oven, and the meal, which took less than an hour to prepare, is complete. A meal is truly transformed when you add a little TLC.

Regarding leftovers—get creative. When I have meat sauce and spaghetti on Monday night, my family is sure to see meat lasagna on Thursday night. It is painless, it is certainly economical, and the family seldom recognizes this meal as leftover.

Many of my friends tell me they hate to cook. I ask them to stop thinking of cooking as a chore and look at it as a way of giving a love offering to their families. When the Lord received a sacrificial offering with which He was well pleased, a "sweet aroma" came forth to heaven: "Then the priest shall take from the grain offering a memorial portion, and burn it on the altar. It is an offering made by fire, a sweet aroma to the LORD" (Lev. 2:9). When you smell the aroma of a meal cooking in your kitchen, think of it as a sweet-smelling sacrifice of love that pleases God the Father.

Honoring family celebrations is another way to bless your family with the gift of hospitality.

2. FAMILY CELEBRATIONS

Birthdays are special occasions in our home. As in many American homes, our tradition is that the birthday person gets to plan his or her favorite menu. Then Mom will prepare it as her gift. When the children were little, I would have to prepare two main meals—spaghetti and meatballs and macaroni and cheese; three side dishes—tater tots, French fries, and mashed potatoes and gravy; and thank heaven, one dessert—chocolate cake—all in the same meal. Not what a nutritionist would call a balanced meal; however, I was nurturing the spirit, not the body, with this special offering.

Another way you can bless your family is to have an open-door policy when it comes to inviting their friends over for a meal. I always had enough for extra guests, and the children saw to it that their neighborhood friends had places at our table. The excitement my children had in their eyes when they would ask if a friend could come to dinner was worth a million dollars. The big question of the day is still, "How many do I set the table for, Mom?"

This policy is in effect today. Last week I invited a church member to come to dinner when his family was out of town. I invited him about two hours before we were to eat, even though I had no time to prepare something out of the ordinary. When he sat down at the table, his eyes opened wide, and he asked, "Do you eat this way every night? This is very fancy!"

I felt honored. My husband and children proudly said they ate like that most nights. I could not have been more pleased. They had felt the love that I had for them through my offering of the meal. The Bible tells us: "God is not unjust to forget your work and labor of love which you have shown toward His name, in that you have ministered to the saints, and do minister" (Heb. 6:10).

Another time that is very special for our family is the holiday season. Thanksgiving and Christmas are occasions for big family gatherings. Since we have the largest home and I am the oldest of our family, the gatherings occur here. I have had an average of twenty-five people for Thanksgiving dinner. One very special year I served our Thanksgiving meal in two shifts, an early afternoon and an evening shift, serving more than fifty people for the day.

I love to plan the menus early and delegate food assignments to those who are attending, but I don't tell them what to bring. I usually just say, "I'm doing ham. Do you have a favorite dish that accompanies ham?" That way they feel comfortable with what they are bringing. Our time together is sweet, and the wonderful memories that we have surrounding these times are priceless.

Several years ago my husband was asked to preach a Thanksgiving camp meeting out of state over the holidays. We told the people at the ministry that we would accept the invitation only if our children could come with us. They agreed and said that they would have a Thanksgiving meal in their banquet hall; there, they assured us, we would be able to eat with our children. We all agreed it would be a new adventure.

What we had planned did not occur. Our hosts were very gracious, but they wanted to spend time with my husband and me, so our seating assignments were placed next to our hosts. Our children were seated all the way across the huge banquet hall. We could hardly swallow our food as our children's sad faces said it all. In our hotel that night we had a family meeting and made a mutual decision: never again!

That was fifteen years ago, and we have had all our Thanksgiving and Christmas holidays at home ever since. It is very important to continue family traditions in your family. Some of my most precious memories of Christmas are of my mother making tamales every year. If you don't have passed-down traditions, then by all means begin to set your own. Don't allow the lack of the past to be perpetuated for future generations. We learn from Scripture: "Only take heed to yourself, and diligently keep yourself, lest you forget the things your eyes have seen, and lest they depart from your heart all the days of your life. And teach them to your children and your grandchildren" (Deut. 4:9).

MI CASA ES SU CASA

With my Mexican heritage, it is second nature for me to equate hospitality with food. "My home is your home" was our family motto as we opened our home to guests when I was a child. Little did I know that this gift of hospitality would influence not only my future home, but also the church I would eventually help pastor with my husband. We take Scripture very seriously when it urges, "Be not forgetful to entertain strangers: for thereby some have entertained angels unawares" (Heb. 13:2 KJV).

John and I have lived in our present home almost sixteen years and have had at least twelve thousand guests for dinner. It's not something I wish to brag about; it's something I have been privileged to do. From family dinners and festive occasions to bridal showers and wedding receptions, we've enjoyed them all tremendously. The number of people at these occasions has ranged from one at a time to three hundred. Our goal has always been to make people feel welcomed when they arrive and satisfied when they leave.

This practice of having guests in our home began more than twenty-five years ago when my husband and I first married. Our church was very small, and my husband wanted to identify the natural leaders so he could begin to train them to win others to Christ. We had absolutely no money to take them out to dinner; therefore, I suggested we invite them over to our home for food and fellowship after church on Sunday evenings.

During the service my husband would spot new couples from the platform and invite them to our home afterward. Gladly they would almost always accept this impromptu invitation to the pastor's house. Once in our home, our guests did not care what they were served or how our house appeared; they were just thrilled to be with us.

I remember my husband and I holding hands and praying a simple, yet powerful, prayer, "Lord, bless our guests as they walk through the door of our home. Let them feel Your presence, Your comfort, and Your joy. If they need healing, heal them through us. If they need companionship, let us fill the loneliness in their lives. We ask that Your love be felt in this home that You have provided for us. Allow each guest to be fed: body, soul, and spirit. Amen."

The Lord has never failed to answer this prayer. The menus I planned for these gatherings were simple crowd pleasers. I used lots of hamburger. Spaghetti and meat sauce, tacos with all the trimmings, and chili and beans were on rotation. These meals were economical and easy to prepare, and I could repeat them as often as I wanted because we had different people every time.

Please don't feel you need to be a pastor's wife to open your home to people you don't know very well or even to those with whom you would like to develop a closer relationship. Whatever your position, hospitality is always well received.

Here are some simple steps to begin your adventure:

1. *Pray.* Ask the Lord to help you with the event you are about to plan. Determine that it is going to be a great adventure.

2. *Decide who you would like to invite to dinner.*

3. *Invite your guests at a time that will be easy on your schedule.* Don't create additional stress for yourself.

4. *Plan your menu several days in advance.* The more elaborate the menu, the farther ahead you need to plan. Planning menus is very enjoyable to me. After my family has gone to bed, I lie in my bed and look through cookbooks for recipe ideas. Make sure to plan a menu that is within your budget. Choose something that is not difficult to prepare, and try not to be too exotic. Home cooking is becoming a rarity.

5. *Make your grocery list.* Be careful not to buy duplicates of items you already have in the pantry; you want to be a good steward of your money. You can do a lot on a tight budget. With the right attitude and a spark of creativity you can make a little go a long way.

6. *Do your shopping early.* Don't wait until you are close to your dinner date to get the necessary items; cutting the lead time will add stress to your day. If you are on a tight budget, you can buy the more expensive items over time so you will not spend all the money from one paycheck. Shopping early will also allow you to make certain dishes ahead of time.

7. *If you can make any part of your menu ahead of time, do so.* Be conscious of the storage space available in your freezer or refrigerator when you make part of your meal early.

8. *Set the table the night before.* This step is almost a must. You would be surprised

how much time this will save, not to mention the peace of mind that comes from knowing that the time-consuming task is done.

9. *Make a time schedule.* To avoid being interrupted while I am cooking that day, I usually call my VIPs—my husband and mom, for instance—and tell them what I'm doing: "I won't be answering the phone this morning, but I will call you back at lunchtime." Then I make a time schedule for all the dishes I'm preparing. Before I begin I put on some inspirational music to help me enjoy the journey.

10. *Be ready early.* I make sure that the meal is in the oven an hour before my guests arrive. Doing this leaves thirty minutes for me to get ready and thirty minutes to check on last-minute details without pressure.

Almost without fail, your guests will ask if they can help you when they arrive. I always say, "Not now, but you can help with the dishes later." I usually find the best visiting time is during the cleanup chores. Friendships develop as my guests feel part of our home during this personal time in the kitchen.

You must know that these are guidelines I have developed to help make dinners easier to prepare. You may have many of your own ideas, and I encourage you to be creative in finding ways to make this time as easy as possible. Also know that I have violated every one of these guidelines, and my dinners have still turned out to be a success. The key is to be flexible and keep your eyes set on the motive of your event. You have just given your guests two of your most valuable gifts: you have opened your home to them, and you have given of your time.

Don't be concerned with what this entertaining might do to your home. Our entry has hardwood floors, and I have only had to strip them professionally twice in the last sixteen years. When the floor specialist was last in our home, he commented, "Ma'am, you're taking very good care of these floors. Obviously not many people have come through your home. These floors are in great shape."

I quickly corrected him, telling him of the thousands who have been to our home. He was shocked. I smiled, knowing that God had cared for my home through the high heels and mud, the spilled punch and cookie crumbs. When you dedicate your home to the work of the Lord, He will see that His angels take care of it.

A SHELTER FOR THE NIGHT

My husband and I have been so grateful for the home God has provided for us that we have always asked family, friends, missionaries, evangelists, and prophets to stay with us. I believe that whatever we offer to God's people is offered to God. The apostle Paul told the first-century Christians, "Receive one another, just as Christ also received us, to the glory of God" (Rom. 15:7).

Believe me, not all the circumstances will be perfect or well planned. When the children were younger, I never left them alone for any reason. On one occasion, however, my husband had an appointment with the optometrist for a pair of new glasses, and he wanted me to help him choose his next pair. The children convinced me that they would be okay watching their favorite video for the hour we would be gone. Sandy, our baby, who was ten at the time, proudly delegated herself the job of official secretary; she would take all phone messages while we were gone—which can be very important at times. We affectionately call her "John Hagee in a skirt." With her at the control panel, I felt that things would be fine.

When we arrived at the doctor's office, I immediately called to see how everything was. My daughter began to efficiently recite the three messages that she received in the fifteen minutes we had been gone. After the third message, I quickly asked her to repeat it.

"Oral Roberts is going to be at our house to spend the night in two hours," she said slowly. "His plane will be landing at Hallmark Aviation."

Half in shock and half in disbelief, I turned to my husband, who was in the middle of an eyeglass fitting, and asked, "You don't know anything about Oral Roberts coming to stay in our home in the next two hours, do you?"

I saw a look of conviction come over his face. Snagged. He had forgotten to tell me that possibility existed. Still, as a man, he could not understand why I was so upset that I had no prior notice. As a woman, I could not comprehend that he could not sympathize with my distress. A classic example of left-brain and right-brain in total collision. Oral Roberts was, in fact, coming to my home in the next hour and forty-five minutes.

Was my home ready for an overnight guest? No! Were the sheets in my guest room ready for Oral Roberts? No!

Unanimously we decided that it was not a good time to choose eyeglasses, and we immediately left the office. For a few minutes our travel time home was silent. Then I knew I had to get into a proactive mode. I needed a plan. My husband and I agreed that he would drop me off at home where the children and I would scramble to get the house ready for our very important company.

John would rush to the airport and be there just in time to meet the private jet. The moment Oral Roberts was in his car John would call me on his cell phone so I had a warning of how soon they would arrive at our home. I asked my husband to be discreet so Oral would not suspect that I was unprepared for a guest.

Some women have their homes ready for out-of-town guests at all times. With five children and their friends at the Hagee Hilton, I am not one of those women. My home may not be neat as a pin 24/7, but there is always an abundance of joy. However, *joy* was not the word to describe my disposition when I set foot inside our door.

I gave the children assignments that resembled a marine drill sergeant's battle plan for the Normandy invasion. Then I set the timer on the microwave to emphasize the importance of the countdown: we had less than an hour to prepare.

Soon my husband called with the special code he had devised: "The eagle has landed and is headed for the nest!"

Good grief! I couldn't believe that he couldn't come up with something more unique. Nevertheless, my home was ready, and the children were all smiles because I had rewarded them with a promise of a movie and burgers. We had a great visit, and my husband agreed to serve on Oral Roberts's Board of Regents, an honor he has cherished for more than ten years.

I shared this story with you because I wanted to show you that it may not be important for your home to be ready in season and out of season, but it is important that your heart and attitude be ready to receive whomever God has put in your path. "He who receives a prophet in the name of a prophet shall receive a prophet's reward. And he who receives a righteous man in the name of a righteous man shall receive a righteous man's reward" (Matt. 10:41).

CAST YOUR BREAD UPON THE WATER

Once you begin to reach outside your home, God will provide more opportunities to minister to others. When new people move into your neighborhood, welcome them into their new home by taking a pie or a cake or maybe a whole meal to them. If you know of someone who is ill on your block, let her know you are praying for her and would like to bring a meal over for the family. You have no idea how that can comfort someone in need.

Through the system of leadership called the Government of Twelve Leaders, our church is able to meet the needs of our congregation in a compassionate and personal manner. This organizational system permits us to aid anyone within the church who is ill or has lost a loved one.

I have chosen twenty-four women to serve with me as members of the Women of Esther; many of them planned the Woman of God conferences with me. When I chose these women, I gave them two gifts: a bottle of anointing oil and an apron. I knew they would use these two tools often as they served the body of Christ.

My husband has taught our congregation that a leader "leads from the front." If there are dishes to wash, the leader washes them first. If there are meals to cook, the leader cooks them first. And God has honored this philosophy.

When my husband chose the leaders of the Government of Twelve, he pondered how to teach them to serve the people they were to lead. After much prayer he had the answer. One Sunday evening he knelt on the platform of our church in the presence of the whole congregation and washed the feet of all of the men he had chosen to work with him. Instantly our church became aware of the importance of service; God's expression of love is shown through servanthood.

Jesus' apostle Matthew told of what Jesus did when He was ready to send His disciples into the world: "When He had called His twelve disciples to Him, He gave them power over unclean spirits, to cast them out, and to heal all kinds of sickness and all kinds of disease" (Matt. 10:1).

We send our leaders out in this way with the added gift of hospitality. I firmly believe that if we don't give the sheep the opportunity to serve one another, we have taken away the equal opportunity for them to be blessed by God, since God's Word says that if you bless others, you will be blessed.

One of the goals I have for our church is to be a "hospitality church." Whenever individuals come through the doors of our church, appointed greeters are there to welcome them. We hear many testimonies of people who were lonely and had not heard a friendly voice in days until they entered our church.

When we have special speakers or singers, we make sure they are greeted at the airport gate with open arms and smiling faces. These appointed hosts volunteer at any opportunity to represent Christ and meet the needs of God's people.

John and I try to eat meals with our guests that have been prepared and served by volunteers who come forward to minister to the men and women of God. I am so proud of our women when they serve others with loving smiles and open hearts. Our church can receive no greater compliment than to hear that the Word of God is preached from our pulpit and the love of God abides within our walls.

We also extend hospitality to the membership of our church. When there is a death in the family of one of our members or congregants, we call the family to let them know that we will bring a meal to them immediately and for the next few days, with the last meal presented after the funeral service.

When we take food to the home, we wear red aprons with the words *Cornerstone Cares*. We make sure the food is served and the kitchen is clean after the company has left. We do this in the name of the Lord as a living example of our love and obedience to Him. This sacrifice of love has never returned void— and it never will. It has proven to be an effective witnessing tool for the unsaved members of these families.

If someone is in the hospital for an extended period of time or family members are waiting in intensive care for news of a loved one for hours on end, we take a "hospitality basket" to them. Knowing that family members will not leave the waiting room and won't have the opportunity to eat, we make sure that the basket contains snack foods and beverages: fruit and cookies, cheese and crackers, juices, and tea bags. (See page 184 for a complete list of items in this hospitality basket.) We always include disposable plates and napkins and utensils for convenience.

Learn to be creative. Ask the Lord to show you how to personalize each basket to make it unique. For instance, you may want to include a small devotional book to help them stay focused on the Source of the healing for their loved one. Your basket could also contain a special note of encouragement for your friends and their family.

Hospitality comes in many forms. It can be as creative and extensive as you want it to be. The main ingredients are love and a pure heart, two ingredients that never fail to bring healing to a wounded heart. The more you extend hospitality, the more you will become like Christ. And the more you are like Christ, the more you will be recognized as a daughter of the King.

THE LOST ART OF ETIQUETTE

Believe it or not, etiquette is a form of hospitality. When you have people to your home for dinner, you need to know the proper etiquette rules so your guests feel as special as they are.

When we had the Woman of God seminar at Cornerstone, we realized that many of the older women, as well as most of the younger girls, had no idea how to properly set a table. You may say, "Who cares?" God, our Father, cares. He wants us to do all we do with excellence. We are not trying to be pretentious, just meaning to put forth our best when we represent our King. (See figures 11.1 and 11.2 on page 186 for formal and informal place settings.)

When you are invited to a party, do you respond as soon as you get the invitation? I have been guilty of assuming that my hosts know I am attending or not attending their function, so I don't give a formal response. Yet they have honored me with an invitation to a very important occasion in their lives, and I need to reply to them as soon as possible.

When you have gone to someone's home for dinner, do you write a thank-you card to thank your host for her graciousness and hospitality? If you receive a gift, do you call the person or send a thank-you card? Our daughter Tish puts all of our family to shame in this area. She is extremely conscientious about sending thank-you cards for all occasions and writes them almost immediately after receiving a gift or attending an event.

HOSPITAL HOSPITALITY BASKET

⌇◌

Small dessert plates
Napkins
Plastic forks, spoons, knives
A paring knife
6-pack of miniature bottled water
4-pack of orange juice (small servings)
Box of mixed teas
One bag of Pepperidge Farms Goldfish
Two bags of Pepperidge Farms Cookies—Milano/Ginger
One box of Ritz crackers
One can of cheese spread
One summer sausage
One block of Cracker Barrel Cheddar Cheese
One bag of Fritos Scoops
One can of bean dip
One bag of trail mix
One bag of Snickers Miniatures
Seven packs of peanut butter cheese crackers
Five plums
Six bananas
Oranges
One small hand cream
One "Thinking of You" card

We live in a thankless society. We seldom thank each other or the Lord for His provision. Yet it is important that we live with thanksgiving in our hearts and praise on our lips as a way of life. "For the administration of this service not only supplies the needs of the saints, but also is abounding through many thanksgivings to God" (2 Cor. 9:12).

In our Woman of God sessions we asked the women to take a short quiz to test their etiquette IQ. How would you answer the five questions?

    1. What is the time frame for sending thank-you cards?
    2. What fork should you use at a dinner party?
    3. What is the "I'm finished" sign?
    4. What is a Christian host?
    5. Is it okay to be fashionably late?

Compare your answers to the ones we gave to the women at our conference.

1. What is the time frame for sending thank-you cards?

Obviously this should be as soon as possible, certainly while the gift or event is still fresh in the giver's mind. Within a week is the usual standard. Thank-you cards can be sent for many different occasions. You may want to thank a teacher at the end of a Sunday school class or the end of a school year, or a favorite coach or Scout leader. Sometimes parishioners send thank-you cards to their pastors for a particularly insightful sermon. Focus on the Family has encouraged parishioners to send notes to their pastors on Pastor Appreciation Day, but a note of encouragement is always appropriate. E-mails and faxes can also be used to thank or encourage others.

2. What fork should you use at a dinner party?

Look at figures 11.1 and 11.2 on the next page, which give you examples of everyday and formal table settings. They also tell you which piece of silver to use. The usual standard is to work from the outside in: the salad fork is first, and the dinner fork is next. The dessert fork or spoon is always placed above the dinner plate; the bread and butter knife and plate are placed above the knives and napkin.

fig. 11.1 A FORMAL DINNER

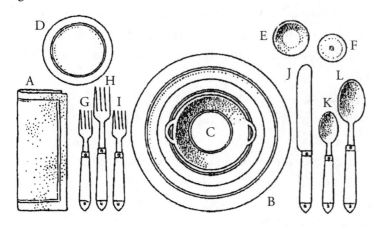

A. Napkin
B. Dinner or service plate
C. First-course bowl
   and liner plate
D. Salad plate
E. Water goblet
F. Tea glass
G. Salad fork
H. Dinner fork
I. Dessert fork
J. Dinner knife
K. Teaspoon
L. Soup spoon

fig. 11.2 AN INFORMAL DINNER

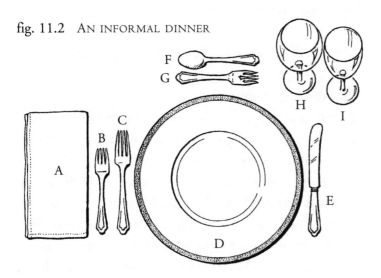

A. Napkin
B. Salad fork
C. Dinner fork
D. Dinner plate
E. Dinner knife
F. Dessert spoon
G. Dessert fork
H. Tea glass
I. Water glass

3. What is the "I'm finished" sign?

When someone is finished with a meal, the person places the fork and knife together with the handles at four o'clock and the tips at twelve o'clock. Crisscrossing the knife and fork on the plate means that the person will be returning.

4. What is a Christian host?

Paul told the Hebrew Christians,

Be kindly affectionate to one another with brotherly love, in honor giving preference to one another; not lagging in diligence, fervent in spirit, serving the Lord; rejoicing in hope, patient in tribulation, continuing steadfastly in prayer; distributing to the needs of the saints, given to hospitality. (Rom. 12:10–13)

Our cell leaders often place a sign outside their homes when they are having a Bible study. The sign says, "A Bible study tonight at 7:30. All are welcome." We mean to make these events open to any neighbors who might enjoy spending some time with friends. Often these people later become group members.

5. Is it okay to be fashionably late?

No. The hostess has gone to a lot of trouble to prepare the food for a particular time. If you are not on time, you are showing a lack of concern for her work and preparation.

It's not acceptable to be late for church either. I am always amazed when we go to the theater; everyone is rushing in on time because the management will not let anyone enter after the first act opens out of respect for the actors. Yet when many people come to church, they walk in late as if it is a privilege for God to have them there. We are to honor His presence as if His physical body were standing at the pulpit. When we are ill, we want His help immediately. When we have financial needs, we ask for His provision to come quickly. When we come to the sanctuary, we must give honor where honor is due.

Then neither is it proper to leave church early. My husband has often witnessed the tragic scene of a person with tears falling down his face almost ready to make the commitment to Christ and another individual interrupts him wanting to pass in front of him as she exits early from her seat. The moment has passed, the composure returns, and the soul is lost. Instead of leaving early to be first to our cars, we should wait, pray, and rejoice as a sinner comes home.

Of all the things we have discussed, one thing is essential to hospitality: a willing heart filled with love. If you prepare food for someone in need, make sure that your attitude is a loving one while you work. The living God will receive this sacrifice as a sweet aroma. My dear friend Quin Sherrer has written *The Warm and Welcome Heart*.[1] It is a great reference for Christian hospitality.

If you entertain in your home, know that the first guest you invite is the Lord in the presence of the Holy Spirit. When you do this, all of the other guests who enter your home will feel welcomed. One of the beauties of serving the Lord is that you will always be blessed when you serve others. You will feel the approval of the Lord like a warm blanket on a cold night. When you minister to God's people, you know there is a smile on His face when He mentions your name.

❧ ACTION POINTS: HOSPITALITY—AN ATTITUDE OF THE HEART

1. As you think about opening your home to do the Lord's work, read through the following scriptures.

You are a daughter of the King who is . . .

- called of God (2 Tim. 1:9).
- His disciple because you have love for others (John 13:34–35).
- a faithful follower (Eph. 5:1; Rev. 17:14).
- elected (Rom. 8:33; Col. 3:12).
- firmly rooted and overflowing with gratitude (Col. 2:7).

Write out your favorite verse.

_____

_____

2. What do you think of when you think of hospitality? Something everyone else does perfectly? Something that you extend only to your friends? Webster's *New World Dictionary* defines *hospitality* as "the act, practice, or quality of being hospitable" or "solicitous entertainment of guests." But what's your definition? Take this handy quiz and see! Check as many of the following responses as you think apply to your life.

To me, hospitality means . . .

__ A. having Ramen noodles for more than one.

__ B. hanging out at someone else's house.

__ C. inviting people over and letting them bring their own food.

__ D. making people feel at home.

To be hospitable, I have to be . . .

__ A. an entirely different person.

__ B. a lot more outgoing than I am.

__ C. Martha Stewart's twin.

__ D. myself—only more relaxed.

Hospitality requires . . .

__ A. way too much time and money to do it properly.

__ B. more energy than I'm willing to give right now.

__ C. less energy and stress than I've given in the past.

__ D. only the effort it takes to make sure my guests feel welcome.

When I think of people to invite, I think of including . . .

__ A. only my friends and family.

__ B. the popular crowd at our club.

__ C. people I'd like to get to know.

__ D. everyone, even strangers.

If you responded to all with *D*, you are an A-, not a D-, student, since those were the right answers.

3. Genuine hospitality begins in the heart, with a giving attitude and a genuine desire to give to and receive from others. What do you give? Your time and effort. What do you receive? Memories that can last a lifetime. What's behind it all? Love!

Hospitality was of major importance during Bible times. Certain rules were built into the laws of God to remind the Israelites to care for others, particularly aliens, poor people, orphans, and widows.

Look up the following scriptures to verify this point:

- Leviticus 19:9–10
- Deuteronomy 24:19–22

Read Romans 12:13 and determine to share with God's people who are in need.

4. Read chapter 10, the final chapter in the book of Esther. End with this prayer:

Father, I come to You in a spirit of gratitude. I thank You for the love, mercy, and grace that You extend to me. Help me to think of others before myself and take on the same mind of Christ, who was equal to You, yet took on the character of a servant.

Lord, use me to bless others. Help me to be creative in ways to extend hospitality and kindness. Let the love of Jesus Christ shine through my stewardship of Your blessings in giving to others, that the needs of the saints are met and a chorus of thanksgiving is given to You.

Father, I am not my own, my home is not my own, my resources are not my own. Everything I have and all that I am is Yours. Guide me and direct me. You have shown me, O Lord, what is good, and what You require of me, which is to show kindness and mercy and to walk humbly with my God. Create in me a new heart that desires to reach out to others and say, "Welcome, my friend."

Father, thank You for an opportunity to grow and serve Your children. Amen.

chapter twelve

Beauty

I have always hated my nose, as I mentioned to you earlier. My mother has a beautiful nose; it is chiseled with a small knot on the bridge added for character. My father has a very distinguished Roman nose. Either one would have been fine, but no, I got a combination of the two. Not pretty.

For years I wanted to go to a plastic surgeon and correct this mistake God had made. One day I gathered up the courage to make an appointment for a consultation. While I was waiting I casually looked through the library in the doctor's office. I was shocked at the extensive surgical work that would be required, but I maintained my seat and my composure.

I knew he would immediately look at my nose and say, "We *know* why you're here!" Several minutes later he entered the examining room. Much to my surprise he walked over to me and put his hand above my brow, raising the skin on my forehead.

Looking at him, I said, "I am *not* in here for a brow lift! I want my nose fixed!"

Obviously embarrassed, he told me he didn't think my nose needed any work. This man was an expert on beauty, and he didn't believe my nose was that bad! Nevertheless, the doctor answered my list of technical questions about the surgery.

Then my eyes began to tear.

He asked what was wrong. I told him I visited with people in the hospital every week and prayed that God would bring healing for their bodies. Most of them had severe surgeries, which were not a matter of choice—rather a matter of life and death. I had been reminded of a verse in Isaiah:

But now, O LORD,
You are our Father;
We are the clay, and You our potter;
And all we are the work of Your hand. (64:8)

I was in the doctor's office, electing to change something God had sculpted as the Master Potter. All along when I complained to the Lord about my nose, He had told me that it was beautiful, yet it took a visit to the doctor's office to make me realize that God doesn't make mistakes.

That day the doctor informed me I was not emotionally prepared for the surgical procedure. Little did he know that surgery *had* occurred during that office visit. The Holy Spirit had supernaturally reversed how I saw myself. He had given me the eyes of a loving King, who thought His daughter was beautiful just as He made her. We must not think we can be beautiful *if and when* certain changes are made to our physical bodies; instead we must enhance what God has already given us.

THE BIBLICAL CONCEPT OF BEAUTY

The outer appearance of various women is recorded throughout the Word of God, and many women in the Scriptures are described as beautiful. Sarah was known as a "woman of beautiful countenance" (Gen. 12:11), Rebekah was "very beautiful to behold" (Gen. 24:16), Rachel was "beautiful of form and appearance" (Gen. 29:17), Abigail was a "woman of good understanding and beautiful appearance" (1 Sam. 25:3), Bathsheba "was very beautiful to behold" (2 Sam. 11:2), and Esther was a young woman who "was lovely and beautiful" (Est. 2:7). Esther's beauty, grace, and character shone, bright and unwavering, against the darkness threatening the Jewish people. Esther even had a beauty regimen that was mentioned in the Bible, which motivated the Woman of God seminar.

God created each one of us with beautiful and unique characteristics. It is not difficult to establish a personal regimen that is individualized to our unique traits. Yet once many women marry, they feel it is no longer necessary to maintain their outer appearance; they assume that their husbands are not going anywhere. Sad to report, this is not the case. We often fall into the adversary's trap and lose much more than our outer beauty when we stop caring about our appearance.

After twenty years of marriage or a single lifestyle, some of us are overwhelmed by the idea of a makeover of our image, but it takes only desire, time, and dedication to become the woman God intended for each of us to be.

The first step in your Woman of God makeover is to pray. Ask God to reveal how He sees you. Often what you consider ugly, He sees as beautiful.

We do not want to be beautiful so that we can gain the approval of man; we want to be beautiful so that we can represent our King with quality and excellence. No matter how cracked the vessel is, it's still a vessel of honor, as Paul called us in Romans 9:21. The light of the world promises to shine through the broken places, but the rest of the vessel should be polished to a sparkling shine. All this is meant to draw lost souls closer to us so we may lead them to the cross of the Savior.

The second step you should take in your makeover is to make sure you are spiritually in balance. I have seen women who were striking outwardly, yet perceived themselves as ugly because their spiritual life was out of God's will. Ask Him what you must do to get back in fellowship with Him. He is faithful and just to complete the good work He has begun in you (Phil. 1:6).

The next step is to make a list of the things that need to be done to enhance your personal appearance. One deterrent in this step is insecurity. *What do I do?* you wonder. *Where do I go?* Take a deep breath and ask yourself, *Do I know someone who always looks great?* Call her, and ask where she goes to have her hair done. She will be more than willing to share this information with you. Or go to a major department store. Almost all of them have a fashion consultant who can answer questions about your personal needs. Keep in mind: buying expensive clothing doesn't make you beautiful. It is how you feel about yourself that radiates the beauty within.

Another obstacle in this step is expense. Most hair salons that employ professional stylists charge higher prices than many women can afford. I tell my class to start a beauty jar, which can hold any extra change they may have after groceries are bought or even loose change in their purses. "Before long you will be surprised by how much you have accumulated," I say, "maybe enough for a professional haircut every six to eight weeks." If you have a good haircut, you can easily manage your hair between visits. Maybe you also have enough for a manicure, a pedicure, or a facial.

If you are interested in updating your wardrobe, know that some of the major discount family stores are carrying great clothing styles at very reasonable prices. And all department stores have inventory-reducing sales twice a year.

Get creative. You will be amazed at all you can do with a willing attitude, linked to a goal that you believe in: making yourself the best representative for Christ you can be.

I would like to share a couple of stories from the makeover session we conducted as part of the Woman of God conferences. One woman, Judy, wrote,

> I am a single mom of three wonderful children. I had been a stay-at-home mom with no education. This class has given me such a new hope and confidence in myself that I have finally begun the classes I need to obtain my GED. I changed my hair color under the encouragement of the professional stylist you had speak to our class. My smile is different, my walk is different, but most of all my hope in my Lord Jesus Christ is different! I know now that He *does* want to bless me, and I can't wait to receive all He has for my kids and me as we serve Him!

Another woman, Connie, was a young wife going to business school. She was desperately trying to get out of a whirlpool of emotional despair and financial lack. Her husband was unemployed, and the house they rented had been condemned by the city. Connie was trying to better herself so she could qualify for a job and contribute to the family income. However, her business teacher told her, "It doesn't matter how many classes you take; if you don't know how to dress, no one will hire you, and you won't be going anywhere!"

When it was time to ask for volunteers to submit their names for makeovers, Connie did not present her name because she was sure she would not be chosen. Nothing else was going her way. Why should this? Her facilitator knew she needed not only the makeover, but also a new hope in the Lord, so the facilitator personally recommended Connie. When she was called forward to be a makeover model, Connie was totally surprised: she could not believe God had chosen *her!*

Instantly her countenance started to change. She had been chosen for something special. Never before in her life had she been chosen, selected, or set apart. Instead of hiding her face with her hair, as was her norm, the stylist framed her face with a brand-new cut. Suddenly Connie's smiling face emerged with hope in her eyes, which replaced the ashen look of someone who was without hope.

We selected Connie to be one of our models for career clothes in the fashion show that was part of our makeover session, and she was able to pick a lovely business suit to complete her new professional look. That evening, when Connie walked down the runway, no one recognized her. We saw a confident woman, a daughter of the King, who now smiled at the future. After the fashion show Connie was additionally blessed as the "Lord kissed her on the forehead." She and the other models could keep the outfits they had chosen because the boutique had donated all the garments. In her letter Connie proclaimed, "My life will never be the same again!" All the specialists did for both women was to enhance what their Father had created; His vessels of honor were finally realizing their worth.

My heart's desire is that you will come to the complete revelation of who you are in Christ. You are the King's daughter, beautiful in His sight. Once you have been released from the bondage of the past, you will never be the same again.

Another very important aspect of beauty is the health of your physical body.

THE TEMPLE OF THE LORD

Paul referred to our bodies as temples of the Holy Spirit:

> Or do you not know that your body is the temple of the Holy Spirit who is in you, whom you have from God, and you are not your own? For you were bought at a price; therefore glorify God in your body and in your spirit, which are God's. (1 Cor. 6:19–20)

References to good health are found throughout Scripture. The Lord gave the Israelites dietary laws to preserve their health (Ex. 15:26), and science has now confirmed that those laws are linked to preventive medicine and long life. James encouraged those who were sick to go to the elders of the church and request anointing with oil and prayer (James 5:14). Solomon stated that the wisdom of the Lord was "health to your flesh, and strength to your bones" (Prov. 3:8). What kind of wisdom are we using to maintain our bodies?

Glowing skin or shiny hair is a clear sign of a healthy body. As a woman grows older, a banner for good health is straight posture. It does not happen overnight; it is the result of years of caring for her body.

If you are over eighteen, it is essential that you go to the gynecologist for an annual exam. If you have been or are currently sexually active, you should go immediately. And again I challenge the single woman to a vow of celibacy until marriage.

If you are over forty, you should have a mammogram once a year or as prescribed by your doctor.

Dental health is significant. You should have a cleaning at least twice a year.

If for some reason you do not have health insurance and cannot afford these exams, call your local teaching hospital; someone there can inform you where these services can be provided. Preventive medicine is a tool the Lord has given us to maintain good health.

You should observe daily principles in order to maintain good health. As mothers, we are responsible for the family's diet. We live in a fast-food society, but these foods are filled with preservatives and other chemicals to compete with other food products. Our children are paying dearly for corporate profit margins. Food allergies are at an all-time high, and Americans are more overweight than ever.

Learn to eat properly. The prevalent advice to drink plenty of fluids daily does not refer to twelve diet sodas. Learn to be wise in your choices. Water is always the best one. Remember, it is the *knowledge* of the truth that will set you free. Dr. Don Colbert has excellent books on health and proper eating habits, such as *Walking in Divine Health* and *What You Don't Know May Be Killing You!*[1] Inform yourself with wisdom from God's Word and His people.

The Bible even refers to exercise (1 Tim. 4:8). I hate to exercise; it is a chore for me. Yet I know I must do it to stay in good health. As time passes, so much of me is responding to the laws of gravity that toning seems to be the only deterrent to sagging body parts. I have friends who love to exercise because their discipline has given them positive results. Some activities that maintain physical health will be harder to do than others, but our efforts will be well worth it.

The most important factor that contributes to a healthy body is a good attitude. Scripture says that "a merry heart doeth good like a medicine" (Prov. 17:22 KJV). We need to learn to laugh again. We must maintain our physical bodies so that our spiritual bodies can be their best for Christ.

As we complete the journey we began eleven chapters ago, I would like to end with two very special stories of two very special women in my life. They are two of the most beautiful women I know.

Her Children Rise Up and Call Her Blessed

The first of these women is my mother. Allow me to tell you a little about her life. She was the third of four children, born Velia Martinez in Charlotte, Texas, on February 26, 1932. We know that her father and most of his ancestors came from Mexico and Spain. Her mother was born in New Braunfels, Texas, and her ancestors came to Texas from the Canary Islands. My mother has a rich heritage.

When she was a child, her family worked in the migrant fields. My mother was no exception; she began to pick cotton at eight years of age. She continued to work in the fields until my grandmother accepted a position as a cook in a local restaurant. At thirteen my mother began working as a waitress in the same restaurant. The money she earned was used to pay her tuition at a private Catholic school, and the balance was given to the family to offset household expenses.

When Mom was fifteen, she started work at a local retail store in San Antonio. She continued to work there until she graduated from high school and married my father on June 10, 1951. I was their first child and came into the family in March 1952. In September of 1954 my sister Rosie was born. Eventually they had two more children, Sandy and Tony.

My mother always fulfilled her destiny of being a gift to her children. My father worked seven days a week, often working two shifts to earn extra income, so he was seldom available for quality time with the family. My parents were intent on keeping my mother in the home to care for their children.

I remember Mom inviting all the neighborhood children to our house. She has always been a fabulous cook, and she would make wonderful meals to bless our friends. I remember living on such a tight budget that we had enough money to buy only one chicken and five pounds of hamburger for the week. Yet the meals she made from such humble ingredients would put any restaurant to shame. Restaurants are not capable of making a meal with love; only mothers can provide that ingredient.

One of her most beautiful characteristics is her laugh, which is contagious. She holds her head back, opens her mouth, and a symphony of joy pours out of her. When she laughed, all was well, and we children could forget all of the day's struggles. My mother is still our spiritual and emotional anchor.

When I was sixteen, Mom didn't laugh as much anymore. Instead pain emanated from her eyes. One day, totally unexpectedly, the doctor called our home. What was suspected to be a cyst on my sister Rosie's hip was instead a rare form of incurable cancer. Rosie, then fourteen, was a beautiful girl who enjoyed life to the fullest.

With the ring of the phone that day, our lives changed forever. My father began to work even longer hours, trying to earn more money to pay all the hospital bills that were accumulating. I began to care for my eight-year-old sister, Sandy, and two-year-old brother, Tony, as well as attend Trinity University. And my mother began a four-year vigil by Rosie's bedside.

During this very trying time, I never saw Mom cry around my sister. She only smiled and made Rosie smile. In fact, she managed to make all of us smile. Again she fulfilled her destiny as a mother who kept the level of hope alive in our home. She would wake at two in the morning and see my father off to work, even though she went to bed long after the rest of her family was asleep. Our home was always immaculate, and when Rosie was in the hospital, the meals were cooked ahead of time for all of us to enjoy.

Throughout those four long years, my mother never left my sister's side. Alone, she would sit with the doctors and listen to the prognosis for my sister's life. The two of them left San Antonio to journey to other medical centers for the latest in cancer treatment. Much of Rosie's treatment was experimental, and my mother would call home with the latest report, which was never optimistic.

I knew something was very wrong when two weeks before my sister's death, my mother left my sister under my care for the afternoon. I did not know until later, but she left Rosie to be at her father's bedside before he died. Three days later she left Rosie again, this time to attend her father's funeral.

Rosie never knew Grandpa passed until she got to heaven because my mother was afraid that she would become depressed and not have hope for her own life if we told her. Somehow Momma came home from her father's funeral with the same smile of hope and healing.

The hardest thing my mother had to do was to leave my sister's bedside after her passing. During the four-year period Rosie was ill, we had all accepted Christ as Savior, so my mother knew her precious daughter was in the arms of Jesus, but she just couldn't bear to leave her side. With His help she lovingly placed Rosie in the arms of God, for "strength and dignity are her clothing" (Prov. 31:25 NASB).

Twenty-one years have passed since Rosie entered heaven, and I have heard my mother laugh again, for time heals many wounds—but a perpetual sadness remains in her eyes, almost like a memorial of her love for her precious daughter. I know it will not disappear until she arrives in heaven, and her Father wipes away every last tear.

If by chance you wonder what this ordeal did to her faith, it has never wavered, and her hope has not faltered. She is faithful, and she believes our God is a promise keeper. She is fulfilling her destiny as one of the best intercessors I know. She is truly a daughter of the King.

Maybe you have ordered my husband's ministry materials for your home. My mother packs almost every request. I am amazed at her constant dedication. She is almost seventy years old, and she stands on her feet eight hours a day, filling the orders with the Word of God. When I encourage her to rest, her answer is always the same: "I can't until the people get their packages; they are depending on God's Word to make a difference in their lives!" As she fills every order she asks the Lord to meet the needs of all those who receive His Word.

Whenever there is a special banquet at our church, Mom often helps me prepare it. She loves to bless others with the gift God has given her—another way she fulfills her destiny as His servant.

I pray that one day you have the privilege of meeting this daughter of the

My mother, Velia Castro, and me

My mother-in-law, Vada Hagee, and me

King. If you want to recognize her in a crowd, she is the beautiful one with the smile on her face. Momma, your children rise up and call you blessed.

The second illustration of a beautiful woman is my mother-in-law, Vada Hagee. From the moment I was grafted into the Hagee family more than twenty-five years ago, I was in awe of my mother-in-law's beauty and confidence. I know the story of her life will inspire many of you to fulfill your destiny.

Mom Hagee was born Vada Swick in Goosecreek, Texas, on May 29, 1913, the third of seven children. To her knowledge, all her ancestors on both sides of her family emigrated from Germany.

When her mother was expecting her seventh child, Mom Hagee's father died at the age of thirty-three. Instantly their lives changed. Mom was nine years old, which was when she accepted the Lord as her Savior.

Her mother was a registered nurse in a town where there was no hospital, and the local doctor would place her in the home of someone who needed constant care. Her duties kept her away from home Monday through Friday as she worked to provide for her family.

Mom Hagee's older sister took care of the children until she married at the age of sixteen, at which time she left home. Then an aunt kept the children who were not yet school age, and my mother-in-law, at the age of eleven, began to care for the household and her three remaining brothers. She went to school, came home, did the household chores, washed all the laundry, and cooked all the meals.

By the time she was sixteen, Mom Hagee worked a part-time job at a soda fountain in a local drugstore as she continued to go to school and care for her family. During this time, she felt she had distanced herself from God, and she rededicated her life to the Lord.

Soon afterward, Mom began to attend Southern Bible College in Baytown, Texas, where she earned a scholarship by becoming a student teacher of homiletics and Old Testament theology. She taught more than eleven classes a week, attended school, and ministered in the pulpit of her church once a week. Within two years she received her bachelor's degree in theology, fulfilling her destiny to become an evangelist.

At twenty-two she met and married my father-in-law. This step caused considerable controversy in her ministry circle because she was scheduled to speak in revivals all over America at the time. Her mentors felt the marriage would hinder her ministry. With the money she had earned preaching revivals in the Southwest, she paid for her wedding dress. My father-in-law worked in the Humble Oil Refinery in Baytown for seven years while he and my mother-in-law evangelized.

They started a ministry in Kenefick, Texas, and began their first church. They eventually moved to Channelview, Texas, and built three different churches and educational facilities. Their first child was born in 1935 and the last in 1955. Mom Hagee told me she always knew she would have four children; she just did not think that they would all be boys and that it would take her twenty years to do it! Her second son is my husband, John Hagee.

My in-laws began their ministry in the middle of the Depression, so Mom Hagee learned to sew all of her own clothes and make all of the boys' shirts out of the feed sacks they bought for their milk cow, Ellie Mae. My husband remembers going to the feed store with his father and choosing the fabric for his next "designer shirt." When haircuts increased to twenty-five cents each, she drew the line in the sand and began to give all her men haircuts with Sears Roebuck home hair-cutting shears. She also obtained her cosmetology license; she wanted to make sure she could care for her four sons if something happened to her husband. She was always thinking of the future.

In the twenty-five-plus years I have known her she has always looked fabulous.

Her favorite color is red, a trait she handed down to my husband. She dresses herself in impeccable style and always adorns her outfits with tasteful accessories such as pearls, earrings, and brooches, many of which she has made herself. When hats were in style, she wanted to wear them. However, they were too expensive, so she enrolled in a millinery class and learned how to make all of her hats.

Her hats were the talk of the church. She has always told me to look the best for Christ: "After all He is the One you represent!" Another bit of advice to me was: don't follow the fashion trends; follow your desires and personal style. She is eighty-eight years old now, and if you walk into her home today, she will have her hair carefully done and will be wearing a lovely coordinated outfit with a string of pearls around her neck. She is beautiful to behold.

While my father-in-law worked a full-time job and led the church, Mom Hagee ran the household, played the church organ, sang in family quartets and the ladies' trio, and played the accordion. She conducted all the vacation Bible school events, including designing and making all the costumes. She directed all the Christmas and Easter programs for the church. In addition, she ran the Missionettes, the girls' missionary council; she was the vice president of the Houston Chapter of the Women's Missionary Council of the Assemblies of God and was the president of her son's PTA organization. She obviously helped her husband with all the pastoral duties, such as making house calls and visiting sick parishioners. She was the special events coordinator of the church and organized the meals for all the church socials, cooking many of the dishes herself. She has always had the ability to walk into a room of strangers and make friends with all of them within the hour. She had more duties than the Proverbs 31 woman.

There was nothing she could not do and do brilliantly. Her greatest skill was that of a Bible teacher, however. Her ability to verbally describe biblical events was like watching a movie. If she described Jesus and the twelve disciples crossing the Sea of Galilee, you could feel the wind on your face and feel the spray of the surf against your skin.

A moment of sacrificial decision came early in her marriage. Because of her brilliant and masterful presentation of the Word of God, crowds would follow her wherever she spoke. Knowing that her husband's calling to the pulpit ministry would never fully develop with her continued unprecedented success, she made a conscious decision to stop speaking and fill the pulpit only when her husband was working shift work at the refinery. The Lord honored her decision; their ministry grew and was fruitful in discipling others and sending out many men and women to minister throughout the country.

She also fulfilled her destiny as she made the decision to invest in her four sons, believing that her investment in their lives would bring a ministry harvest of a hundredfold. Her sacrificial life is the foundation of my husband's worldwide media ministry. All that she taught him, all that she instilled in him, has germinated in his heart and produced a harvest of souls.

When Mom Hagee gave up her place in the teaching ministry, God gave her something even greater: the ability and the power to intercede for others in prayer. Prayer moves mountains, and she is a woman who addresses God with confidence in His power and promise. She kneels on arthritic knees and prays for hours for someone in need. She will call on the name of God, and He will answer. They have an intimate relationship as Father and daughter. She has one deep desire, and that is to see Him face-to-face.

One day she had a distant look on her face, and I asked her what she was thinking. She responded, "I long to go to heaven and see my Lord. I never thought I would live as long as I have, but He must still have continued purpose for my life. If one day you get a call that I have passed from this life to the next, don't cry for me. Rejoice, for I am exactly where I want to be. I have waited a long time, and I can hardly wait to get there!"

I am so blessed to know and love Vada Hagee. And I am blessed to receive her love. Mom Hagee, you have fulfilled your destiny as a daughter of the King: you were a wife of noble character; you are worth more than rubies; you have brought good to all who come in contact with you all the days of your life.

Beauty is more than a professional haircut, a facial, or a new dress. Think about Ruth in the field of Boaz. She and Naomi, her mother-in-law, were literally homeless, without income or a future because both their husbands were dead. Yet Ruth's beauty shone through her dusty and tattered garments. When Naomi wanted Ruth to have the security of being married again, Naomi didn't tell Ruth to buy a new dress. Naomi's only advice was "wash yourself and anoint yourself, put on your best garment and go down to the threshing floor" (Ruth 3:3). Naomi knew Boaz would be struck by Ruth's natural beauty if she only made these few preparations.

As I mentioned before, Cornerstone is called the "people's church" because our members come from various races and economic levels. A few years ago a woman came to me weeping. "I don't have the money to buy nice clothes," she said. She went on to explain how inferior she felt to some of the women in the congregation who had expensive clothes. "I don't feel good enough to walk in the door of this church," she added.

"Look at your face," I immediately replied. "The gleam in your eyes . . . your beautiful skin . . . All you need to do is make sure your dress is clean and well-pressed." That was simple advice, but so true. She now radiates every Sunday.

Beauty has deep roots, which begin in the soul. When the soul is secure in Christ, the roots produce the fruit of peace, joy, kindness, and ultimately beauty. We have discussed some practical applications to making our outer vessels more attractive. The most important makeover lessons we will ever receive are those that will draw us closer to the Light of the World; then we will be able to shine to our fullest potential.

YOUR DIVINE DESTINY

If you want to reach your divine destiny, remember these requirements:

1. *Show absolute obedience to the voice of God.* You know His voice by reading His Word and by listening to Him speak to you through prayer.

2. *Rely on faith over feeling.* Despite the pain in my mother's life as she watched her daughter die, her faith in God never failed. She knew God was too good to be unkind and too wise to make a mistake.

3. *Be persistent.* The kind of persistence dictated in Ephesians 6 was to stand, stand, and having done all, stand again. Both my mom and Mom Hagee persisted despite the obstacles in their lives.

4. *Take bold action.* You must be proactive in acquiring what you want from God. The woman with the issue of blood wanted healing from Jesus. Yet she was an outcast because according to the Law, she was considered unclean; she should

not have been at a public gathering for any reason. Touching a rabbi was punishable by death, but she wanted Jesus to heal her.

When she received what she needed from God, the Master asked her, "Who touched Me? . . . Somebody touched Me, for I perceived power going out from Me" (Luke 8:45–46). Despite any fear she might have felt for her life, she answered by proclaiming that she had touched Jesus, and she gave her healing testimony to the multitude. She was not ashamed to proclaim the healing power of the Lord Jesus Christ. Once you have received God's direction, act on what He has commissioned you to do, and watch miracles happen before your eyes.

5. *Know that you are a very important person in the kingdom of God.* You have been chosen for such a time as this, just as Esther was. The purposes of God will prevail in your life when you surrender yourself to His will. King Solomon experienced this in his life: "There are many plans in a man's heart, nevertheless the LORD's counsel—that will stand" (Prov. 19:21)

Your speech will proclaim your salvation, your actions will demonstrate your faith, your prayers will move mountains, and your character will influence others for Christ, which is the ultimate destiny of a woman of God. Hear Jesus speak to you directly through the Great Commission: "Go therefore and make disciples of all the nations, baptizing them in the name of the Father and of the Son and of the Holy Spirit, teaching them to observe all things that I have commanded you; and lo, I am with you always, even to the end of the age" (Matt. 28:19–20).

FACILITATOR'S APPENDIX

Introduction

*M*ordecai's challenge to Esther revealed God's destiny for her life as she saved the people she loved: "Yet who knows whether you have come to the kingdom for such a time as this?" (Est. 4:14).

In these sessions we are patterning ourselves after Esther. Once she put others before her, she discovered her destiny. From the beginning of time God appointed her to become a queen, an intercessor, and a deliverer of a nation. Before she accomplished God's purposes in her life, however, she had to prepare herself, and that's the intent of these sessions.

As we began our Woman of God conferences, I prayed for the women of our congregation according to Colossians 1:9–11:

- They would be filled with the knowledge of God's will in all wisdom and spiritual understanding.
- They would walk worthy of the Lord, fully pleasing Him, being fruitful in every good work and increasing in the knowledge of God.
- They would be strengthened with all might, according to His glorious power, for all patience and long-suffering with joy.

With these goals in mind I began to plan this curriculum with other members of the Women of Esther, my women's leadership committee.

Each chapter in this book represents one session in the course, so you already know the extent of the curriculum. This appendix provides details to help make this program a part of your church ministry. As you know, at Cornerstone we conducted two different conferences—one for adult women and one for teens.

This book reflects the adult women's course, but the teen course covered the same topics, except finances. Also the teens' questions for Dr. Farhart were obviously different. When the member of one church staff heard about this curriculum, she decided to conduct one course for the moms and the teens, an experience they could share together. I encourage you to adapt this program to your own situation.

Now to the details that work behind the scenes to make a program like this a success.

IMPLEMENTATION

CLASS REQUIREMENTS

We charged a small fee for the class to help offset the cost of the supplies and to give the women a financial investment in the class. (A few of the women could not afford this cost, so we made scholarships available.) The early registration fee was set at twenty-five dollars; we added ten dollars during the regular registration period. Many of our ladies did register early, which helped us determine how many facilitators and child care workers were needed. After the second session, we did not accept any additional registrations. I wanted the small groups to bond, and I did not want to disrupt what the Lord started doing in the group dynamics.

Attendance was stressed. We told the women that they were required to attend all classes to qualify for graduation. If they could not attend certain classes, they were to get their facilitators to approve their excuses. They were then responsible to submit papers on those sessions. (See page 245 for the makeup assignments.) The purpose was to make the women realize it wasn't just another class or Bible study. We were serious about this commitment to them, and we needed them to be committed to this journey.

We also asked that they maintain a good attitude and turn in all required assignments. Obviously we expected them to attend graduation. Less than 5 percent of the enrollees dropped out of our class for various reasons.

SPEAKERS

Don't feel that you have to conduct all of these sessions by yourself. Sometimes I introduced the topic from my own experience and then brought in special speakers, such as Dr. Scott Farhart, the gynecologist who taught the sessions on sex. Other times I was the cohost for the session, presenting part of the material with another person who was a recognized and qualified leader in our church. This approach is scriptural, since Paul told the early Christians: "We urge you, brethren, to recognize those who labor among you" (1 Thess. 5:12).

FACILITATORS

Facilitators are essential to this program. The interaction and sharing that occur within these groups ensure that the women will carefully consider the teaching and express their feelings about the subject matter. Here are the qualifications that I used to determine who might act in this capacity:

1. They were leaders in our church and had a strong belief of who they were in Christ. When they applied, we asked them to give a spiritual reference from someone within the church.
2. If they were married, they had strong marriages. If they were single, they were pure in their walk with Christ.
3. They were passionate about the class and excited to impart the principles of being a daughter of the King.

We assigned each facilitator to a specific age-group, based on the data from the registration forms. I chose to break into age-based groups because our participants spanned such a wide age range, from eighteen years to seventy-six years. I felt that they would be better able to discuss their experiences and situations with their peers.

FACILITATOR DUTIES

We challenged these women to fulfill the following duties:

1. Be responsible for five to ten women.
2. Follow the instructor's directions for the class, and walk the women in their group through the action points.
3. Commit to the program for the entire twelve-week session.
4. Call the women under their care throughout the week to encourage them and pray with them.

5. Collect the women's makeup assignments, and help maintain attendance records for the class coordinator.
6. Assist in the graduation/consecration service.
7. Read the Scripture references for each class prior to that session.
8. Find a replacement who fulfilled our qualifications if they could not attend a class.

Each facilitator should be given a copy of this book and a folder with attendance sheets. I was pleased that the groups that were established during the Woman of God sessions did not end with graduation. These women had truly become sisters in Christ and are still sharing each other's lives in regular small group meetings.

FACILITIES

We held our sessions in the church sanctuary because we had more than five hundred participants. At the beginning of the sessions I noticed that some of the women were entering the sanctuary as they would enter a restaurant or a Wal-Mart. They just kept laughing or talking rather than entering with an attitude of reverence and a sense of expectation. We reminded the women that the dictionary defines *reverence* as "profound awe," "respect," and "an act of showing respect." Sometimes we think of God in such casual and familiar terms that we forget who He is. We learn from Hebrews 12:28–29: "Therefore, since we are receiving a kingdom which cannot be shaken, let us have grace, by which we may serve God acceptably with reverence and godly fear. For our God is a consuming fire."

I told the women, "We don't want to be so formal and legalistic that we think we need to have an appointment to meet God, yet we need to remember that He is holy. We need to separate ourselves from the busyness of this life to seek His holiness. One way is to come before Him in reverence and love, seeking Him, not our friends or conversation, but His presence. The Lord told us in Leviticus 19:30: 'You shall keep My Sabbaths and reverence My sanctuary: I am the LORD.'"

Soon after we reminded the women about their conduct, I noticed them coming into the sanctuary and beginning to kneel in prayer, read their Bibles, or sit silently before the Lord.

SPECIAL SESSIONS AND EVENTS

DAYS OF FASTING

We held two sessions of prayer and fasting, one at the beginning and one at the end of the conference, both in the evening at seven o'clock. The first was held on the Feast of Purim, which is a Jewish feast in the month of March that reminds the Jews of God's faithfulness through His daughter Esther. The women were asked to undertake a water fast, which meant no food at all, only water. We told them that they could add lemon or lime to their water, but that was all. No tea, coffee, juice, or sodas. If for health reasons they felt they could not do the water-only fast, we asked them to do a "pleasant bread fast," abstaining from anything with sugar. The fast began at sundown (when they went to bed) on Wednesday to sundown on Thursday when we had our prayer meeting.

During the day, they were asked to pray for the following:

- Our president, for wisdom and discernment, that he would nominate God-fearing men and women to the Supreme Court, and for godly, wise advisers and counselors
- Our U.S. Supreme Court, that the men and women seated there would fear the Lord and hunger and thirst for God's righteousness
- Our federal, state, and local government leaders, that they would fear God and desire to serve their constituents
- Our pastors and the ministry God has given them, that they would fear God so much that they would fear no man
- Revival in our church and city
- Our desire to have a great fire and passion for the lost
- Our families and personal needs

On the first day of prayer and fasting, we broke our fast following the prayer service with the traditional Feast of Purim cookies—Hamantaschen cookies—and punch.

On the second day of prayer and fasting, we broke our fast with a Communion ceremony using French bread and grape juice, which was served by the facilitators.

Before we partook of the Communion, a teaching on Communion was presented, and we corporately proclaimed the Benefits of Walking in God's Favor on page 164 of this book. We ended with our usual prayer time.

These prayer and fasting days were beneficial to the women as well as to the spiritual strength of the church, the families within the church, and eventually our city. After returning from the second day of fasting, one of the women heard a message from her sister on her answering machine. "Happy birthday," her sister said. "Call so I can give you this wish in person."

When the woman called her sister, she learned that between the time the message was left and the time she returned her sister's call, someone had led her sister to the Lord. One of this woman's greatest petitions during this time of fasting had been for her sister's salvation, a prayer she had repeated fervently for the last ten years.

I received many other notes of the blessings God provided during these two days of prayer and fasting:

- A woman's husband had to take the night shift at work and was told that once he switched from days to nights, he couldn't get the day shift back. He particularly wanted the day shift so he could spend time with his son and wife. The Friday after our Thursday prayer and fasting day, his supervisor called to let him know he needed to be in at 7:00 A.M. on Monday. He was back on the day shift!
- A woman whose husband had been unemployed for four months found a job the Friday after the Thursday fast.
- A daughter, fasting and praying for her mother's salvation, received the news that her mother had accepted Christ as Savior.

I feel that these special days released the power of the Holy Spirit to these women in ways that would not have been possible without the fasting and prayer.

MAKEOVERS

As I mentioned in the first chapter, the owner of a local beauty salon donated her stylists' time to perform makeovers for the participants. We then asked each facilitator to refer one or two ladies from her small group to us as possible models. They were to write each woman's name and any special need or helpful information on an index card and return it to us.

The facilitators were to choose these ladies based on the following criteria:

- Someone who had perfect attendance
- Someone for whom a makeover would be a special treat
- Someone who was going through a difficult time
- Someone who was willing to have a totally different look: haircut or makeup

We then drew thirty names from these cards as our makeover models. We took "before" and "after" pictures of these women and used a few of these pictures as part of our graduation presentation. Oprah would have been proud!

Some churches may not want to approach a salon. However, a cosmetic consultant might be willing to perform some makeovers for the class, knowing that she will probably get some business from this exposure. The speaker for this evening used the questions on the participant surveys (see p. 223) as an outline for her presentation. I have also included an outline of this class on page 242.

MOBILE MAMMOGRAMS

I believe that God calls us to take care of our bodies, which are temples of the Holy Spirit. We included a session on health in our curriculum, in which Dr. Farhart reminded women of the importance of yearly checkups and mammograms.

Because many women were either too busy or unable to afford mammograms, we provided this opportunity one Saturday for women who were forty and older at a special rate of eighty dollars. If the women had insurance, we asked them to bring their cards so the company could file for reimbursement. If the women didn't have insurance and could not afford the cost, we issued vouchers to cover the screening mammogram. Our church provided this service from its benevolence fund.

GRADUATION AND CONSECRATION

We held graduation ceremonies during our Sunday evening service. (An outline of this service is on p. 243.) We provided graduation robes for the women in the royal colors of red, blue, purple, gold, silver, and emerald. After the graduation the gowns were collected, cleaned, and boxed for further use. Obviously graduation can be personalized to each particular church. It might be a special event for just the members of the class, or it might be part of a Mother's Day celebration during a Sunday evening service, as was ours.

A MEMENTO

Each woman received a diploma and a gift at graduation. A jeweler found an intricate silver box pendant in which we placed a scroll with the words from the prayer of Jabez in 1 Chronicles 4:10: "Oh, that You would bless me indeed, and enlarge my territory, that Your hand would be with me, and that You would keep me from evil that I may not cause pain!" We gave these to the women on silver chains so they could wear them around their necks, always remembering Jabez's prayer for their lives. We also gave them a copy of *The Prayer of Jabez* by Bruce Wilkinson.

I pray that this King's Daughter course will be as beneficial to the women of your church as it was to the ladies at Cornerstone. As the main facilitator, I shared my most inner thoughts, desires, goals, and insecurities with my class. This vulnerability allowed the Holy Spirit to operate in the lives of the women. We laughed together. We cried together. We called on the name of the Lord together. Together, we took the journey.

Every journey will be different, but the destination of the journey will be the same: to help the women find their destiny as daughters of the King. Let me give you an example from one of many letters we received after the course was completed:

On February 18, 2001, I decided to rededicate myself to the Lord and agreed to accompany my sister to "Becoming a Woman of God." The very next day, on the 19th, my landlord came down from Corpus Christi, and all of a sudden announced that he was going to sell the house I was renting. He wanted me out on the 28th of February. I feel Satan tried to use this against my rededication.

So I had nine days to find somewhere to go with my two children and had no money. I am a single mother. My sister prayed that God would provide—and He did! My landlord granted me a thirty day stay so that I'd have enough time to find somewhere to live.

In the midst of trying to find a house, my son, who's always had a behavior problem began getting good reports from school. Then the Lord blessed me with a truck that my dad had put his blood, sweat, and tears into. It's just like a new vehicle, only better because God gave me His best.

Then I started going to Wednesday prayer in the chapel. I got not one, not two, but three promotions at work and a prophecy that God was going to teach me what I need to know—and He's going to give me my own business!

So by now, I'm witnessing at work and waking up with my children every morning at 6 A.M. to have Bible study. Then God brought me the perfect house. I kept going to "Women of God" and kept battling with cigarette addiction, then I won one of the makeovers. I moved into my new home and as I got rid of things—movies and clothes that are not of God—He delivered me from cigarettes!

Where my children were lacking structure and discipline before, they have now gained it through Christ in me. My son is making A's and B's, my daughter, who always had an attitude and was always unhappy, now has joy. Her attitude has turned into witnessing to children at her school; she is just a ray of sunshine.

As for me I am eternally blessed and eternally saved and will serve the Lord Jesus Christ with all that I have in me. I want to thank you for being obedient to the Lord and for wanting to share God's wisdom, love, and understanding to those like me who desperately need Jesus. There is none like Jesus!

I almost forgot to mention. God provided the money and the transportation and the people [to help me] move. When you lay everything down for Jesus, He will move mountains.

I'm sure the Lord is pleased that His daughter has come into an intimate relationship with Him. We also received letters from some of the husbands, thanking us for this program. Here is one of them:

My wife went to the meetings in awe of you all. However, she does not realize that she is a great woman, a great wife, a great mother, and a great new grandmother in her own right. All the little things that she has done and continues to do make her so very special to us. She is one of the Lord's blessings and representatives on earth.

I praise the Almighty Lord for His love and faithfulness. We are so undeserving of such beauty that is my wife. I am living proof of her love in action as I witnessed the way she related to her children, grandchildren, and me during twenty-seven years of marriage.

May the Lord bless all of you women in your endeavor to become Women of God. My wife has been one for quite some time; she just doesn't know it.

How pleased we were to realize that we had helped this daughter of the King see herself as God and her family see her.

The following curriculum has been inspired by the Holy Spirit as an instrument to instruct and guide women in this journey. I will begin with an enrollment form and an instruction letter for facilitators and then go into each session's instructions for facilitators.

Facilitator Registration Form

NAME:_____

ADDRESS:_____

CITY/STATE/ZIP:_____

PHONE: Home_____ Work_____

E-MAIL:_____ MOBILE #:_____

AGE:_____

CHURCH REFERENCE (A pastor or church leader):_____

_____

_____

Participant Registration Form

NAME:_____

ADDRESS:_____

CITY/STATE/ZIP:_____

PHONE: Home_____ Work_____

E-MAIL:_____ MOBILE #:_____

AGE:____ MARRIED/SINGLE

NEED CHILD CARE: YES/NO

CHILDREN'S AGES: (1)_____ (2)_____ (3)_____ (4)_____

EARLY REGISTRATION (available through   /   /   ) $_____

REGISTRATION (after   /   /   ) $_____

PAID: CASH/CHECK #_____

(Make checks payable to:_____)

LETTER TO FACILITATORS

First let me express my appreciation to you for your commitment to this God-inspired program. My prayer is that God will bless you as you bless others, over and above what you can imagine. We are about to begin a journey, and our destination will lead us closer to Jesus Christ. As we begin this journey, know that our God is faithful and just to complete the good work He has begun.

In serving as a facilitator, you are committed to do the following:

- Attend the program for the entire twelve-week session.
- Be responsible for five to ten women.
- Follow the instructor's directions for the class, and walk the women in your group through the action points.
- Not counsel but give direction to the Word of God.
- Refer anyone in need of immediate help to the leadership of this class.
- Pray for your group and the leadership on a regular basis.
- Assist in the graduation/consecration service.

There is so much to do in such a short time; your participation is critical. Here's an overview of what will transpire each session:

1. Meet prior to each session at _____ A.M./P.M. in _____ (location) for prayer and instructions, which will include a review of action points. (I recommend meeting thirty minutes before class begins. Always open in prayer.)

2. Pick up your group folder, which will contain an Attendance Sheet. Fill it out and return your folder to the folder box at the designated place following your small group. It is important to turn in your folder each session to assist the coordinator in keeping attendance.

3. The main facilitator will open each session in prayer, make announcements, and introduce the evening's speaker.

4. The speaker will make a presentation.

5. Following the speaker, the main facilitator will instruct the class on the

action points and then ask the participants to go to their small groups. (At the first session I will call each facilitator forward and then read the names of the women in their respective groups.)

6. In the small group, everyone is to respond to the action points. Start with yourself; we all learn by example. Discuss the action points, reminding the women that everything said in these groups remains confidential. Do not allow this to become a counseling session. No one should speak more than two or three minutes. Take prayer requests and pray for each need. As we progress, please ask the women to pray for one another within the group.

7. Do not allow anyone to control or dominate the group.

8. Do not allow criticism. Under no circumstances should you allow a critical spirit to arise. Criticism will only breed criticism.

9. You will receive the phone and address lists of the women in your group. If possible, call and encourage them during the week and tell them you will see them at the next session.

10. Should someone in your group present a serious situation, pray with her and notify the leader of your class. Refer this person to our counseling department or to a good Christian counseling center.

11. Pray for your group and the leaders weekly.

Thank you for sowing your valuable time into the kingdom of God.

chapter one

The King's Daughter

This is an opening session. The main facilitator will introduce The King's Daughter sessions and then give her testimony.

ACTION POINTS

1. *Guidelines.* You will use some of your group time to review the guidelines, rules, and commitments. A handout of these guidelines follows this session outline so you can go through these points with your group.

2. *Surveys.* Hand out the survey that follows this session outline, and ask each participant to complete it and return it to you tonight. Turn in the surveys, your attendance sheet, and your folder before leaving this evening.

3. Now explain the plan of salvation and the fact that Jesus Christ will write our names in the Lamb's Book of Life once we pray the sinner's prayer. Pray the following prayer, and ask the members of the group to join with you:

> *Dear Lord, I have made many mistakes in the past. I have sinned against You and Your Holy Spirit. I am sorry for all I have done. Please forgive me. I accept Jesus Christ as my Savior and ask that You will be with me in the days ahead. Amen.*

NEXT WEEK: MY VALUE IN GOD'S EYES

GUIDELINES FOR THE KING'S DAUGHTER SESSIONS

- Please plan to attend every session. Any missed class will require a written paper.
- Remember the sanctuary is where we come together to meet God. Please enter with an attitude of prayer and reverence.
- Please be prompt. We need to start on time and end on time.
- Remember, no food or drink in the sanctuary.
- Turn off all pagers and cell phones.
- Give total respect to everyone.
- Do not interrupt or speak when someone else is speaking.
- During group discussion, stay on the focus point. We are discussing you, not your children or spouse. We will be addressing different issues in each session.
- Anything said here is to stay here. Please do not gossip.
- We will lift your need in prayer, but we are not here to counsel.
- Please remember to pick up your children immediately after our sessions. Then feel free to visit.
- If someone else is to pick up your child, please confirm that your child has been picked up before you leave. We do not want a child to be left behind.

Participant Survey

Please assist us by filling out this survey and returning it to your facilitator before you leave this evening. You do not need to put your name on it. Please print.

Your age: _____

If you had your own personal consultant, what questions would you ask her about the following?

Hair:

_____

_____

_____

Makeup or skin care:

_____

_____

_____

Fashion:

_____

_____

_____

If your best friend was a doctor, what two questions would you ask her about your body and/or your sexuality?

1. _____

_____

2. _____

_____

~

My Value in God's Eyes

*W*asn't that a great beginning? There is such an expectation that invites the Holy Spirit to minister to our lives. Thank you for your willingness to participate and serve. Your role is critical, since the small group sessions are a key to the success of this program.

ACTION POINTS

1. Talk to the women about self-esteem. Say, "The me I see is the me I will be." Then ask the women:

- Do you see yourself as ugly? This can represent low self-esteem.
- Do you feel unworthy? This can represent rejection in your childhood or now.
- Do you often feel angry? This can represent self-hatred.
- Do you feel guilty? This can represent emotional, physical, or sexual abuse.

2. Counter these emotions with the Word: "I, therefore, the prisoner of the Lord, beseech you to walk worthy of the calling with which you were called, with all lowliness and gentleness, with longsuffering, bearing with one another in love" (Eph. 4:1–2).

Before this session, read the material about Ephesians 4:1–2 on page 20 in this book. Then use this outline as you discuss the material with your group:

Lowliness of mind. "I accept all things that God says about me without argument. It enables me to accept myself."

Meekness. "I accept all of God's dealings with me without resistance or bitterness. It enables me to accept God."

Long-suffering. "I accept all of man's dealings with me without retaliation. It enables me to accept my enemies."

Forbearance. "I accept people with all their faults and differences. It enables me to accept my friends."

3. Ask the women to turn to page 24 in this book. Then tell them what you feel is ugly about yourself, which will help them to feel comfortable talking about their own weaknesses. This discussion identifies the self-esteem problem we wrestle with daily, but when we confront the enemy, we disarm him. Then ask the women to mention the traits that bother them. Finally look at the scriptures on pages 24–25.

4. Now list all the things you believe are beautiful about yourself. Again invite the women to do the same thing. (Doing this will be more difficult than listing the things that we don't like about ourselves.)

5. Proclaim that the precepts of the Lord are intentional and in good order. He has made everything beautiful in its time. Quote these scriptures: "I am fearfully and wonderfully made" (Ps. 139:14), and "I have called you by your name; you are Mine" (Isa. 43:1).

6. Ask a member of the group to read the "letter from God," which is on pages 21–22 of this book.

7. State: "I am beautiful. You are beautiful. We have value in God's eyes. We are daughters of the King!"

8. End with prayer.

ᗄ NEXT WEEK: I AM NOT ASHAMED OF THE GOSPEL

chapter three

~

I Am Not Ashamed of the Gospel

ACTION POINTS

1. Follow the outline as you discuss a Christian's call to evangelize:

Presenting Our Testimony

- We are witnesses the moment we become Christians
  (Eph. 4:21–24; 5:1).
- Witnessing is more about who I am than what I say
  (Eph. 4:25–32; 5:3–6).
- Being God's person is more important than doing God's work
  (Acts 11:26; Rom. 2:21–24; Titus 3:1–7).

2. Use this scripture in Proverbs to guide you for the next part of this session:

> Trust in the LORD with all your heart,
> And lean not on your own understanding;
> In all your ways acknowledge Him,
> And He shall direct your paths. (Prov. 3:5–6)

My part. Trust Him, casting on Him all hopes now and in the future and finding shelter and security in Christ.

My part. Do not lean on my own understanding. Avoid finding solutions for my problems through my own knowledge.

My part. Acknowledge Him. Recognize that once we are Christians, we are never alone. Jesus is present and concerned about each circumstance of our lives.

His part. He will walk with me. The Lord will have full control of my situations. He will make my paths straight and guide me through each obstacle along the way.

3. Give your testimony in one minute. It doesn't have to be your entire life story. Just tell about your life before Christ and your life after Christ. Mention that our testimony is always to glorify the Son and draw attention to the Father.

End your testimony with two questions: "Has Jesus come into your life? Would you like to pray the sinner's prayer?"

Instruct the group to turn to page 34 and write their own testimonies. They will be amazed by what the Holy Spirit will bring to their minds, much of which will be blessings God has given them. Tell group members to remember to keep their testimonies short, simple, and to the point. Then request that each member share her testimony with the group.

4. Ask someone to read "Releasing the Word in Your Life" on pages 23–24 of this book.

5. End with prayer.

ᴄᴏ NEXT WEEK: THE HOLY SPIRIT AND ME

chapter four

The Holy Spirit and Me

ACTION POINTS

1. Ask about whether participants have prayed to receive the baptism of the Holy Spirit. If some have prayed, but not received, lead them in the following prayer:

> *Father, I ask that You reveal Yourself to me in a way I have never known before. If there is something You have for me that I have not experienced, then show me now. I ask You to pour Your Holy Spirit into my heart. With this infilling, I ask You to impart in me the passion to witness as Your disciples did on the day of pentecost. I ask that You help me with my prayer life, lifting me to levels far beyond my natural strength and understanding. When I pray, I want the authority and the power of the living God.*
>
> *Guide me, through Your Holy Spirit, in the path You would have me go. Father, I ask that You pour into my heart a love so rich that it can be described only as agape love. A love that is so pure that its only source can be the throne of the living God. Lord, if there is more of You, then I want to have it. Amen.*

2. Go through the scriptures that are part of the action points on page 46 of "The Holy Spirit and Me" chapter, pointing out the position we have as daughters of the King.

3. Ask a member of the class to read "Releasing the Word in Your Life," which is found on pages 23–24.

NEXT WEEK: DREAMS WITH A HAPPY ENDING: SETTING GOALS

chapter five

Dreams with a Happy Ending: Setting Goals

ACTION POINTS

1. Take your group members through the goal-setting process in this book. First, tell them to turn to page 55 in Chapter 5 where readers are instructed to list their talents and skills. They are not to be overly humble here. Honesty is the best policy for accurate goal setting. Instruct them to list their talents and skills on this page.

2. Now ask them to think of how they might use these skills in their lives. For instance, someone who is good in math might want to become a bookkeeper, an accountant, or an engineer. Someone who is gifted in hospitality might want to use this gift at church or in her home. Ask members to mention their gifts and talents, and encourage the group to talk through how these talents might be used.

3. Now tell the group members to turn to pages 55–58, where readers list their goals for tomorrow. Remind them that it is important to train themselves to be successful in the smaller things first. They should fill in their spiritual goals, personal goals, career goals, and educational goals. Then share some of them with the group.

4. Turn to pages 58–60 where the readers list their goals for the future. Again, ask members of your group to list their future goals and share some of them with the group.

5. Turn to the goal-setting sheets on pages 65–66. Instruct group members to take the goal that is most important to them and work through this process to reach that goal. Then ask them to share this goal and the process with the group.

6. End the session today with a prayer that God will help all members of the group to know His will for their lives and to help them fulfill these goals.

Urge them to pray for each other and encourage each other to reach for their goals.

⌒ NEXT WEEK:
TEN COMMANDMENTS FOR WOMEN IN THE WORKPLACE

chapter six

Ten Commandments for
Women in the Workplace

ACTION POINTS

1. Begin the session today with a general discussion of work: what, why, where, and whose idea was it anyway?

Work is a part of God's plan for us. All of God's creation works. In fact, He Himself worked in the beginning and continues to work today: "In six days the LORD made the heavens and the earth, the sea, and all that is them, and rested the seventh day" (Ex. 20:11).

The basic definition of *work* clearly indicates that it requires effort and action on our part, and that it is supposed to yield a positive result, including our personal satisfaction and ultimately God's blessing. We work because we were created to work:

Six days you shall labor and do all your work. (Ex. 20:9)

You will eat the fruit of your labor;
blessings and prosperity will be yours. (Ps. 128:2 NIV)

Diligent hands will rule,
but laziness ends in slave labor. (Prov. 12:24 NIV)

A [woman] can do nothing better than to eat and drink and find satisfaction in [her] work. (Eccl. 2:24 NIV)

Work happens in a lot of places: at a job and in a home. The problem with work? It usually turns out to be work!

2. Now discuss the benefits of work, beginning with this verse: "Give her the reward she has earned, and let her works bring her praise at the city gate" (Prov. 31:31 NIV).

Excellence in work brings us great rewards: God's blessings, an outstanding reputation, a raise in pay, or a promotion. Above all, it is pleasing to the Father as we use every gift that He has given us. Work can be glorifying to Him!

3. Ask the members to mention four things they can do to be better examples and witnesses in their workplace or home.

4. Attitude is critical for a daughter of the King. See the action points on pages 90–93 for help with cultivating a godly attitude.

5. End with prayer.

❧ NEXT WEEK: WOMEN AND COURTSHIP

chapter seven

Women and Courtship

ACTION POINTS

1. Ask the women to begin by writing their own proclamations on page 116 of this book. Then encourage them to share these proclamations with the class, asking for prayer for specific items within the proclamation. Reemphasize the confidentiality of the group experience. Anything that is said during these sessions is to remain confidential. Tell the women we want to make sure we do not dishonor our husbands as we share our hearts' desires with one another.

2. Devote five minutes for the women to examine themselves. Each woman should think about her life and what God is calling her to do. (See p. 116.)

3. Ask the married women to fill out the O.W.E. (One Way Everyday) form on pages 118–119 for their husbands. Single women may fill out the form for a special friend or loved one—a parent or a sibling who needs special love at this time.

Ask a member of the group to read "Releasing the Word in Your Life," which is found on pages 23–24 of this book.

Designate two members of the group to begin and end the prayer time.

NEXT WEEK: AND GOD SAID . . . "LET THERE BE SEX" *AND* TEN QUESTIONS YOU'RE AFRAID TO ASK YOUR GYNECOLOGIST

And God Said . . . "Let There Be Sex"

and

Ten Questions You're Afraid to Ask Your Gynecologist

*W*e will not have small groups tonight. The itinerary for this evening will be as follows:

The main facilitator will welcome the participants and open with prayer.

The doctor will give a ten-minute slide presentation, followed by answering some of the questions from our surveys.

If a leader in your congregation has been sexually abused and is willing to share her testimony, take this time to do so now. Choose this person carefully because she has to discern what to share, and make sure she can testify to the healing, hope, and restoration of the blood of Jesus Christ. There has to be evidence of her healing from pain and the victory in her life since then. You will remember that after I told Teresa's story, I mentioned that God redeemed her life. He gave her a marriage of thirty-two years to one man, He gave her four children who love the Lord, and most of all, He gave her His mercy and grace.

Altar calls for three groups can then be given, but these calls should be made simultaneously so that it will not be obvious which person is answering each call. The women should be told to wait to come forward until all three groups have been called.

The three groups include these:

1. A call for those who have been sexually molested or abused. You might want to lead them in the following prayer:

> *Father, I acknowledge the violation that was committed against me. I place it right now in Jesus Christ's nail-pierced hands. I ask You to give me grace to forgive _____, who violated me. I have been held hostage to this offense and will no longer be held captive.*
>
> *Your Word says, "If you forgive men their trespasses, your heavenly Father will also forgive you" (Matt. 6:14). What the person did was not right; it was wrong. It was sin, but I choose no longer to be held in bondage. No weapon formed against me shall prosper, and You will quiet every tongue that rises up to accuse me, for that is my inheritance as a daughter of the King.*
>
> *In the name of Jesus I choose to forgive _____ for what he/she did to me, and I ask You, Father, to forgive him/her. I pray that he/she will come to the saving knowledge of Jesus Christ and seek Your forgiveness and healing in his/her broken life.*
>
> *Thank You for Your healing power working in my life right now; heal my memory, heal my emotions, and heal my body by the blood of Jesus Christ. I bind up the spirit of rejection that was imparted to me through this violation. I receive the spirit of adoption extended to me by the Cross of Jesus Christ. Restore to me the hope of my salvation and the blessings that come with that hope. Father, You see me with the robe of righteousness that Your Son purchased on my behalf. You see me as pure and whole. Father, I am completed in You in Jesus' name. Amen.*

2. A call to those who have been promiscuous to confess their sins, repent before the Lord, and pledge themselves to remain pure and sin no more, consecrating themselves to the Lord. Again you might want to lead them in a specific prayer:

> *Father, forgive me, for I have sinned against You and Your temple. In*

Jesus' name I ask that You forgive me of all my sins and transgressions. I want to walk in Your fellowship and blessings. I repent of my sins and ask that You renew my mind daily. Create in me a pure heart, Lord. Change me; mold me into a woman of God. I desire Your righteousness. I consecrate myself to You, Lord, for You are a holy God. In Jesus' name. Amen.

3. A call for married women who want their marriages to reflect God and His glory. Pray this prayer over these women:

Father, bless my marriage bed. Let no impurity taint what You have joined together. I thank You for my husband and our sexual union. I pray that neither of us will ever look elsewhere to meet our needs. Help me to remember that it is my ministry as a wife to meet the sexual needs of my husband. I desire to make myself attractive to him as I would for the King.

Lord, show me each day a way to let my husband know he is special to me. My desire is that he will see Your love for him through me. In Jesus' name. Amen.

Before these altar calls every facilitator should come to the front. If any participant begins to open up about incest or other abuse, pray with that person, and then take her to a counselor or a member of a support group for victims of abuse.

ᴄᴑ NEXT WEEK: THE FAVOR OF GOD

chapter ten

The Favor of God

ACTION POINTS

1. Ask the following questions, and use the following scriptures as you talk to the members of your group about the favor of God.

How do we withhold God's provisions?
- We do not ask, according to James 4:2.
- We are disobedient, according to Malachi 3:8–12.

What is God's plan?
- To prosper His children (3 John 2).
- To supply all our needs (1 Kings 17:12–15; Phil. 4:19).
- To rebuke the devourer for our sake (Mal. 3:11).
- To urge us to be the lender and not the borrower (Deut. 28:12).

How do I get into God's favor?
- Receive Jesus Christ as my personal Lord and Savior (John 3:16).
- Recognize I am a child of the King, a joint heir with Christ Jesus (Eph. 1:5).
- Obey God's Word (1 Sam. 15:22; John 14:15).
- Ask in faith believing, according to His will (Matt. 21:22; Mark 11:24; Luke 11:9).
- Receive my inheritance (Deut. 28:1–14; Eph. 1:3–20).

2. Ask a member of the group to read "Releasing the Word in Your Life" on pages 23–24 of this book.

3. End with prayer.

ᴄᴏ NEXT WEEK: HOSPITALITY—AN ATTITUDE OF THE HEART

chapter eleven

Hospitality—An Attitude of the Heart

ACTION POINTS

1. Ask the women to look up the scriptures on page 188, under the action points in the hospitality chapter. Discuss what these scriptures mean to each person and how they affect her attitude toward hospitality.

2. Then go through the questions in number two of that section, and tell the women to take the fun quiz.

3. Talk about hospitality in Bible times, and read the scriptures listed there.

4. Encourage each woman to mention a way that she can reach out in hospitality in the next week or month.

5. Close with prayer.

∾ NEXT WEEK: BEAUTY

chapter one

Beauty

ACTION POINTS

1. Begin this session by handing out "My Body, a Temple of the Lord," which follows the action points here. Work through the points on this handout with the group.

2. Ask each member to mention one or two women who epitomize the Scripture's definition of beauty and are fulfilling their destiny as daughters of the King. Each person should tell why this woman is beautiful in God's sight and also how the person is fulfilling God's plan for her life.

3. Ask each member to tell what she believes is God's purpose for her own life—and how she can fulfill that purpose.

4. Designate a member of the group to read "Releasing the Word in Your Life," pages 23–24.

5. End with group prayer.

My Body, a Temple of the Lord

If anyone cleanses [herself] from the latter, [she] will be a vessel for honor, sanctified and useful for the Master, prepared for every good work.

—2 Timothy 2:21

1. *Repent* from using food as a substitute for a relationship with God and/or others or as a way to comfort or soothe your hurts and fears.

2. *Implement.* Read the Word, pray, and ask.

3. *Be accountable.* Ask a friend or someone in your group to pray for you, and you will also pray for her. As you pray for each other, be sure to talk to each other regularly to give encouragement.

4. *Exercise.* You don't have to join a health club; just walk. Brisk walking is the ideal exercise for everyone, regardless of age or health. Remember to always check with your physician before starting any exercise program.

5. *Read the labels.* Know what you are eating. Eliminate sugar from your diet and see the difference. Cut back on white flour and fat.

6. *Choose.* You have to want to be healthy. Do this for yourself, so you will live a healthy, happy, and long life. That is what your heavenly Father wants for you, just because He loves you!

Extra Session: Makeovers

～

$\mathcal{W}$e held two sessions on makeup and appearance, but you might be able to do this in one session.

PART ONE: SKIN CARE AND MAKEUP

First, a professional aesthetician or makeup artist demonstrated the importance of taking care of our skin, discussing protection from overexposure to the sun, daily cleansing, facials, waxing, brow shaping, exfoliating, and moisturizing. She also explained how to shop economically and even described skin care items that are available in everyone's kitchen pantry. At the back of the sanctuary we had sample items from local stores, such as Bath and Body Works.

Then a professional makeup artist presented the looks for the season; she discussed colors and face shapes and demonstrated makeup application on a model chosen from the participants. Again, this can be considered biblical: "Behold, you are fair, my love! . . . You have dove's eyes behind your veil . . . Your lips are like a strand of scarlet, and your mouth is lovely. Your temples behind your veil are like a piece of pomegranate" (Song 4:1, 3).

Then a professional nail technician discussed nail care, foot care, and pedicures.

PART TWO: HAIR STYLING AND MAKEUP

A licensed hair stylist began by introducing the women who were receiving complete makeovers, which included haircuts, brow waxing, makeup application, and styling. She had each model tell a little bit about herself—her lifestyle, her hobbies, her hair type. Then the makeup team gave an analysis on each model.

A member of our congregation talked about fashion dos and don'ts, which included our definition of modesty: If you have trouble putting it on or off, it's not modest. If you bring attention to anything other than your face, it's not modest.

Then the models went to the stylists for wet cuts and to the makeup team for makeup.

Graduation

Each church's graduation will be unique to that particular congregation and women's ministry. I will tell you the agenda for our graduation, just to give you an outline of what might be done.

Upon completion of The Woman of God sessions, we presented the women to the congregation.

I explained the purpose of the conference and gave an overview of each session and thanked the businesses that had contributed to our program.

Then I read four letters of testimony, which had been written by participants, telling how their lives had changed during the course.

My sister Sandy sang "Mercy Saw Me."

After that we showed a video that presented various parts of the Woman of God conference, shots from the days of fasting and prayer, from some of the sessions, and from the makeovers.

Then the graduates were introduced. (You might want their facilitators to present them.) At this time the participants received their diplomas, the silver box pendants, and copies of *The Prayer of Jabez.*

My daughter Tina sang "The Potter's Hand."

Finally my husband prayed a prayer of blessing over the women, which included the prayer of Jabez.

At the end of this service the facilitators met with their groups and encouraged the ladies to stay in touch and to visit their cell meetings. The leaders also reminded them to visit the tables in our center narthex, which are assigned to the different ministries of the church. We wanted the women to consider signing up for one of these ministries.

Makeup Assignments

SESSION TWO: MY VALUE IN GOD'S EYES

Reference a minimum of ten scriptures that describe how God sees us, His relationship toward us, and His desire for us. Then write the story of your salvation experience.

SESSION THREE: I AM NOT ASHAMED OF THE GOSPEL

Reference a minimum of ten scriptures that define what a testimony should be and what was said of the witness of early believers. Write your own testimony.

SESSION FOUR: THE HOLY SPIRIT AND ME

Reference a minimum of ten scriptures that describe the work of the Holy Spirit and why you should seek the baptism of the Holy Spirit.

SESSION FIVE: DREAMS WITH A HAPPY ENDING: SETTING GOALS

Reference a minimum of ten scriptures that refer to God's plan and purpose for our lives. Define goals. Write out one of your goals and the steps you need to take to achieve it.

SESSION SIX: TEN COMMANDMENTS FOR WOMEN IN THE WORKPLACE

Reference a minimum of ten scriptures that tell what God's Word says about the works of our hands. List four things you can do at home or in the office to share Jesus with those around you.

SESSION SEVEN: WOMEN AND COURTSHIP

Reference a minimum of ten scriptures that list God's priorities for us. Single women should write two sentences on why they feel they need a relationship, then four sentences on who God is in their lives. Married women should write ten things they can do One Way Everyday to show their love for their spouses—and do them.

SESSIONS EIGHT AND NINE:
AND GOD SAID . . . "LET THERE BE SEX"
AND
TEN QUESTIONS YOU'RE AFRAID TO ASK YOUR GYNECOLOGIST

Reference ten scriptures that give God's plan for marriage and His opinion on promiscuity and adultery. List three sexually transmitted diseases and how they are transmitted.

SESSION TEN: THE FAVOR OF GOD

Reference a minimum of ten scriptures that present God's view of our finances. Then tell how these scriptures will affect your financial planning.

SESSION ELEVEN: HOSPITALITY—
AN ATTITUDE OF THE HEART

Reference a minimum of ten scriptures that define hospitality and graciousness and God's desire for us to minister to others through the gift of hospitality. List ten ways you can show hospitality to others.

Notes

CHAPTER 2
1. Carl Jung, as quoted in Cecil Osborne, *The Art of Understanding Yourself* (Grand Rapids: Zondervan Books, 1967), 28.

CHAPTER 4
1. Derek Prince, *The Spirit-Filled Believer's Handbook* (Orlando, FL: Creation House, 1993). Used by permission.

CHAPTER 6
1. Rabbi Yechiel Eckstein, *What You Should Know About Jews and Judaism* (Word: Waco, 1984), 126–7.
2. Arnold G. Fruchtenbaum, *Israelology: The Missing Link in Systematic Theology* (Tustin, CA: Ariel Ministries Press, 1989), 594.

CHAPTER 7
1. Michelle McKinney Hammond, *If Men Are Like Buses, Then How Do I Catch One?* (Sisters, OR: Multnomah, 2000).
2. Drawn from Josh McDowell's soon-to-be-released *Why True Love Waits* (Wheaton, IL: Tyndale House, 2002).
3. Adapted from the proclamation in *If Men Are Like Buses, Then How Do I Catch One?* by Hammond.

CHAPTER 8
1. Chart provided by Why kNOw® Abstinence Education Program. Used by permission.

CHAPTER 9
1. Kevin Leman, *Sex Begins in the Kitchen* (Grand Rapids: Revell, 1999).
2. Dr. Jerry R. Kirk, *The Mind Polluters* (Nashville: Thomas Nelson, 1985), 60.

CHAPTER 10

1. Jerry Savelle, "How to Get Out of Lodebar," one in the sermon series The Favor of God, presented at Southwest Believer's Convention, 6 August 1997. Used by permission.

CHAPTER 11

1. Quin Sherrer, *The Warm and Welcome Heart* (Ventura, CA: Regal Publications, 2002).

CHAPTER 12

1. See Don Colbert, *Walking in Divine Health* (Lake Mary, FL: Siloam Press, 1999) and *What You Don't Know May Be Killing You!* (Lake Mary, FL: Siloam Press, 2000).

ABOUT THE AUTHOR

Diana Hagee is the wife of Dr. John Hagee, founder and Senior Pastor of the Cornerstone Church in San Antonio, Texas. She serves as Chief of Staff for John Hagee Ministries television ministry, as well as Special Events Coordinator and leader of Women's Ministries at Cornerstone Church. Diana is the author of *Not by Bread Alone*, a cookbook encouraging creative ministry through food. She was presented the prestigious Lion of Judah award by the Jewish Federation of Greater Houston. Diana and Pastor John Hagee have five children and one granddaughter.